Resurrection
and Renewal

"This is the most important and, indeed, exciting book on the resurrection to have emerged in half a century. Whereas many focus on the associated historical debates, very few explore in depth the central place of the resurrection in God's purposes of reconciliation and transformation. Rigorous biblical scholarship and profound theological insight define the discussion throughout. Intellectually rigorous and incisive, it is also lucid and accessible. This is obligatory reading for theologians and an ideal seminar text. But it should also be read by all those who are serious about understanding the defining affirmation at the heart of the Christian faith and its radical significance."

—**Alan J. Torrance**, University of St. Andrews (emeritus)

"In this beautifully written, biblically rooted, and theologically rich work, Murray Rae explores the demand the bodily resurrection of Jesus Christ places on scholars and Christians alike. Highlighting God's agency and the work of the Spirit in this 'utterly new starting point for our understanding of what is going on in the world,' Rae offers a refreshing vision for the academy and the church. His compelling insights into the grace and power of God for renewal through the resurrection bring life, light, and hope to the conversation."

—**Lucy Peppiatt**, Westminster Theological Centre

"Jesus's resurrection marks the transformation of all things. How this is so is the focus of Murray Rae's refreshing study, which works intimately with Christian Scripture to show what we might say and how we might live because Jesus has been raised from the dead. *Resurrection and Renewal* is both learned and theologically formative, even edifying, as befits theological engagement with the central claim that 'Christ is risen.'"

—**Joel B. Green**, Fuller Theological Seminary

"Dogmatically and scripturally rich, Murray Rae's *Resurrection and Renewal* traces the cosmic logic of life that the resurrection of Jesus brings. Written in an accessible style, this book edifies as much as it educates, reminding and demonstrating to readers that the resurrection of Jesus has truly changed everything."

—**Christa L. McKirland**, Carey Baptist College; executive director, Logia International

"Accepting Murray Rae's invitation to read this book not as an apologetic for the resurrection but as an exercise in faith seeking understanding, one is treated handsomely to biblical exegesis and theology that resonate with the practice of the theological interpretation of Scripture. Most importantly, one is reminded afresh of the cruciality of the resurrection of Jesus Christ for all that God is doing in this world, in its past, present, and future."

—**Edmund Fong**, Trinity Theological College

Resurrection and Renewal

JESUS

AND THE TRANSFORMATION

OF CREATION

Murray A. Rae

𝕭

Baker Academic

a division of Baker Publishing Group

Grand Rapids, Michigan

Published by Baker Academic
a division of Baker Publishing Group
Grand Rapids, Michigan
BakerAcademic.com

Printed in the United States of America

Library of Congress Cataloging-in-Publication Data
Names: Rae, Murray, author.
Title: Resurrection and renewal : Jesus and the transformation of creation / Murray A. Rae.
Description: Grand Rapids, Michigan : Baker Academic, a division of Baker Publishing Group,
    2024. | Includes bibliographical references and indexes.
Identifiers: LCCN 2023046047 | ISBN 9781540966209 (paperback) | ISBN 9781540967824
    (casebound) | ISBN 9781493446261 (ebook) | ISBN 9781493446278 (pdf)
Subjects: LCSH: Jesus Christ—Resurrection.
Classification: LCC BT482 .R335 2024 | DDC 232/.5—dc23/eng/20231130
LC record available at https://lccn.loc.gov/2023046047

Cover image © Nomad Studio / Stocksy United

24   25   26   27   28   29   30   7   6   5   4   3   2   1

To the faculty and students
at Trinity Theological College, Singapore,
where much of the material for this book
was first presented as the 2023 Trinity Lectures
and
To Alan Torrance,
extraordinary theologian, teacher, and friend

Contents

Introduction

I f Christ has not been raised, then our proclamation has been in vain and your faith has been in vain" (1 Cor. 15:14). With these words the apostle Paul emphatically affirms that the Christian gospel stands or falls with the resurrection of Jesus from the dead. Were Jesus not raised, then the grieving friends and disciples who had followed him around Galilee and then on to Jerusalem, where he was crucified at the hands of the religious and political authorities of the day, would have retained, no doubt, their fond memories of Jesus's companionship and continued to nurse their sorrow at his tragic demise, but Jesus himself, one imagines, would have largely been forgotten as human history continued on its way.

Because Jesus was raised, however, the world is not the same as it would otherwise have been. The whole course, and indeed the very nature, of human history has been radically transformed. Human life, and all of history with it, is not, after all, merely "one damn thing after another," as Henry Ford is supposed to have once remarked, but the terrain upon which God is drawing humanity, and indeed the whole creation, into reconciled communion, overcoming thereby the deadly consequences of humanity's efforts to determine its own course in defiance of the one who is the sole creator and sustainer of life. This book is an attempt to give an account of that transformation. It is not, let me be clear, an attempt to investigate whether the resurrection really happened. Much ink has been devoted to that project, with, I might say, inconclusive results. That inconclusivity does not mean, however, that the ink has been wasted. Historical investigation, for example, of the circumstances surrounding the original proclamation that Jesus had been raised from the dead, has yielded genuine insight into what the first followers appear to have meant by declaring that Jesus had been raised, and indeed what difference it made to their own lives and to the lives of others who received and believed the news. Historical inquiry has also made clear that the Christian proclamation of Jesus's resurrection cannot be simply dismissed as nonsense. Something happened that generated a movement that has been remarkable in its subsequent impact and extent. It is not my purpose, however, to pursue that kind of historical exploration; the work has been well done by others. I remain convinced, furthermore, that the recognition that Jesus has been raised depends, ultimately, not on the well-considered results of historical inquiry (valuable though those otherwise may be) but on encounter through the Spirit with the risen Lord himself. It is in consequence of such encounter, as the apostle Paul's own biography makes clear (e.g., 1 Cor. 15:8–10; Gal. 1:11–17), that minds and hearts are converted to a new understanding of the world, an understanding that is founded upon, and is shaped in its distinctive particulars by, the resurrection itself.

I am convinced as well that the divine agency that is the subject of the claim "God raised Jesus from the dead" cannot be confirmed by any process of verification that regards as finally authoritative our own (limited!) intellectual capacities. Such agency is recognized only under the guidance of God. Objections to this claim are certainly possible. The most common focuses on the possibility (some would say the likelihood) that persons claiming to have encountered God are simply deluded. This objection identifies a genuine possibility—human beings can be wrong about many things—but the possibility of being wrong does not exclude the further possibility that claims of encounter with God may in some cases be true.

The purpose of this book, then, is not to enter into an argument about whether the resurrection really happened but to explore what has changed and what may be affirmed as true in light of the fact (so I believe as a Christian) that it *has* happened. Any readers demanding or seeking proof of the resurrection should set this book aside, for I offer none. It was no part of the New Testament writers' purpose to offer proofs that the resurrection had happened. Their purpose was simply to proclaim the good news that Jesus is risen, to explore how the world had changed in light of that fact, and, above all, to understand the call upon us to participate in the emerging reality of a world transformed. Those who hear the proclamation that Jesus has been raised from the dead and confess that they too believe have a lifetime then to discover what it means. This book is offered as a contribution to that process of discovery.

One of the consequences of the fact that the resurrection is to be proclaimed rather than proven is that theological speech about the resurrection will often have a homiletic tone. That is true of the chapters that compose this book. I cannot avoid the fact that the biblical proclamation of the resurrection is *good news* and that its reception makes an existential demand on us. I am in full agreement here with N. T. Wright, who explains that the person who claims that "Jesus of Nazareth was bodily raised from the dead" is committed to living in accordance with the "newly envisioned universe of discourse, imagination and action" that this claim entails.[1] The discourse of theology, and indeed of biblical studies, is profoundly shaped, for those who believe, by their acceptance of the news that God raised Jesus from the dead.

I wish to be clear from the outset: when I refer to the resurrection in the pages that follow, I am referring, as I think is undoubtedly the case for all the writers of the New Testament, to the bodily resurrection of Jesus. The reality they speak of requires that when a group of women went to the tomb of Jesus on Easter morning, they found that the tomb was empty. We must also be clear, however, that resurrection is not the same as resuscitation; it is not a "coming back" to the same form of bodily existence that preceded death, such as is reported to have occurred with Lazarus and with Jairus's daughter. It is, rather, a "going forward" to a transformed kind of bodily existence that is no longer subject to death. We will explore such matters more fully in the pages that follow.

Finally, some thanks are in order. Although I did not start out with this intent, some of the chapters of this book were delivered as the Trinity Lectures, a biannual series sponsored by Trinity Theological College, Singapore. The lectures would have been delivered much sooner had the COVID-19 pandemic not disrupted many plans for travel and scholarly collaboration around the world. Had they been, the critical engagement from the audience at Trinity would undoubtedly have had a constructive impact on the content of this book. I am no less grateful, however, for the invitation extended by the college to deliver the Trinity Lectures and for the engagement that the lectures made possible. The warm and generous hospitality extended to my wife, Jane, and me during our visit to Singapore and the stimulating theological conversation

---

1. See Wright, *Resurrection of the Son of God*, 714.

I enjoyed with the faculty of Trinity, the students, and others who attended the lectures is deeply appreciated. Anticipation of that engagement kept me always mindful, as I wrote these chapters, of my concern to communicate not just with the academy but also with the wider community of believers who likewise confess with joyful hearts that Jesus is risen.

I am grateful too for the opportunity to deliver the annual international lecture hosted by the Logos Institute at the University of St. Andrews in February 2020. The content of that lecture, titled "'Behold, I Am Making All Things New': Resurrection and New Creation," has found its way into this book in scattered form, though mostly in chapter 5. Again, the warm and generous hospitality shown by students and staff at St. Andrews is deeply appreciated, especially that of Alan Torrance, Andrew Torrance, Oliver Crisp, and the late Christoph Schwöbel. Various parts of the book have been tried out in the staff and postgraduate seminar of the Theology Programme at the University of Otago. My colleagues here at Otago and the vibrant community of postgraduate students are a constant source of joy and encouragement. They constitute together a community of theological scholarship that is enthusiastically interdisciplinary in its conception of theological scholarship and committed to serving both the academy and the church.

Bob Hosack at Baker Academic deserves special commendation for his patience and persistence in shepherding this book toward publication. He first expressed interest in it more than ten years ago, and he has been willing to accept my excuses along the way for not delivering it as soon as might have been hoped. I am deeply grateful for his patience and for his trust that it would eventually arrive on his desk in a form suitable for publication. His advice and support throughout have been invaluable.

Finally, I wish to mention again Alan Torrance, who extended the invitation to deliver the Logos Institute international lecture at St. Andrews in 2020. Alan was my teacher at Knox Theological Hall in Dunedin, New Zealand, where I first embarked upon formal theological study. He was also my doctoral supervisor at King's College in London. He has become a lifelong mentor, adviser, and friend. I am one of many students whom Alan has encouraged, inspired, and supported in their pursuit of theological study. His passion for the subject matter of theology, his own considerable gifts as a theologian, and his generous encouragement and praise, unworthy though I have been of it, have meant more to me than I can possibly express. It is with deep gratitude and admiration that I dedicate this book to him.

1

The Evangelical Witness

On the first day of the week following Jesus's crucifixion, so we are told, some women went to the tomb where the dead body of Jesus had been laid. The four Gospel writers offer mixed testimony as to who the women were and how many there were. The one figure who consistently appears in all four Gospels is Mary Magdalene. So let us follow her story as it is variously told across the four Gospels. We do not know much of Mary. She appears only once in the Gospel accounts of Jesus's public ministry. In Luke 8:1–2 she is identified as one of a group of women who "had been cured of evil spirits and infirmities" and who now traveled with Jesus and the "twelve" as he made his way "through cities and villages, proclaiming and bringing the good news of the kingdom of God." The proximity of this mention of Mary to the immediately preceding story of a "woman who was a sinner" bathing Jesus's feet with her tears and anointing them with ointment (Luke 7:36–50) led the Western (though not the Eastern) church to erroneously conflate Mary Magdalene with the woman who anointed Jesus and whose "sin" was widely regarded as prostitution.[1] Mary Magdalene's reputation suffered much in consequence, and she became in medieval imagination an archetype of "the loose woman"; a penitent sinner; and in some extreme renditions that persist in present-day fables like Dan Brown's *The Da Vinci Code*, the secret lover of Jesus himself and mother to his children.[2] None of this colorful rendering of Mary's identity

1. On which see Leyser, "Mary Magdalene," 416–17.
2. This history of (mis)representation is thoroughly examined in Haskins, *Mary Magdalen*.

is true, but it has left its mark nevertheless on the popular imagination. We will do well to stick to what the biblical narratives about her actually say.

Beyond the passing reference to her in Luke 8, Mary becomes prominent in the biblical narrative only when she is named as one of the women who had "followed Jesus from Galilee," had "provided for him," and was present at his crucifixion (Matt. 27:56; cf. Mark 15:40–41). John also names Mary Magdalene as one of the women who was present at the crucifixion but makes no mention of Mary or the other women having followed him from Galilee. Luke tells us that there were women present during Christ's passion who followed him as he made his way toward the place of crucifixion (Luke 23:27). These women are not named, but it is possible given the Markan and Matthean accounts that Mary was among them. Then in Luke 23:55 we learn that the women who had come with him from Galilee, still unnamed by Luke, followed Joseph of Arimathea to the tomb and saw how Jesus was laid. A series of further actions undertaken by these women is described by Luke, until finally in 24:10 he names three of the group as Mary Magdalene, Joanna, and Mary the mother of James.

Luke's report that the women saw the tomb where Jesus was laid is supported by Matthew (27:61) and by Mark (15:47), both of whom name Mary Magdalene as one of the two women who witnessed Jesus's burial, the other being "Mary mother of Joses," in Mark, and "the other Mary," in Matthew. The witnessing of the burial by these women is a detail omitted by John, but the Synoptic authors may have considered it an important detail in order to counter allegations that on Easter morning the women, now convinced that the tomb was empty, had gone to the wrong tomb. Perhaps at the time of John's writing that allegation was no longer circulating.

We have learned of Mary Magdalene thus far, largely on the basis of the Synoptic testimony, that she was among the women who had followed Jesus from Galilee and had provided for his needs, had been present at the crucifixion, and had seen where Jesus was buried. John, for his part, as noted above, offers confirmation that Mary was present at the crucifixion.

The Empty Tomb

We now follow Mary's story through to Easter morning, beginning with the Synoptic accounts. While there are many parallels in John's account, there is also some distinctive detail that we will consider further below. The Synoptics jointly testify that "when the Sabbath was over" (Matthew and Mark), on the first day of the week (Matthew, Mark, and Luke), Mary Magdalene with some other women went to the tomb.[3] Their intent in going, Mark tells us directly and Luke by inference, was to anoint Jesus's body with spices, as was the Jewish custom. Only Mark has the women pondering how they would gain access to the tomb, given that its entrance had been sealed with a large stone. When the women arrived, however, they discovered, according to Mark and Luke, that the stone had already been rolled away. In Matthew's account, there was an earthquake and the women saw an angel descend from heaven and roll the stone away. Mark and Luke are noncommittal at this point, but Matthew is wanting to stress, apparently, that there are features of the events he is narrating that cannot be explained in merely human terms. The earthquake has been invoked before in Scripture as a sign of divine presence (Exod. 19:18; Ps. 114:7), while the angel, having descended from heaven, is clearly a divine emissary. Matthew's insistence that the women saw the stone being rolled away is a detail coherent with his concern about the security of the tomb (see Matt. 27:64–66). Floyd Filson observes that in Matthew's account the grave was not opened until the women came, "so no one could have removed the body by stealth. [Jesus] must have risen and left before the tomb was opened."[4] Matthew's reference to the guards who had been stationed at the tomb precisely to prevent any such stealthy removal of the body (28:4) further bolsters his insistence that a surreptitious removal of the body could not have occurred.

Whatever the means by which the stone had been rolled away, the effect was that Mary and her companions were able to enter the tomb and see that it was empty. The empty tomb, attested in all four Gospels, does not in itself offer any explanation of what happened. The most natural explanation—that someone removed the body—is the one that, as we have seen, Matthew takes pains to discount (e.g., Matt. 28:6–17). But in John's Gospel, that is precisely the explanation that comes most readily to Mary's mind. Mary Magdalene comes to the tomb alone, in John's account, and upon discovering it empty, she runs to tell Simon Peter and the other disciple "whom Jesus loved" that "they have taken the Lord out of the tomb, and we do not know where they have laid him" (John 20:2).

3. In Luke, as already noted, the women were not named until later in the story.
4. Filson, *Gospel according to Matthew*, 301.

This is an interpretation of the empty tomb that lies wholly within the bounds of human comprehension. It was the most plausible conclusion to draw given what Mary knew, and what we know, of the everyday realm of historical occurrence. Despite Jesus having indicated, according to the Synoptic record, that he would suffer and be killed and on the third day be raised (Matt. 17:22; Mark 8:31; Luke 9:22), the prospect of resurrection seemed so far beyond the realm of possibility that neither at the time of Jesus uttering those words nor in the days immediately following his crucifixion was any such hope generated among those who followed him. It was a grieving Mary Magdalene, rather than a hopeful one, who went to the tomb with her companions at dawn, after the Sabbath, in order to complete the rites of burial and anoint Jesus's body with spices. That Jesus's body had disappeared could mean only that somebody had taken his corpse away. Faultless human logic could offer no other explanation.

Human logic and human estimations of the way things work in the realm of historical occurrence is constrained, understandably, by the cumulative record of human experience and by what the human mind can comprehend of everyday causal relations. This was the constraint insisted upon by Ernst Troeltsch, who formulated in the late nineteenth century a set of principles by which could be determined, so it was argued, the likelihood of a reported event having actually taken place. The first was the principle of analogy, according to which the probability of an event having happened is proportionate to its agreement with "normal, customary, or at least frequently attested happenings and conditions as we have experienced them."[5] In other words, our readiness to accept an account of something having happened—or in the case of Mary and the other women discovering the empty tomb, the explanation we offer for a particular state of affairs—is determined by our prior experience of how things work in the world. In order for us to find something believable it must be a repetition of or similar in kind to other things that we have experienced in the past. This Troeltschian principle is applied instinctively as we make our way in the world and helps us to distinguish fact from fantasy within reasonable margins of error and to guard against foolish gullibility. Yet this constraint, reasonably applied in most circumstances, can blind us to the possibility of anything radically new and unprecedented ever occurring. Our minds are programmed to expect the

5. Troeltsch, "Historical and Dogmatic Method in Theology," 11–32. The principle of analogy is described on pp. 13–14.

same sort of things happening again and again. Upon discovering the empty tomb, therefore, Mary Magdalene, according to John's account, can only imagine that someone has removed Jesus's body and laid it somewhere else. Such an explanation conforms to all that Mary has known of the world thus far.

However, human judgment is not infallible. Our capacity to discern the true nature of things is limited, and our judgments on many matters must be regarded as provisional—hence the oft-heard plea that we must approach the world with an open mind. Just as an open mind is recommended within the realms of art and of scientific inquiry, in case the objects of apprehension reveal aspects of themselves that are not anticipated, so too an open mind is required in biblical studies and in theology. The consideration of previously unimagined possibilities is often prompted, as Thomas Kuhn has explained, through the recognition of anomalies, through the mind's encounter with things that simply cannot be accommodated within our previous explanations of the world.[6] Such anomalies that defy customary modes of explanation demand a revolution in our thinking and new ways of understanding the world. The Copernican revolution through which human beings gradually came to terms with the counterintuitive and nonsensical[7] claim that the earth was not the stationary center of the solar system around which the sun and all the planets revolved, but is itself in motion hurtling around the sun at the rate of thirty kilometers per second, is offered by Kuhn as a classic example of a scientific revolution that required a radical transformation of human knowledge and understanding. It required a wholly new point of reference for our understanding of how the solar system works.

The New Testament offers us some helpful terminology for this radical transformation of our thinking. It uses the Greek word *metanoia*, variously translated as "conversion" or "repentance," but literally meaning "the transformation of one's mind." Such a transformation was about to begin for Mary and the other women who visited the tomb where Jesus was laid and found that it was empty. To suggest that the reality Mary and her companions came upon that morning at the tomb was an anomaly—in the Kuhnian sense

---

6. See Kuhn, *Structure of Scientific Revolutions*.

7. I use the term *nonsensical* here to indicate that the Copernican claim that the earth revolved around the sun contradicts regular sense experience. Our senses tell us quite plainly that the sun rises in the east and sets in the west while we remain firmly fixed in space. That we continue to speak of the sun rising and setting, even though we know better, reveals an enduring fondness for our own immediate perceptions.

of being something that could not be accommodated within the women's previous experience and understanding of the world—is true but also an understatement of considerable magnitude. The reality before them required an explanation that their common human experience of the world had not equipped them to provide.

The Angelic Announcement

The extraordinary nature of the news being conveyed required an extraordinary mode of disclosure. The Gospel writers here introduce the angels who reveal to the women the true nature of what has taken place. Mark's Gospel describes the messenger as "a young man, dressed in a white robe" (Mark 16:5). Lamar Williamson explains that "traditional designation of him as an angel (messenger) is quite appropriate, for the message he brings is the heart of this unit and the key to the entire Gospel."[8] Matthew describes "an angel of the Lord" whose "appearance was like lightning, and his clothing white as snow" (Matt. 28:2–3). Luke speaks of "two men in dazzling clothes" (Luke 24:4), later identified as angels (24:23), and John of "two angels in white" (John 20:12). This is not the place to develop an account of the ontological status of angels, but it is important to take note of Karl Barth's insistence that while we may be dealing here with "a particular form of history which by content and nature does not proceed according to ordinary analogies," the Bible presents the angels as an essential, though subsidiary, part of the story.[9] That the presence of the angels cannot be verified by the ordinary analogies of world history means, according to Barth, that they can be seen and grasped only imaginatively.[10] The angels are an instance of "the incommensurable reaching into the commensurable, of mystery [reaching] into the sphere of known possibilities."[11] What we can say with confidence, however, is that whenever the Bible speaks of angels, it is the message they bring, the *euangelion*, which is the central focus of attention. That will also be the focus of our attention then as we consider the role of the angels encountered at the empty tomb.

8. Williamson, *Mark*, 284.

9. See Karl Barth's discussion of angelology in *Church Dogmatics* III/3, 369–418. The quotation is taken from p. 374.

10. See Barth, *Church Dogmatics* III/3, 375.

11. Barth, *Church Dogmatics* III/3, 375.

In the Synoptic accounts, the angel (or angels in Luke) initially strike fear or alarm into the hearts of those present at the tomb. The consternation of the women upon discovering the empty tomb now turns to alarm as they become aware of the heavenly messenger. Mark's Gospel renders the angelic announcement as follows: "But he [the young man] said to them, 'Do not be alarmed; you are looking for Jesus of Nazareth, who was crucified. He has been raised; he is not here. Look, there is the place they laid him" (Mark 16:6). What is announced here changes the course of world history. It demands of those who hear and understand a reorientation of their hearts and minds. It radically transforms our understanding of the way the world works and prompts recognition of the fact that the world is a project established and governed by God, whose intent remains, as it has been from the beginning, that the creature should have life. The empty tomb and the risen Christ confirm once and for all that sin and death will not have the last word. The difference the resurrection makes will be the subject of the remaining chapters of this book. For now, however, let us continue our investigation of the story of Mary Magdalene and her companions who first bore witness to the news.

Mary and her companions have heard the angelic declaration that Jesus is not here; he has risen. But as we have noted, the women's prior experience of the world left them ill-equipped to comprehend the news. In each of the Synoptic accounts, therefore, the angelic messengers remind the women that Jesus himself had spoken of his rising from the dead. In Matthew and Mark it is just a glancing reference: "But the angel said to the women, 'Do not be afraid; I know that you are looking for Jesus who was crucified. He is not here; for he has been raised, *as he said*'" (Matt. 28:5–6, emphasis added). "But go, tell his disciples and Peter that he is going ahead of you to Galilee; there you will see him, *just as he told you*" (Mark 16:7, emphasis added). In Luke the reference to Jesus's prior teaching is more fulsome: "'Remember how he told you, while he was still in Galilee, that the Son of Man must be handed over to sinners, and be crucified, and on the third day rise again.' Then they remembered his words, and returning from the tomb, they told all this to the eleven and to all the rest" (Luke 24:6–9). Jesus said to them, according to Mark's report, "But after I am raised up, I will go before you to Galilee" (Mark 14:28).

There had been other times too when Jesus had spoken of his resurrection, but, as Mary Healy observes, the import of "Jesus' prophecy of his resurrection ([Mark] 8:31; 9:9, 31; 10:34) had completely eluded their grasp, just as it had for the male disciples."[12] Indeed, on two of the occasions when Jesus spoke of his being raised up after his death, the incomprehension of those listening to Jesus is explicitly remarked on by the Gospel writer. On the first occasion when Jesus spoke of his death and resurrection, "Peter took him aside and began to rebuke him" (Mark 8:32), while on a subsequent occasion Mark reports that "they did not understand what [Jesus] was saying and were afraid to ask him" (9:32). The same predictions and comparable reactions, including Peter's rebuke, appear also in the Gospel of Matthew (16:21; 17:23; 20:19; 26:32).

Consistent with Matthew's and Mark's reports, in Luke's Gospel too the words in question had met with silence or incomprehension when they were first uttered by Jesus. There are two predictions in Luke's Gospel of Jesus being raised from death. The first occurs in 9:21–22: "He sternly ordered and commanded them not to tell anyone, saying, 'The Son of Man must undergo great suffering, and be rejected by the elders, chief priests, and scribes, and be killed, and on the third day be raised.'" The audience on this occasion is "only the disciples" (9:18), and no response is recorded. It is worth noting here that the episode at the tomb assumes that the women, and not just "the twelve," were among the disciples who had been told by Jesus that he would suffer and die and on the third day be raised. As Fred Craddock points out, "This information places the women in the inner circle of disciples with whom such a prediction had been shared."[13]

The second occasion of Jesus sharing such news is, by contrast, confined to just the twelve: "Then he took the twelve aside and said to them, 'See, we are going up to Jerusalem, and everything that is written about the Son of Man by the prophets will be accomplished. For he will be handed over to the Gentiles; and he will be mocked and insulted and spat upon. After they have flogged him, they will kill him, and on the third day he will rise again'" (Luke 18:31–33). Here the reaction of the disciples is recorded: "But they understood nothing about all these things; in fact, what he said was hidden from them, and they did not grasp what was said" (18:34).[14] The incapacity to comprehend continues when in Luke's account the women return from the

---

12. Healy, *Gospel of Mark*, 328.

13. Craddock, *Luke*, 282. Craddock observes further that in contrast with Mark and Matthew, the women are not instructed to go and tell the disciples: "The women are not errand runners for the disciples; they are disciples" (283).

14. The incomprehension here pertains not just to the resurrection but also to Jesus's predictions of his suffering and death (see Luke 9:44–45).

tomb and tell the apostles of what they had seen and heard. Luke reports, "But these words seemed to them an idle tale, and they [the apostles] did not believe them" (24:11). It is misleading to assign, as some commentators have done, a naive credulity to the early Christians on the basis of their allegedly primitive worldview. The Gospel narratives make clear that the news of the resurrection was no less astounding for them than it is for us. As Eduard Schweizer remarks, "In the entire tradition, even in the accounts of Jesus' appearances to the disciples, we can sense that the truth of Jesus' resurrection had to prevail against men [sic] who were very critical and who did not anticipate that such a thing would ever occur."[15]

What then does prompt people to recognize the truth that Jesus has been raised from the dead? How do the first witnesses to the resurrection come to believe what common sense deems impossible? The first hint that the women who visited Jesus's tomb had taken a step toward comprehension and belief comes with their reaction to the angel's reminder, in Luke's account, of what Jesus had said to them while they were with him in Galilee: "Then they remembered his words" (Luke 24:8). The phrase is reminiscent of Luke's nativity narrative, in which Jesus's mother, Mary, "treasured all these words and pondered them in her heart" (2:19). Joel Green picks up a similar resonance: "'To remember' consists of more than cognitive evocation. 'To remember' includes as well the nuance of understanding or insight, and is the threshold of response apropos what is recalled."[16] The perplexity and the fear experienced moments earlier by the women is giving way now to a dawning recognition of what has taken place. That recognition, furthermore, fires within them a compulsion to tell all this to the eleven and to the rest (24:9). It is at this point that Luke sees fit to name the women: "Now it was Mary Magdalene, Joanna, Mary the mother of James, and the other women with them who told this to the apostles" (24:10). The women assume preeminence now as the first witnesses, the first proclaimers of the news delivered by the angels that Jesus had been raised.

The first hint in Matthew's Gospel that the women are beginning to understand comes again in response to the angel's words. "So they left the tomb quickly with fear and great joy, and ran to tell his disciples" (Matt. 28:8). The fear signifies, no doubt, that something profoundly out of the ordinary has happened, while the joy surely indicates that the women had begun to

15. Schweizer, *Good News according to Mark*, 373.
16. Green, *Gospel of Luke*, 838.

believe that the angelic announcement of Jesus's resurrection could actually be true. What happens next abundantly confirms their joyous inkling: "Suddenly Jesus met them and said, 'Greetings!' And they came to him, took hold of his feet, and worshipped him. Then Jesus said to them, 'Do not be afraid; go and tell my brothers to go to Galilee; there they will see me'" (28:9–10).[17] Encounter with the risen Christ is the decisive turning point and generator of belief. The cumulative evidence of the empty tomb and the angelic testimony had begun to open the women's minds to the unimaginable possibility of the resurrection, but it was the encounter with Jesus himself that removed any lingering doubt. This pattern of cognitive transformation brought about through encounter with the risen Christ repeats itself, as we will see further below, in each of the episodes recorded by Luke of the disciples coming to believe. (We will see this same pattern in John as well.)

Go and Tell

We have come to the point in the Synoptic accounts where, some differences in detail notwithstanding, Mary Magdalene and her companions have discovered that the tomb where Christ's body had been laid is empty; they have heard the angelic announcement that Jesus has been raised, and according to Mark and Matthew, they have been instructed by the angel to go and tell the other disciples. What happens next? Here the Synoptic accounts begin to diverge—not in their central testimony that the tomb was empty and that Christ had been raised but, rather, in their reports of what then transpired as the first witnesses left the tomb with news of the resurrection burning in their hearts.

Let's start with Matthew. In Matthew's account, as we have seen, the women are instructed by the angel to "go quickly and tell the disciples" (Matt. 28:7). They are to tell the disciples that Jesus has been raised and that the disciples will see him in Galilee. That instruction is repeated by Jesus himself when the women encounter him on their way back into Jerusalem: "Go and tell my brothers to go to Galilee; there they will see me" (28:10). Rather than continuing immediately with the women's story, however, Matthew's Gos-

---

17. Margaret Davies suggests that "the gesture of holding his feet indicates that the women were determined to prevent Jesus' departure (compare the woman's holding Elisha's feet, 2 Kgs 4.27, and see John 20.17). Perhaps, therefore, 'they took hold of his feet' should not be taken literally but as an idiomatic expression of their desire to keep him with them." Davies, *Matthew*, 234.

pel then returns our attention to the guards who were at the tomb and who "shook and became like dead men" at the appearance of the angel (28:4). By now, apparently, they have revived and some of them went into the city and told the chief priests everything that had happened. Upon hearing the news, the priests "devised a plan to give a large sum of money to the soldiers, telling them, 'You must say "His disciples came by night and stole him away while we were asleep." If this comes to the governor's ears, we will satisfy him and keep you out of trouble.' So they took the money and did as they were directed" (28:12–15).

W. D. Davies and Dale C. Allison assert that the purpose of Matthew's report about the guards is "transparently apologetical."[18] The apologetic character is evident enough, but differing accounts can be offered of Matthew's apologetic purpose. We note first that the report of the guards is unique to Matthew. His inclusion of the episode indicates, as Matthew himself claims (Matt. 28:15), that he was seeking to counter a story that was in circulation at the time that the Gospel was written—namely, that the body of Jesus had been removed from the grave by the disciples. As R. T. France observes, precisely because of its currency in Jewish circles, "as a countermeasure to Christian preaching of Jesus' resurrection, . . . it was important for Christians to set the record straight."[19]

The proposition that the disciples stole the body is unlikely for reasons well documented elsewhere,[20] but given the story's apparent acceptance by some, Matthew is concerned to assure his own audience that it has no credibility. The story exists, he asserts, because the chief priests wanted to suppress any notion that Jesus had been raised from the dead and so bribed the guards to offer an alternative explanation of the empty tomb. Be that as it may, there are two points of interest for my purposes. First, the reality of the empty tomb itself was apparently not in dispute—otherwise no explanation to counter the

18. Davies and Allison, *Gospel according to St. Matthew*, 3:670.

19. France, *Gospel of Matthew*, 1104. France cites Justin, who claims that the story of the grave robbery was still being propagated in the middle of the second century. France, *Gospel of Matthew*, 1093.

20. These reasons include the following: (1) The disciples' subsequent and costly proclamation of the resurrection is unlikely to have been sustained as it was if the disciples themselves knew that the proclamation was false. (2) The disciples had fled in fear from Jesus's cross, and from the authorities presumably, and would have been unlikely to muster the courage to commit what was a capital offense. (3) It is improbable that the disciples would have been able to roll away a heavy stone from the entrance of the tomb and then make off with the body of Jesus without waking the guards. For further discussion, see Keener, *Gospel of Matthew*, 713–14.

belief that Jesus had been raised from the tomb would be necessary. Second, the empty tomb by itself permits a variety of plausible explanations. It is, in my view, an essential component of what it means to say that Jesus has been raised from the dead, but, as has already been suggested above, the fact of the empty tomb does not by itself prove that Jesus has been raised.

Ulrich Luz, who thinks that Matthew's story about the guards is a "narrative fiction largely created by the evangelist Matthew,"[21] proposes that Matthew may have constructed the story in order to draw attention to the contrasting reactions of faith and unbelief. On the one hand, the women run to tell the disciples that Jesus has risen; on the other hand, at the very same time different forces are at work to suppress belief in the resurrection. "The simultaneity of the events emphasizes their polarity; while the women obey the command of the angel and Jesus and 'announce' their message to the disciples, the guards 'announce' to their 'chiefs' what has happened."[22]

We need not enter the debate here about the historical provenance of the guards' report to the chief priests,[23] but Luz rightly identifies a recurring contrast in Matthew's Gospel between faith and the conspiracies of unbelief.[24] The same contrasting response is evident at the beginning of the Gospel, where the faith of the magi visiting the infant Jesus is contrasted with the conspiratorial scheming of King Herod (Matt. 2:1–18). Matthew makes clear that from his birth through to his death and resurrection Jesus represents a threat to the existing order. We will explore further in subsequent chapters why that is so. Here, however, we simply note that the conspiratorial forces of religious and political power recognize the threat and do all that they can to suppress the news that Mary Magdalene and her companions bear with them from the empty tomb.

The telling of this news to the disciples is not actually reported in Matthew's Gospel. Matthew records that the women ran to tell the disciples, but their errand is interrupted by their encounter with Jesus himself, following which Matthew's narratival attention is diverted to the episode with the guards. When again he takes up the story of belief in the resurrection, the focus has shifted to Galilee and to the eleven disciples who encounter Jesus there

---

21. Luz, *Matthew 21–28*, 609.
22. Luz, *Matthew 21–28*, 609.
23. For a contrary view to that of Luz, see Wright, *Resurrection of the Son of God*, 636–40.
24. R. T. France likewise highlights the contrast between the respective announcements of the women and the guards: "The women have a message of hope and victory for the disciples, the guards one of confusion and failure for the priests." France, *Gospel of Matthew*, 1104.

just as Jesus had directed them. By comparison with the women's discovery that Jesus had been raised from the dead, the disciples' own engagement with the news is somewhat fleeting. Matthew notes only that the eleven saw and worshiped Jesus, though some doubted, but his real interest lies not in the disciples' coming to believe, nor in anything comparable to the turmoil of fear and joy that accompanied the women's encounter with the reality of Jesus's resurrection, but rather in the commission given to the disciples: "And Jesus came and said to them, 'All authority in heaven and on earth has been given to me. Go therefore and make disciples of all nations, baptizing them in the name of the Father and of the Son and of the Holy Spirit, and teaching them to obey everything that I have commanded you. And remember, I am with you always, to the end of the age'" (Matt. 28:18–20). The angelic commission to the women, "Go quickly and tell" (28:7), is now extended by Jesus's own commission: "Go therefore and make disciples of all nations" (28:19). That Jesus has risen is news that must be shared, for it is news that establishes a new order, a new way of being in the world that is entered into through baptism, characterized by obedience to all that Jesus has commanded, and sustained by the promise of his presence. We will explore further this new way of being in the chapters that follow.

We turn first, however, to Luke's report of what happens after the women's discovery of the empty tomb and their encounter with the angels. We have already noted that Luke has the women returning from the tomb to tell the eleven and "all the rest" all that they had experienced. It is clear, however, that the women's testimony falls on "cynical and unbelieving ears."[25] It is possible, as many commentators propose, that the testimony was met with skepticism because of "the fact that those doing the reporting are women in a world biased against the admissibility of women as witnesses,"[26] but we must also take account of the prima facie implausibility of what the women had to say and, more importantly, of the consistent message of the New Testament that discernment of the truth concerning Jesus is a gift bestowed through divine action. Human witness matters; to put it in terms proposed by Søren Kierkegaard, human witness may well become the occasion through which one may learn the truth, but faith—the condition for learning the truth—is ultimately given by God.[27] It is no surprise, therefore, that the women's testimony is not

---

25. Green, *Gospel of Luke*, 839. For a contrary view, see Craddock, *Luke*, 283.
26. Green, *Gospel of Luke*, 840.
27. See Kierkegaard, *Philosophical Fragments*, 14–15 and passim.

immediately accepted by those with whom it is shared. As Craddock observes, "Their faith waits on a confirming experience of the risen Christ."[28]

The word ἔλεγον used at Luke 24:10 is the imperfect form of the verb λέγω ("to tell"), which indicates that in the face of skepticism the women go on telling. Joseph Fitzmyer emphasizes the point by translating the verb as "kept repeating."[29] As I have noted elsewhere,

> One can well imagine that the news was greeted with disbelief and so had to be repeated again and again. We can imagine too that every last detail was inquired after and clarified through incessant questioning. Disbelief is the most natural immediate reaction. What the women are saying is very much out of the ordinary. It is something much harder to swallow than the relatively inoffensive suggestion that Jesus' influence will somehow carry on. Thus in verse 11 we read that the words of the women seemed to the [apostles] to be an idle tale, and they did not believe them. Luke makes no attempt to disguise the fact that what he is trying to tell us is very hard to believe.[30]

Peter, ever ready to take matters into his own hands, decides to go to the tomb to see for himself what has been reported by the women. Upon arriving at the tomb, he looks inside and sees the linen cloths by themselves. Just as was the case for the women, however, the tomb emptied of Jesus's body does not by itself confirm that Jesus has been raised from the dead. Peter returns home "amazed at what had happened" (Luke 24:10), but it is not clear yet that he knows what to make of it.

The resurrection of Jesus from the dead is an event that takes place in the terrain of human history; it leaves traces in the fabric of time and space. The grave clothes in which his dead body was wrapped are left as a pile of folded linen. The reality of the empty tomb could be confirmed by those who went to visit. Indeed, if we are to believe that Matthew's story of the guards was not simply fabricated for polemical purposes, those fearful of what the empty tomb could mean hasten to promulgate a story that would quash the spreading news that Jesus had been raised from the dead. Historical inquiry can assess the plausibility or otherwise of these claimed alterations to the world. Those like Peter who were purportedly present at the time could verify

---

28. Craddock, *Luke*, 283.
29. Fitzmyer, *Gospel according to Luke X–XXIV*, 1532.
30. Rae, *History and Hermeneutics*, 82.

them if they chose to, but again, these pieces of evidence, should they be confirmed, do not by themselves prove that Jesus has been raised. Peter, we are told, was amazed by what he discovered at the tomb, but the text does not say that he knew what to make of it or that he believed. Just as Mary Magdalene and her companions required divine assistance in the form of angelic emissaries to understand what had taken place, so too, Luke's Gospel makes clear, the disciples came to understand through encounter with the risen Christ himself.

Encounter with the Lord

There follows then in Luke's Gospel the story of a journey to Emmaus made by two of the group who had heard the testimony of the women. As they were walking, a stranger encountered them and asked what they were discussing. The travelers explained all that had taken place in Jerusalem during the past few days right up to the story of the women returning from the tomb and astounding them with news that Jesus was alive. Those who told this tale did not recognize that it was Jesus who had joined them on the road. Luke tells us that "their eyes were kept from recognizing him" (Luke 24:16). They were not equipped conceptually, it seems, to countenance the possibility that Jesus had been raised from the dead, and their perceptions readily complied with what they considered to be possible.[31] Jesus, however, opened up for them an entirely different conceptual world informed by the prophets and by "the things about himself in all the scriptures" (24:27). It is the story of God's long involvement with Israel, of the promised Messiah, of eschatological hope, and of redemptive suffering, that is the framework within which the two disciples and all who follow after them may begin to make sense of what had been discovered at the empty tomb. Jesus reminded the travelers of that conceptual framework and so provided them with the hermeneutical tools to interpret what had taken place. Yet it was not until the travelers rested from their journey and shared a meal with Jesus that the decisive moment of recognition took place: "When he was at the table with them, he took bread, blessed and broke it, and gave it to them. Then their eyes were opened, and they recognized him; and he vanished from their sight. They said to each

---

31. Francis Watson observes that "as yet . . . there was no framework available within which the message of Jesus' resurrection would make sense." Watson, *Text, Church and World*, 290.

other, 'Were not our hearts burning within us while he was talking to us on the road, while he was opening the scriptures to us?'" (24:30–32).

Let us gather up at this point the evidence we have concerning how the first witnesses to the resurrection came to believe. The empty tomb is an important piece of evidence, but, as we have noted, it does not by itself confirm that Jesus has been raised from the dead. For the women at the tomb, it was the guidance of the angels that set them on the path to belief. Then we come to the eleven and all the rest who heard the women's testimony. The testimony gave them much food for thought, certainly, but there is no indication that any of those who heard, including the two who subsequently made their way to Emmaus, had yet come to believe. Peter set off for the tomb in order to gather such evidence as an eyewitness—or subsequent historian—might discover, but even upon finding it, Peter offers no consequent confession of belief. The travelers to Emmaus were reminded of the scriptural framework within which the suffering of Jesus and his resurrection are to be understood, but none of these contributing factors seem to be sufficient conditions for belief in Christ. What appears to be the essential condition is the divine act of self-disclosure, either through the angels or through direct encounter with the risen Christ. Even then, however, recognition and belief are not immediate. As with the travelers to Emmaus, so also with the disciples back in Jerusalem to whom Jesus subsequently appeared: it took time and further explanation of the Scriptures by Jesus himself before their minds were opened (Luke 24:45) to the astonishing reality of Jesus's resurrection from the dead. It remains true in our own time and place, I suggest, that historical inquiry, the witness of others, and study of the Scriptures may become the *occasion* for belief, but the necessary *condition* for the transformation of hearts and minds is ultimately the revelatory work of God.

The Markan Ending

We have explored the accounts in Matthew and in Luke, but we must attend as well to Mark's Gospel, which tells of a different outcome, at least initially, following the women's encounter with the angel. When we look back at the Gospel of Mark, upon which both Matthew and Luke draw, we find broad agreement about what happened when the women visited Jesus's tomb on that first Easter morning. They find the tomb empty but are encountered by an angel who tells them not to be alarmed. "[Jesus] has been raised," the angel says, "he is not here" (Mark 16:6). Next comes the instruction, much like that found in Matthew: "But go, tell his disciples and Peter that he is going ahead of you to Galilee; there you will see him, just as he told you" (16:7). But then comes a striking departure from the accounts offered in the other three Gospels. According to Mark, the women "fled from the tomb, for terror and amazement had seized them; and they said nothing to anyone, for they were afraid" (16:8).

Since the latter half of the nineteenth century, there has been widespread agreement among biblical scholars that Mark's Gospel breaks off at this point. The two endings appended in modern translations—a shorter ending, tacked on to the end of 16:8, and a longer ending, found in 16:9–20—are clearly additions, so it has been argued,[32] that do not come from the original author's hand. These "additional" verses do not appear in Codex Vaticanus or Codex Sinaiticus—which, dating from the fourth century, are the oldest complete (Sinaiticus) and near complete (Vaticanus) extant manuscripts of the New Testament. It is commonly argued, in addition, that the awkwardness of the transition from verse 8 to verse 9 and the distinctive literary features of verses 9–20 clearly indicate that the so-called longer ending is not original to Mark. The question then discussed is whether Mark intended to end his Gospel at verse 8, intended to add more but never did, or did write more but what was written was later lost.[33]

This is not the place to explore the intricacies of the debate concerning Mark's ending. It is sufficient for my purposes to note the agreement across all four Gospels that Jesus's tomb was found to be empty by Mary Magdalene and some other women, and that the news that Jesus had been raised from the dead was conveyed to the women by a messenger or messengers. We may note, further, that although Mark reports that the women "said nothing to anyone, for they were afraid" (16:8), their initial silence must have been short-lived, for otherwise the evangelists, including Mark himself, would never have learned of the women's experience at the tomb. And another detail of Mark's account also indicates that the women's (initial) silence does not mean that the news of Jesus's resurrection will spread no further. The angel says to the

32. This assumption is widespread, but for an extended defense of the claim see Kelhoffer, *Miracle and Mission*; and Williams, "Bringing Method to the Madness," 397–418.

33. There have been some recent attempts to argue for the authenticity of the longer ending. See, e.g., Lunn, *Original Ending of Mark*. But this remains a minority view.

women, "Tell his disciples and Peter that he is going ahead of you to Galilee; there you will see him, just as he told you" (Mark 16:7; see also 14:28). Mark is aware of further appearances of the risen Christ, even though his Gospel, in the truncated form that has come down to us, offers no report of those further appearances. Even in this form, however, Mark leaves us with a profound theological challenge: "He is going ahead of you . . . ; there you will see him" (16:7). It is an invitation to discipleship, an invitation to set out on the journey of faith, trusting in the promise that as we do so, we will encounter the risen Lord.

Why Are You Weeping?

We return finally to John's Gospel in order to examine the differences between John's rendering of that first Easter morning and the reports offered by Matthew, Mark, and Luke. Of particular interest is the even greater prominence given by John to the experience of Mary Magdalene. In contrast with the Synoptics, John records two visits to the tomb by Mary. There is no mention in John of other women accompanying her. Mary goes to the tomb on the first day of the week, while it is still dark. Her first visit is very brief. Upon discovering that the stone covering the entrance to the tomb had been rolled away, Mary runs to tell Simon Peter and "the other disciple, the one whom Jesus loved" (John 20:2).[34] Her explanation indicates that she had also ascertained that the tomb was empty: "They have taken the Lord out of the tomb and we do not know where they have laid him" (20:2). The first person plural verb (οὐκ οἴδαμεν, "we do not know") may indicate that Mary had not gone to the tomb alone, but John's interest is clearly focused here, and in what follows, on Mary's experience. Perhaps in order to provide some further verification of the reality of the empty tomb,[35] however, John tells of Peter and the beloved disciple running to the tomb and also finding it empty save for the linen cloths in which Jesus's body had been shrouded. Their reaction to the disappearance of Jesus's body is confusingly portrayed by John. Peter entered the tomb

---

34. There are six passages in John's Gospel that refer to "the disciple whom Jesus loved." In 21:24 (referring back to v. 20) we are told that this beloved disciple is the one whose testimony the Gospel of John records. For a brief discussion of who the "beloved disciple" may have been, see Brown, *John I–XII*, xcii–xcviii. A more extensive survey is offered by James Charlesworth in *Beloved Disciple*.

35. This possibility is espoused by Charlesworth, for example, in *Beloved Disciple*, 97–98.

first followed by "the other disciple" (20:4). The latter, John says, "saw and believed" (20:8)—a recurring theme in John. But immediately thereafter we are told, "for as yet they did not understand the scripture, that he must rise from the dead" (20:9). The conjunction of these two claims is awkward, for the pronoun *they* refers presumably to the beloved disciple along with Peter. Peter and the beloved disciple are the only two proximate subjects. Here I merely note the ambiguity concerning what was believed by the beloved disciple and what had yet to be understood, and by whom. The ambiguity remains unresolved.

In John's treatment of Mary Magdalene, however, ambiguity becomes a feature of the story that resolves into an unmistakable disclosure of the risen Lord. Mary remains in the background as Peter and the other disciple run to see the tomb, but when John turns our attention again to Mary, we find her weeping outside the tomb (John 20:11). Two angels then appear to Mary and ask her why she is weeping. As previously noted, Mary responds, "They have taken away my Lord, and I do not know where they have laid him" (20:13). It is at this point that John's story takes a turn not found in the Synoptic Gospels. Mary turns and sees Jesus standing there, but she does not recognize him. Instead, she mistakes him for the gardener. Jesus too poses the question: "Woman, why are you weeping? Whom are you looking for?" (20:15). Mary continues to believe at this point that the body of Jesus has been removed from the grave, and she says to the "gardener," "Sir, if you have carried him away, tell me where you have laid him, and I will take him away" (20:15). There is a certain poignancy in Mary's supposition that Jesus is the gardener. At one level, of course, she is mistaken. She has failed to recognize her Lord. But given John's concern throughout his Gospel to portray Jesus as the one who ushers in the new creation, restores its fruitfulness, and truly tends the earth as humanity was commissioned to do (Gen. 2:15), his identification as the gardener here is entirely apposite. We will return to this point in subsequent chapters.

Meanwhile, however, we have come to the point of dramatic transformation for Mary. In answer to her forlorn plea, Jesus simply says "Mary!" (John 20:16). He calls her by name, and with that word of personal address Mary sees the truth. She turns and says to Jesus in Aramaic, "Rabbouni!," which means Teacher (20:16). Carla Ricci describes the moment well: "Mary, after the uncontainable sorrow of losing, is now completely filled with the joy of finding what she sought."[36]

---

36. Ricci, *Mary Magdalene and Many Others*, 143.

It is important to draw attention once more to the way in which recognition of the risen Christ comes about. John's Gospel is not an outlier here. Recognition that Jesus has been raised from the dead takes place across all four Gospels, without any clear exception, in the moment when Jesus makes himself known.[37] Recognition of the truth takes place through personal encounter with the risen Lord. The empty tomb is an indispensable condition of the appearance of Jesus in person. But as I have stressed earlier, the empty tomb by itself does not generate faith. Nor, as it turns out, do reports from others that they have seen the risen Lord. Thomas's skepticism in the face of his fellow disciples' testimony confirms the point, as does the disbelief still evident in the minds of the two disciples who pondered the women's testimony as they walked the road to Emmaus. The testimony of others may become the occasion through which faith is generated, as has been the case many times since, but these early reports suggest that recognition of Jesus's resurrection from the dead depends on personal encounter with Christ himself.[38] That is indeed the pattern repeatedly seen in the subsequent appearances of Jesus to the other disciples as reported in Matthew, Luke, and John, and briefly noted in the "longer ending" to Mark's Gospel (16:9–20).

After Mary Magdalene's moment of recognition, Jesus commissions her: "'Go to my brothers and say to them, "I am ascending to my Father and your Father, to my God and your God."' Mary Magdalene went and announced to the disciples, 'I have seen the Lord'; and she told them that he had said these things to her" (John 20:17–18).

Why have I focused on Mary Magdalene's participation in this story? It is because she is the first consistently named witness to the most momentous event in all human history, and the first who was commissioned by Jesus to bear witness to this news. She is, as Ann Graham Brock has made clear, the very first apostle.[39] Befitting this status, there is evidence in extracanonical

---

37. The ambiguity surrounding the "belief" of the beloved disciple in John 20:8–9 renders his experience unconvincing as a contrary example. It is not clear what he believed; John immediately points out "they did not yet understand"; the other disciple's return home after visiting the tomb is a rather anticlimactic sequel to the discovery that Jesus had risen; and Peter's companion who visited the tomb is presumably among the collection of fearful disciples who gathered behind locked doors that evening, apparently unsure about what to make of the events of the day.

38. We may properly claim on the basis of Jesus's words reported elsewhere in John's Gospel that it is the Spirit who draws people into communion with Christ and who guides the believer to the truth (John 16:13).

39. See Brock, *Mary Magdalene, The First Apostle*.

sources to indicate that Mary went on to play a leading role in the early church. In the second-century Gospel of Mary, for instance, we find Mary consoling the disciples after Jesus's ascension. Peter initially invites Mary to say more about what she remembers of Jesus, but when Peter later resists Mary's testimony, Levi admonishes him: "Peter, you are always angry. Now look, you are treating this woman as you would treat an enemy. If the Lord has made her worthy, who are you to reject her? Certainly the Lord knows her very well. Because he loved her more than us."[40]

Was it chauvinism that prompted Peter's resistance to Mary's words, or jealousy, or perhaps a combination of both? We may speculate. The resistance to Mary's testimony has persisted down through the ages, however, especially because her proclamation that Christ has risen calls for a radical transformation of our hearts and minds and opens up a wholly new understanding of the nature of reality itself. The required transformation is so radical and so thoroughgoing that it remains a work in progress, even for those of us who say we believe.

40. Quoted in Ricci, *Mary Magdalene and Many Others*, 147.

2

Promise Fulfilled

Then he said to them, "Oh, how foolish you are, and how slow of heart to believe all that the prophets have declared! Was it not necessary that the Messiah should suffer these things and then enter into his glory?" Then beginning with Moses and all the prophets, he interpreted to them the things about himself in all the scriptures.

—Luke 24:25–27

These words are spoken by Jesus to Cleopas and another, unnamed, disciple—who were journeying from Jerusalem to Emmaus on that first Easter day. The two disciples had heard the women's testimony that Jesus's tomb was empty and that angels had appeared to them and had declared that Jesus had been raised. They were aware that others had gone to the tomb and had confirmed that it was empty of Jesus's body (Luke 24:22–24). Yet they were despondent. They had heard the testimony, but they did not yet believe that Jesus had been raised from the dead.

As the two disciples journeyed toward Emmaus, discussing as they went all that had happened in Jerusalem, they were joined on the road by the risen Lord himself. As Luke puts it, however, "their eyes were kept from recognizing him" (Luke 24:16). Immanuel Kant has taught us that percepts without concepts are blind.[1] The evidence of our sense experience, in other words, makes no sense unless we have the conceptual resources to interpret that which lies before our eyes. The undeveloped and unprepared conceptual resources of the two disciples were not up to the task of recognizing the presence of the risen Christ, whom they knew to have been crucified and laid in a tomb just three days earlier. In their minds, the hope that Jesus "was the one to redeem Israel" (24:21) had come to naught. It had been crushed by Jesus's death. Jesus's rebuke—"Oh, how foolish you are, and how slow of heart to believe all that the prophets have declared!"—indicates, however, that the conceptual resources needed to comprehend "all these things that had happened" (24:14) are at hand. They are to be found in the record of God's dealings with Israel. And so Luke tells us, "beginning with Moses and all the prophets," Jesus proceeded to "interpret to them the things about himself in all the scriptures" (24:27).

That Israel's story provides the conceptual framework for comprehending what has taken place was emphasized again when, a short time later, Jesus appeared "to the eleven and their companions," now reunited with the two disciples who had encountered Jesus on the road to Emmaus. "Then he said to them, 'These are my words that I spoke to you while I was still with you—that everything written about me in the law of Moses, the prophets, and the psalms must be fulfilled.' Then he opened their minds to understand the scriptures, and he said to them, 'Thus it is written, that the Messiah is to suffer and to rise from the dead on the third day, and that repentance and forgiveness of sins is to be proclaimed in his name to all nations, beginning from Jerusalem. You are witnesses of these things'" (Luke 24:44–48).

Interpreting the Scriptures

There is no proof text from the Scriptures in which we find written precisely what Jesus says here. Luke may echo Isaiah 53, for example, or Deuteronomy 18:18, or Hosea 6:2, but as David Tiede points out, "Luke does not seem to be groping for a 'proof text' here"; the point, rather, is that "the risen Messiah undertakes a reinterpretation of **all the scriptures**."[2] Or as Arthur Just Jr. puts it, "Luke's method is to portray Jesus as the final consummation of *the*

---

1. In the original German, Kant wrote "Anschauung ohne Begriffe sind blind." Kant, *Kritik der reinen Vernunft*, B 75.
2. Tiede, *Luke*, 436. Emphasis original.

pattern set by Moses, the prophets and the psalmists."[3] Christopher Seitz's commentary on the Pauline and creedal claim that Jesus "was raised in accordance with the scriptures" (1 Cor. 15:4) is equally applicable here:

> This accordance is not about scattered proof texts, but about a much broader skein of convictions. In a word, these involve God: the agency of God, the relationship of God to Jesus, and the present life of Jesus in relationship to the Father until the Second Coming. "In accordance with the scriptures" means: related to claims about God and God's promises as presented in the Old Testament scriptures—not to individual proof texts about the details of Jesus' death, burial, and resurrection. To speak of God raising Jesus is to ask how such raising fits into a larger scriptural depiction of God's plans with the world.[4]

Tiede further observes that Jesus's scriptural explanation of all that has gone on is the "beginning of a kind of 'messianic exegesis,' or post-Easter reading of the Scriptures."[5] Such exegesis is indeed prevalent in the Gospels themselves and throughout the New Testament. The Hebrew Scriptures are read in the light of the resurrection and provide in turn the conceptual and narrative framework within which the early church sought to make sense of what had taken place among them through the life, death, and resurrection of Jesus. Frank Crüsemann aptly observes that "the encounter with the resurrected Christ evokes a faith that can then be, and surely must be, subsequently identified with the faith of Israel as it is witnessed to in the Scriptures."[6]

The four Gospels provide abundant evidence of the early Christian community applying the framework of the Hebrew Scriptures to their interpretation of who Jesus is and the role he plays in taking forward and bringing to fulfillment the promise that God had declared to Israel. Matthew, for example, begins his Gospel by immediately linking Jesus's story to Israel: "An account of the genealogy of Jesus the Messiah, the son of David, the son of Abraham" (Matt. 1:1). Mark likewise begins with immediate reference to Israel's story: "The beginning of the good news of Jesus Christ, the Son of God. As it is written in the prophet Isaiah, 'See, I am sending my messenger ahead of you . . .'" (Mark 1:1–2). Luke's Gospel conforms to the same pattern but offers a more gradual disclosure of Jesus's relationship with Israel's story. Luke sets

---

3. Just, *Luke 9:51–24:53*, 1022. Emphasis original.
4. Seitz, *Word without End*, 55.
5. Tiede, *Luke*, 436.
6. Crüsemann, "Scripture and Resurrection," 90.

the story of Jesus's birth within the framework of Israel's temple tradition, beginning with the story of Zechariah, a faithful temple priest, and his wife, Elizabeth, an equally faithful participant in Israel's covenant with the Lord (Luke 1:5–6). He then continues with Zechariah's prophecy:

> Blessed be the Lord God of Israel,
>   for he has looked favorably on his people and redeemed them.
> He has raised up a mighty savior for us
>   in the house of his servant David,
> as he spoke through the mouth of his holy prophets from of old.
>
> (Luke 1:68–70)

Finally, John's Gospel begins with words that deliberately echo the opening words of Israel's Scriptures: "In the beginning was the Word, and the Word was with God" (John 1:1; cf. Gen. 1:1).

Creation Renewed

The evangelists' shared conviction that the life, death, and resurrection of Jesus is the fulfillment of "everything written about [him] in the law of Moses, the prophets, and the psalms" (Luke 24:44) informs and pervades their respective efforts to make known who Jesus is and what has been accomplished through him. While the four evangelists frequently cite or allude to particular texts from the Hebrew Scriptures as they tell the story of Jesus, it is the overall trajectory of the biblical story that ought to be attended to. That story begins, in the canonical ordering of Scripture, with creation. "In the beginning when God created the heavens and the earth, the earth was a formless void and darkness covered the face of the deep, while a wind from God swept over the face of the waters. Then God said, 'Let there be light'; and there was light" (Gen. 1:1–3). Among the multiple theological claims embedded in this text we learn that God is a God who brings forth light from darkness; we learn that the heavens and the earth—that is, "all things"—are the product of God's creative agency; we learn here and in the subsequent unfolding of the story of creation that God is a God who brings order to the formless void and is the giver of life. This is the God who is at work on Easter morning bringing forth light and life from the darkness of the tomb. It is in the context of this biblical faith in the creative agency of God, repeatedly affirmed throughout the Hebrew Bible, that the reality of the resurrection becomes compellingly apparent.

One might say that there is an irresistible necessity about the resurrection, so long as it is also made clear that the "necessity" is predicated entirely on the constancy of divine love and not, as Karl Barth has rightly insisted, on any constraint or obligation placed on God.[7] The raising of Jesus from the grave was an utterly free act of divine grace. The God who gives life to the world as an act of sheer unmerited love will not be dissuaded from the divine purpose that the creature will have light and life even when, as at Calvary, humanity chooses the chaos, the formless void, and the darkness of the tomb. The resurrection of Jesus from the dead is the utterly consistent outworking, repetition, and eschatological fulfillment of the divine declaration "Let there be light." It is God's refusal to abort the project that was begun when "the LORD God formed man from the dust of the ground, and breathed into his nostrils the breath of life" (Gen. 2:7). There is, as Barth again has noted, an exact correspondence between what is going on in the death and resurrection of Christ and what God "did as Creator when He separated light from darkness and elected the creature to being and rejected the possibility of chaos as nothingness."[8] Barth had noted earlier that "to raise (ἐγείρειν) the dead, to give life (ζωοποιεῖν) to the dead, is, like the creative summoning into being of non-being, a matter wholly and exclusively for God alone, quite outside the sphere of any possible co-operating factors (Heb. 11:19; 2 Cor. 1:9; Rom. 4:17). And this is primarily and particularly the case in the resurrection of Jesus Christ."[9]

The "believability" of the resurrection, as it were, rests on the fact that it is an act of the God who is the giver of life.[10] There is no other conceivable basis for the resurrection of Jesus from the dead.

The Promise to Abraham

The God who is the creator of all things and who gives life to the creature does not cease to take an interest in the creature once life has been given. God is not satisfied with the mere biological existence of the creature but intends,

---

7. See Barth, *Church Dogmatics* IV/1, 307.
8. Barth, *Church Dogmatics* IV/1, 349.
9. Barth, *Church Dogmatics* IV/1, 301.
10. A fuller articulation of this point requires attention to the nature of this God who has life in Godself (John 5:26). We shall return to the point in chap. 4, below.

rather, that the creature should flourish and exist in a state of shalom, enjoying the blessing of God in loving relationship with God and with all that God has made. Thus it is that God elects a particular people and makes them the stewards and the bearers of a divine promise: "Now the LORD said to Abram, 'Go from your country and your kindred and your father's house to the land that I will show you. I will make of you a great nation, and I will bless you, and make your name great, so that you will be a blessing. I will bless those who bless you, and the one who curses you I will curse; and in you all the families of the earth shall be blessed'" (Gen. 12:1–3).

The apostle Paul, in his letter to the Romans, takes up this promise and links it explicitly to the resurrection of Jesus from the dead. Abraham lived by faith, Paul contends, and that "faith was reckoned to him as righteousness" (Rom. 4:3). It was through faith that Abraham was enabled to live in right relationship with God and to live within the realm of divine blessing. Of interest here, however, is the link Paul makes to the resurrection. His argument deserves to be quoted at length:

> For this reason it depends on faith, in order that the promise may rest on grace and be guaranteed to all his descendants, not only to the adherents of the law but also to those who share the faith of Abraham (for he is the father of all of us, as it is written, "I have made you the father of many nations")—in the presence of the God in whom he believed, *who gives life to the dead* and calls into existence the things that do not exist. Hoping against hope, he believed that he would become "the father of many nations," according to what was said, "So numerous shall your descendants be." He did not weaken in faith when he considered his own body, which was already as good as dead (for he was about a hundred years old), or when he considered the barrenness of Sarah's womb. No distrust made him waver concerning the promise of God, but he grew strong in his faith as he gave glory to God, being fully convinced that God was able to do what he had promised. Therefore his faith "was reckoned to him as righteousness." Now the words, "it was reckoned to him," were written not for his sake alone, but for ours also. *It will be reckoned to us who believe in him who raised Jesus our Lord from the dead*, who was handed over to death for our trespasses and was raised for our justification. (Rom. 4:16–25, emphasis added).

Abraham trusts in the God who overcomes death: "He did not weaken in faith when he considered his own body, which was already as good as dead . . . or when he considered the barrenness of Sarah's womb" (Rom. 4:19).

Paul does not mention it specifically, but Abraham persisted in faith even when commanded to sacrifice his own beloved son, the one through whom the promise of blessing to all the families of the earth was to be maintained and extended (see Heb. 11:17–19). Abraham learned and trusted that life is God's gift and that the fulfillment of the promise is God's gift. There is no human capacity nor causal logic deriving from the operations of the natural world that can give life to the dead or call into existence the things that do not exist. The resurrection is rather, however astonishing it remains, an action of the God in whom Abraham had put his trust.[11] It fulfills, as Douglas Campbell has put it, "the great story of faithfulness that lay at the inception of Israel in its founding father Abraham."[12]

We may note further here that the God in whom Abraham had faith is identified precisely as the one "who gives life to the dead and calls into existence the things that do not exist" (Rom. 4:17). God is also identified this way in the second of the Eighteen Benedictions, which forms the second section of daily prayers for Jews and to which Paul also refers in 2 Corinthians 1:9:

בָּרוּךְ אַתָּה יהוה מְחַיֵּה הַמֵּתִים
Blessed are you, O LORD, who gives life to the dead.[13]

God is identified as the one who gives life to the dead because, again and again through the course of its own history, Israel had experienced God as the giver of life. God is, of course, the one who gave life to the creation "in the beginning." But God is also the one who gave life to Abraham and Sarah when, "considering his own body," Abraham was "as good as dead," and when from out of the lifelessness of Sarah's barren womb, the child of promise was born (Rom. 4:19). God is the one who gave life to a child in answer to Elijah's prayer (1 Kings 17:17–24) and again in answer to Elisha's prayer (2 Kings 4:32–37). The same pattern of divine action is also celebrated in Hannah's prayer:

> The LORD kills and brings to life;
>   he brings down to Sheol and raises up.

11. I have benefited in formulating this point from the work of Crüsemann, "Scripture and Resurrection," 90.

12. Campbell, *Pauline Dogmatics*, 308.

13. Although there is some uncertainty about how widespread the use of the Benedictions may have been prior to AD 70, Klaus Haacker contends that they would have been part of Paul's Pharisaic tradition. See Haacker, *Römer*, 108. Cited in Jewett, *Romans*, 333.

> The LORD makes poor and makes rich;
>   he brings low, he also exalts.
> He raises up the poor from the dust;
>   he lifts the needy from the ash heap,
> to make them sit with princes
>   and inherit a seat of honor.
>
>   (1 Sam. 2:6–8)

Deliverance from Bondage

This confidence in God to give life, to exalt, to raise up the poor from the dust, and to lift the needy from the ash heap is founded on Israel's long history of covenantal relationship with the Lord, and especially on God's deliverance of Israel from bondage in Egypt.[14] In Israel's Scripture, this divine action is the preeminent event by which God defines who God is. Repeatedly we hear, "I am the LORD your God who brought you out of the land of Egypt" (e.g., Exod. 20:2). Outside of the book of Exodus itself, "the Exodus theme is mentioned in Scripture approximately one hundred and twenty times, more than any other historical event or theological concept."[15] Walter Brueggemann observes that "the Exodus grammar of Yahweh saturates the imagination of Israel. The Exodus recital, either as a simple declarative sentence enacting Israel's primal theological grammar or as a fuller narrative, becomes paradigmatic for Israel's testimony about Yahweh. It becomes, moreover, an interpretive lens to guide, inform, and discipline Israel's utterances about many aspects of its life. As the paradigmatic function of the utterance is unmistakable, it is equally unmistakable that the entire field of grammar never departs from the concrete, specific reference point rooted in Israel's memory."[16]

14. I recognize that there is considerable debate about the historicity of the exodus story. It is undoubtedly the case that the story has been crafted, embellished, and interpreted through generations of telling and retelling in ways determined not so much by a concern for "historical accuracy" but by Israel's self-understanding as a people chosen by God. It seems probable as well, however, given its foundational and pervasive place in the Hebrew Bible, that the story was generated by some experience in Israel's past of liberation from hardship and escape from the hands of its oppressors. A relatively recent exploration of the historical provenance of the exodus narratives in the Bible can be found in Levy, Schneider, and Propp, eds., *Israel's Exodus in Transdisciplinary Perspective.*

15. Avery-Peck, "Doctrine of God," 214–15.

16. Brueggemann, *Theology of the Old Testament*, 178.

It is reasonable to suppose that when Jesus encountered the two disciples making their way to Emmaus and when "beginning with Moses and all the prophets, he interpreted to them the things about himself in all the scriptures" (Luke 24:27), he used this same grammar of exodus and divine deliverance. He might have said something to this effect: "My victory over death should be recognizable as an action of the same God who delivered Israel from the bondage of slavery in Egypt and who acted in like manner again and again through the course of Israel's history. And yet, how foolish you are, and how slow of heart to believe all that the prophets have declared!"

This grammar of exodus saturates the New Testament witness—which was written, of course, in light of the resurrection. The story of Jesus is told by those for whom the penny had dropped: the recurring pattern of redemptive and life-giving divine action is recognizable now in the person of Jesus himself. Thus, as Brueggemann again explains, the exodus tradition, though appealed to explicitly in places by the Gospel writers (e.g., Matt. 2:13–15; Luke 9:31), is found especially "in the larger affirmation that Jesus acts transformatively in solidarity with the bound and bonded, the weak and the marginalized (Luke 7:22). Thus it is possible to see that the narratives of Jesus's powerful transformative acts (miracles) are in effect enactments of exodus, whereby a gift of power decisively transforms the circumstance of the subject."[17]

The "enactments of exodus" throughout Jesus's ministry—and that most decisive enactment of the same in the resurrection of Jesus from the dead—confirm the identity of Jesus as the one who enacts once more, but now for all nations, the divine work of delivering God's people from bondage. Equally, however, it confirms the identity of God as the one who raised Jesus from the dead. Robert Jenson makes much of this point: "To the question 'Who is God?' the New Testament has one new descriptively identifying answer: 'Whoever raised Jesus from the dead.'"[18] That God's raising of Jesus from the dead becomes in the New Testament a means of identifying God is supported by Dale C. Allison's observation that the New Testament affirmation "God raised Jesus from the dead," repeated in various forms, "is structurally similar to the Hebrew confession that prefixes the decalogue: 'I am the Lord your God who brought you out of Egypt.'"[19] Allison notes further that for

---

17. Brueggemann, *Theology of the Old Testament*, 179.
18. Jenson, *Systematic Theology*, 1:44.
19. Allison, *Resurrection of Jesus*, 26.

Jürgen Becker "the parallel reveals that Jesus' followers 'regarded the Easter experience qualitatively as on the same level as God's classical act, the Exodus of Israel from Egypt.'"[20] Jenson explains, however, that the identification of God as the one who raised Jesus from the dead "neither replaces nor is simply added to identification by the Exodus; the new identifying description *verifies* its paradigmatic predecessor. For as the outcome of the Old Testament it is seen that Israel's hope in her God cannot be sustained if it is not verified by victory also over death."[21] This victory over death is the final exodus, as it were—the release of the creature from the ultimate consequence of sin and the final realization of God's promise that the creature shall have life. That promise is realized just insofar as the creature is united with Christ in his death and resurrection (see Rom. 6:3–11; Gal. 2:19–20; Col. 2:12–13; 1 Tim. 2:11).

The Suffering and Exalted Servant

Among the early church's attempts to understand the life, death, and resurrection of Jesus as the fulfillment of the Old Testament witness to God's creative and redemptive purposes for the world, the so-called servant songs of Deutero-Isaiah (Isa. 40–55) feature prominently. That Jesus was identified with the suffering and exalted servant is attested at the outset of all four Gospels, each of which presents John the Baptist as the forerunner and herald of the coming Messiah and quotes various portions of Isaiah 40:3–5:[22]

> A voice cries out:
> "In the wilderness prepare the way of the LORD,
>   make straight in the desert a highway for our God.
> Every valley shall be lifted up,
>   and every mountain and hill be made low;
> the uneven ground shall become level,
>   and the rough places a plain.
> Then the glory of the LORD shall be revealed,
>   and all people shall see it together,
>   for the mouth of the LORD has spoken."

20. Allison, *Resurrection of Jesus*, 26n7, quoting Becker, *Jesus of Nazareth*, 362.
21. Jenson, *Systematic Theology*, 1:44.
22. Matt. 3:3; Mark 1:2–3; Luke 3:4–6; John 1:23.

By quoting this text, the four evangelists clearly intend that Jesus is to be understood as the coming Lord and suffering servant whose glory will be revealed and as the one who fulfills the vision of restoration and redemption laid out in Isaiah 40–55. This conviction predates the four Gospels, however. Already in the letters of Paul, Jesus is understood in light of Isaiah 40–55. In Romans 4:25, Paul speaks of Jesus Christ as the one "who was handed over to death for our trespasses and was raised for our justification." C. E. B. Cranfield speaks for many commentators when he writes, "That the influence of Isaiah 52:12–53:13 is to be seen here is hardly to be doubted."[23] The allusions are thought to appear also in 1 Corinthians 15:3–5, where Paul explicitly invokes the Scriptures: "For I handed on to you as of first importance what I in turn had received: that Christ died for our sins *in accordance with the scriptures*, and that he was buried, and that he was raised on the third day *in accordance with the scriptures*" (emphasis added). Richard Hays notes that "the confessional statement does not stipulate *which* Scriptures are in view"; however, "the description of Christ's death as having been 'for our sins' calls to mind the suffering servant in Isaiah 53," albeit "the allusion is not very explicit (cf. Isa. 53:5–6, 11–12)."[24] That Jesus was "raised on the third day" can be seen in turn as a fulfillment of Isaiah 52:13: "See my servant shall prosper; he shall be exalted and lifted up, and shall be very high." We find further allusions to Isaiah 52 and 53 in 1 Peter 2:22–25 and Hebrews 9:28.

It is evident that the early church appealed to Deutero-Isaiah's presentation of the suffering servant in seeking to understand who Jesus was and what had been accomplished through his life, death, and resurrection. Some scholars have argued that the church was prompted to do this precisely because Jesus himself understood his mission and ministry in this way. Peter Stuhlmacher thus writes, "The Christological interpretation of Isaiah 53 that comes to the fore in Romans 4:25; I Corinthians 15:3b–5; I Peter 2:22–25; Hebrews 9:28 and so forth was not first and foremost the fruit of post-Easter faith; its roots lie rather in Jesus' own understanding of his mission and death. He himself adopted the general messianic interpretation of Isaiah 53 current in early Judaism."[25] Stuhlmacher continues: "Jesus taught his disciples this

23. Cranfield, *Romans*, 96. Note that Cranfield suggests that the allusions are most obvious when read in the light of the Septuagint text of Isaiah. Among many others who make the same point we find, for example, Käsemann, *Romans*, 128; and Jewett, *Romans*, 342.

24. Hays, *First Corinthians*, 256.

25. Stuhlmacher, "Isaiah 53 in the Gospels and Acts," 148. Stuhlmacher cites in support of this claim J. Jeremias, H. W. Wolff, O. Betz, and L. Goppelt.

understanding of his messianic mission and sufferings in private in various settings. Testimony to such private instruction is found above all in Mark 9:31 par.; 10:45 par.; 14:22, 24 par.; and also in Luke 22:35–38."[26]

While there is room for some debate about the strength of the particular allusions adduced by Stuhlmacher, and indeed about the claim that they go back to Jesus himself, there is no doubt that the early church, whether through Jesus's own prompting or not, did apply the servant songs in Deutero-Isaiah with particular poignancy to the person of Jesus himself.[27] He is the one, so the church believes, who "was wounded for our transgressions, crushed for our iniquities; upon him was the punishment that made us whole, and by his bruises we are healed" (Isa. 53:5). He is also the one who has been "exalted and lifted up" (Isa. 52:13) through resurrection and ascension.

Can These Dry Bones Live?

The biblical story begins with the gift of life, with God bringing forth light and life from the formless void, separating the waters from the dry land, and summoning the earth and waters to put forth vegetation and living creatures of many kinds. That story of creation culminates in God's creation of humankind in God's own image, according to God's likeness (Gen. 1:26–27). Those who first told this story of the goodness of God did so, however, in the midst of suffering. They wrote in the context of their own exile, in the context of their estrangement from the land that God had given them and the temple in which they had worshiped God, but which had now been reduced to rubble at the hands of their enemies. So Israel tells its story of the goodness and the trustworthiness of the Lord in full awareness that the human story has gone awry. Humanity's vocation to live in faithful relationship with the Lord, and thus to enjoy the fullness of divine blessing, has not been honored. The biblical accounts of creation in Genesis 1 and 2 are followed immediately in chapter 3, therefore, by a story of human defiance and disobedience. From that

26. Stuhlmacher, "Isaiah 53 in the Gospels and Acts," 150.
27. It is essential to point out that the legitimacy of such christological readings can be affirmed without diminishing in the least Israel's conviction in the midst of their own suffering that God had made *them* to be a servant people who would bear the sin of many. I have defended this point at length in my article Rae, "Texts and Context." For further discussion of the christological interpretation of Isaiah 53, see Bellinger and Farmer, eds., *Jesus and the Suffering Servant*.

defiance comes struggle and suffering, alienation from God, enmity between God's creatures, and finally death.

The long tale of Israel's fluctuations between faithfulness to Yahweh and the worship of other gods, between obedience and defiance, between life and death, is told through the course of Israel's Scriptures. Very often, it is the prophets, speaking the word of the Lord, who chastise Israel for its wayward-ness and call it back to its true identity as the people elected by God to be the bearer and herald of God's promised blessing to all the families of the earth. The prophets invite Israel, and all subsequent readers, into a searching theological exploration of what has become of the divine promise in the face of human defiance and of what will become of humanity itself when alien-ated from God. They summon Israel to repentance and call it to return to righteousness, to right relationship with God and with one another. Ezekiel is one of those prophets.

Ezekiel in exile knew that Jerusalem had fallen (Ezek. 33:21) and that it was because of Israel's rebellion (Ezek. 5). In the midst of exile, the Lord takes Ezekiel and shows him a vision of Israel's desolation; it is a vision of a valley full of dry bones. The Lord leads Ezekiel all around the bones. "There were very many lying in the valley, and they were very dry. He said to me, 'Mortal, can these dry bones live?'" (37:2–3). Ezekiel responds that only the Lord knows. Then the Lord commands him, "Prophesy to these bones, and say to them: O dry bones, hear the word of the LORD. Thus says the Lord GOD to these bones: I will cause breath to enter you, and you shall live. I will lay sinews on you, and will cause flesh to come upon you, and cover you with skin, and put breath in you, and you shall live; and you shall know that I am the LORD" (37:4–6).

Christians are those who believe that God in Christ has come to the valley of dry bones and found in that valley not just Israel but all of humankind, and God has breathed new life into the creature, declaring once more, "You shall have life." The resurrection of Jesus, who has taken our death upon himself, is God's definitive declaration, once and for all, that the dry bones shall live and that death will not triumph in the end. Walter Brueggemann writes in response to the divine promise of life entrusted to Ezekiel, "The load is lifted. We begin again. The bones rattle. The air stirs. We could be on our way back home to our true community."[28]

---

28. Brueggemann, *Hopeful Imagination*, 87.

Blessed Be the Lord

One last story will serve to illustrate the principal claim of this chapter—namely, that the resurrection of Jesus from the dead is the utterly consistent outworking of a pattern of divine action well established throughout the course of Israel's Scriptures. This last example is the story of Naomi, Ruth, and Obed. The book of Ruth is an exquisitely crafted story, and its crafting serves a profound theological purpose. It is a story of the God who replaces nothingness with plenitude, and emptiness with abundant life. That theme is introduced in the opening verse: "In the days when the judges ruled, *there was a famine in the land*" (Ruth 1:1, emphasis added). The land lies desolate and so is unproductive. Life itself is under threat. That is the first level of emptiness—the emptiness of the land.

We are told then of a certain man of Bethlehem, Elimelech, who went to live in Moab with his wife Naomi and their two sons, Mahlon and Chilion. The family left Bethlehem in Judah, we suppose, in search of a land that would yield food. But then a second level of emptiness is introduced: "Elimelech, the husband of Naomi, died, and she was left with her two sons" (Ruth 1:3). D. F. Rauber writes, "Here is the same theme on the social level: fullness is the complete and harmonious family, and emptiness is the loneliness of the widow."[29] Yet there are still greater depths of desolation that leave Naomi even more deeply bereft. Naomi's two sons took Moabite wives, but "when they had lived there about ten years, both Mahlon and Chilion also died, so that the woman was left without her two sons and her husband" (1:4–5).

In response to this further experience of emptiness and desolation, Naomi decides that she will leave Moab and return to the land of Judah. Initially, the two daughters-in-law, Orpah and Ruth, decide that they will go with her, but Naomi says to them, "Go back each of you to your mother's house" (Ruth 1:8). She knows that there is no future for them with her. "Turn back, my daughters," she says, "why will you go with me?" (1:11). When a woman was widowed, she would then, according to Jewish law, be taken into the household of her husband's brother. But in this case there are no brothers, and Naomi's words hammer home the point: "Do I still have sons in my womb that they may become your husbands?" (1:11). The answer, of course, is no. Thus, we have a third level of emptiness. Naomi's womb is empty, and so,

---

29. Rauber, "Book of Ruth," 165. Much of my discussion of the book of Ruth follows Rauber's lead and that of an unpublished sermon preached in 2003 by Alister Rae.

with her sons dead, she can offer nothing to Orpah and Ruth, and she herself no longer has reason to live.

The land is empty. The earth languishes, and the fruits wither on the vine. The family is empty; the men are all dead. And Naomi's womb is empty. There is no future and so no reason for hope. The scene of emptiness and desolation is complete. Rauber observes,

> There is added power in our sensing that the beginning and the end of the series bend around to meet. Our minds sweep from the intense point of personal grief back to the opening as we recognize the parallel between the barrenness of the old woman and the barrenness of the exhausted earth. We see the similarity, and then the difference. The cycle of nature is endlessly repeated, but Naomi is old and for her, or so to her it seems, there will never come a time in which the Lord will visit her again as he will visit "his people in giving them bread."[30]

Naomi thus says to Orpah and Ruth, "It has been far more bitter for me than for you, because the hand of the LORD has turned against me" (Ruth 1:13). Orpah, we are told, does then turn back, but Ruth will not leave Naomi. "Do not press me to leave you," she says, "or to turn back from following you! Where you go, I will go; where you lodge, I will lodge; your people shall be my people, and your God my God" (1:16). When Naomi sees that Ruth will not be dissuaded, she says no more to her. "So the two women went on until they came to Bethlehem. When they arrived, the whole town was stirred because of them, and the women said, 'Is this Naomi?' She said to them, 'Call me no longer Naomi, call me Mara'" (1:18–20). Naomi means "pleasant," while Mara means "bitter." Naomi prefers the latter, she says, "for the Almighty has dealt bitterly with me. I went away full, but the LORD has brought me back empty; why call me Naomi when the LORD has dealt harshly with me, and the Almighty has brought calamity upon me?" (1:20–21). The emptiness and desolation is made explicit here: "*I went away full, but the LORD has brought me back empty.*"

This first chapter has set the scene. The problems have been posed. The movement of the chapter "has been a skillfully managed downward spiral, a sinking to the very depths."[31] And so the chapter comes to an end—almost! There is one last sentence that provides an intimation of things to come: Naomi

---

30. Rauber, "Book of Ruth," 166.
31. Rauber, "Book of Ruth," 166.

and Ruth "came to Bethlehem *at the beginning of the barley harvest*" (Ruth 1:22, emphasis added). The chapter has told a story of famine, desolation, and emptiness, but here at the last there is a hint of the replenishment to come. It is "at the beginning of the barley harvest" that Naomi and Ruth return to Bethlehem.

We proceed to chapter 2: "Now Naomi had a kinsman on her husband's side, a prominent rich man, of the family of Elimelech" (Ruth 2:1). The second level of emptiness in chapter 1 was the emptiness of Naomi, bereft of family following the death of her husband and two sons. Now, we are told, Naomi has a kinsman! "And Ruth the Moabite said to Naomi, 'Let me go to the field and glean among the ears of grain'" (2:2). Note that her identity as a foreigner is emphasized. Naomi answers, "Go, my daughter" (2:2). Although Ruth is a foreigner, with no blood ties to Naomi, Naomi calls her "my daughter." The storyteller is working now toward the renewal of the family, the overcoming of the second level of emptiness with which Naomi has been stricken.

So Ruth goes into the field and begins to glean. "As it happened," the storyteller says, making it sound like a coincidence, Ruth "came to the part of the field belonging to Boaz, who was of the family of Elimelech" (Ruth 2:3). Boaz notices Ruth working in the field behind the reapers. He inquires of his servants who this woman is, and when he learns that she is the daughter-in-law of Naomi, Boaz instructs his men to let her glean and not to bother her. Then Boaz himself speaks to Ruth, telling her to stay within his field and that if she gets thirsty she should go to the vessels of water and drink. Overcome by the kindness shown to her, Ruth "fell prostrate, with her face to the ground, and said to him, 'Why have I found favor in your sight, that you should notice me, when I am a foreigner?'" (2:10). That she is a foreigner renders Boaz's favor, in Ruth's mind at least, all the more remarkable—and undeserved! And yet, as Rauber points out,[32] there is also here a subtle identification of Ruth with Israel's frequent plight in its history—especially in Egypt and in Babylon. Ruth is identified with Israel, particularly with Israel in its need for deliverance and redemption.

The story continues: Ruth gleans from the field until evening and goes home to Naomi with the barley from the field (Ruth 2:17–18). Upon seeing the grain and hearing Ruth's report of the events of the day, Naomi inquires further: "Where did you glean today? And where have you worked? Blessed

---

32. Rauber, "Book of Ruth," 168.

be the man who took notice of you" (2:19). So Ruth explains, "The name of
the man with whom I worked today is Boaz" (2:19). Naomi sees something
here that Ruth does not, and her spirit begins to be lifted from the depths.[33]
She responds with gratitude for the Lord's provision: "Blessed be he by the
LORD, *whose kindness has not forsaken the living or the dead!*" (Ruth 2:20,
emphasis added). Rauber notes, "We know that Naomi, who was herself
among the dead, now lives again."[34]

Naomi then explains to Ruth, "The man is a relative of ours, one of our
nearest kin [מִגֹּאֲלֵנוּ]" (Ruth 2:20). That kinship is vital, for when a woman is
left a widow, it is the obligation of kinsfolk to care for her. The Hebrew word
used here is גֹּאֵל, a kinsman who can redeem. It is a word with rich theological
overtones, suggesting that Boaz will be the one through whom we will see
the saving work of God.[35] The "coincidence" of Ruth gleaning in the field of
Boaz is no coincidence after all: God is at work here. Naomi sees and begins
to hope that the fortunes of the family will be restored. The story then plays
out according to "the custom in former times in Israel" (Ruth 4:7) whereby
kinsfolk take responsibility for women left widowed. The obligation to care
for Naomi is exercised through Boaz taking the land that was Elimelech's and
that was the inheritance of Chilion and Mahlon, and then by taking Ruth to
be his wife so that the family name will remain with the inheritance (4:5).
The earth has been replenished; the barley harvest is good—thus the first level
of emptiness has been replaced by the fruitfulness of the land. Then, following the initiative of Naomi, Boaz takes Ruth to be his wife, and the loss and
emptiness of the family is overcome.

But there is one level of emptiness still to be overcome: the emptiness of
Naomi's womb. Thus, we move on to the final act. "So Boaz took Ruth and
she became his wife," we are told. And "when they came together, the LORD
made her conceive, and she bore a son" (Ruth 4:13). The local women "gave
him a name, saying, 'a son has been born to Naomi'" (4:17)—note, to *Naomi*,
the one whose womb had been empty. Through this son of Ruth, Naomi's
daughter, and her kinsman Boaz, the emptiness of Naomi's womb is overcome.
She will have descendants after all.

33. I take the point from Rauber, "Book of Ruth," 170.
34. Rauber, "Book of Ruth," 170.
35. There are passages in the Old Testament in which the concept of the kinsman redeemer
is applied even to God (e.g., Isa. 63:16). As T. F. Torrance argues, it is an especially apt description of Jesus who became bone of our bone and flesh of our flesh precisely in order to redeem
humanity from its sin and shame. See Torrance, *Atonement*, 44–50.

Again, it is the women who recognize the work of the Lord: "Then the women said to Naomi, 'Blessed be the LORD, who has not left you this day without next-of-kin; and may his name be renowned in Israel! He shall be to you a restorer of life and a nourisher of your old age; for your daughter-in-law who loves you, who is more to you than seven sons, has borne him'" (Ruth 4:14–15). Observe especially the phrase "He shall be to you a restorer of life." This captures the central theme of the book of Ruth as a whole. The pronoun *he* refers to Ruth's child, but it has already been made clear that God has been at work throughout the course of this drama. The gift of new life comes from God. The storyteller encourages us to see here a much larger drama playing out. When Boaz agrees to take Ruth as his wife, the witnesses to this new commitment declare, "May the LORD make the woman who is coming into your house like Rachel and Leah, who together built up the house of Israel" (4:11). Thus we see it is not just Naomi's life that is restored; it is also the life of Israel. The story concludes with a final affirmation that God is at work here restoring the life of Israel: the women of the neighborhood name the child Obed. "He became the father of Jesse, the father of David" (Ruth 4:17–22).[36] The name Obed means "one who worships."[37] Worship is precisely what is due to the God who has rescued God's people from emptiness once more and established the royal line.

Conclusion

Throughout the Old Testament texts considered in this chapter, an unmistakable pattern is evident. God is the giver and the restorer of life. From darkness, God brings forth light; in the midst of despair and resignation, God gives hope; from bondage, God offers deliverance; and from barrenness and desolation, God gives new life. In light of this narrative thread running through the Scriptures, the resurrection of Jesus from the dead may be understood as the consistent outworking of the divine promise that the creature shall have life in all its fullness. Francis Watson puts it well: "Having momentarily glimpsed the risen Christ, the disciples [on the road to Emmaus] recall how their hearts

---

36. E. John Hamlin points out that the fact that it was the women of Bethlehem who named the child, rather than the parents, "suggests that the birth of this child was an event that concerned all the citizens of Bethlehem, as well as the people of Judah and the entire nation." Hamlin, *Ruth*, 72.

37. Brown, Driver, and Briggs, *Hebrew and English Lexicon*, 714.

burned within them 'while he talked to us on the road, while he opened to us the scriptures' (Luke 24:32). The fire is the light and warmth of the dawning of faith in the resurrection, understood not as an isolated marvel but within the comprehensive context established by holy scripture."[38]

Luke does not specify any particular texts to which Jesus may have referred when "beginning with Moses and all the prophets, he interpreted to them the things about himself in all the scriptures" (Luke 24:27). But the Scriptures provide, for those with eyes to see, abundant confirmation that the raising of Jesus from the dead is an action of the same God who has been at work in the world from the dawn of time.

---

38. Watson, *Text, Church and World*, 291.

3

Life Transformed

I have argued in chapter 2 that the appropriate way to understand Jesus's life, death, and resurrection in the light of Israel's Scriptures is not to go looking for proof texts that might provide prophetic anticipations of particular details of Jesus's story but, rather, to recognize that what takes place in and through Jesus is a fulfillment of the consistent pattern of divine action in the Old Testament. That action reveals the God of Israel to be the one who brings forth life from nothingness, who delivers God's people from bondage, and who rescues them again and again from desolation and despair. What takes place in Jesus is the fulfillment of this trajectory of divine action inasmuch as his resurrection represents, in anticipation of the final consummation of all things, the overcoming of death, the final enemy. The hermeneutical lead given by Jesus in his conversations with the disciples after his resurrection shapes then the writing of the New Testament. Israel's Scriptures provide the theological framework within which the New Testament writers offer their testimony concerning the good news of Jesus the Christ. As the culmination of the story, so Christians believe, it is true as well that the life, death, and resurrection of Jesus casts light backward onto the witness of the Old Testament and reveals that the promises made there have been kept.

The hermeneutical principle noted here is twice affirmed by the apostle Paul in 1 Corinthians 15:3–4: "For I handed on to you as of first importance what I in turn had received: that Christ died for our sins *in accordance with the scriptures*, and that he was buried, and that he was raised on the third day *in accordance with the scriptures*" (emphasis added). This accordance with the Scriptures of the good news that Paul has proclaimed to the church in Corinth is the basis upon which he also affirms that the gospel of Jesus Christ is that "in which . . . [they] stand" and "through which also [they] are being saved," as long as they "hold firmly to the message that [Paul] proclaimed" (1 Cor. 15:1–2). The death and resurrection of Jesus "in accordance with the scriptures" are here presented by Paul as the foundation of a new identity and a new form of life for those who believe. Christopher Seitz aptly observes that "'in accordance with the scriptures' is a shorthand for 'in accordance with the reality for which God requires our conformity and our obedience.' As Jesus was in accordance with scripture, so the church lives in accordance with the Jesus canonically presented and shared with believers through the work of the Holy Spirit."[1]

The church's oldest extant witness to this accordance is, of course, Paul himself, some of whose letters are preserved in the New Testament. My purpose in this chapter is to explore the witness of the Pauline letters[2] to the new identity and form of life established through the resurrection of the one who died for our sins. It must be noted to begin with that Paul takes the resurrection of Jesus as a given. Writing a decade and more after Paul, the Gospel writers consider it prudent to provide a written account of the career of Jesus for those who will no longer have the advantage of temporal proximity to the living memory of the events involving Jesus. Paul, on the other hand, apparently assuming that his audiences will already know the story, adopts the role of the historical narrator only occasionally and then with the purpose, it seems, of picking out details that are especially pertinent to the theological

---

1. Seitz, *Word without End*, 52.
2. I do not intend, nor do I have the expertise, to engage in the debate about which of the "Pauline letters" came from Paul's own hand and which may have been authored by others under the purported authority of Paul. As has been the case with chapters 1 and 2 as well, the biblical study engaged in here is focused on the theological claims being advanced through the canonical witness rather than on the multitude of historical-critical questions that are worthy of more detailed attention in other contexts. I confess also to venturing somewhat warily into what Douglas Campbell calls the "confused roiling complexity" of Pauline studies. See Campbell, *Quest for Paul's Gospel*, 1. I can offer only an inexpert perspective on what insight on the resurrection is available to the church through the Pauline witness, but I appeal in doing so to the doctrine of the perspicuity of Scripture, which holds that expertise in biblical scholarship is an extremely valuable aid to, rather than a necessary condition of, God's self-disclosure to the church through Scripture. Such an understanding of Scripture is expounded in, for instance, Webster, *Holy Scripture*.

argument he is constructing. Paul's primary purpose throughout his writings is not to provide a historical narrative of Jesus's life, which he largely takes as read,[3] but to explain what it now means for the church to confess that "Christ died for our sins in accordance with the scriptures, and that he was buried, and that he was raised on the third day."

Jesus Is Lord

The first and most important thing that Paul has to say concerning the resurrection of Jesus from the dead is that "Jesus is Lord." That is the dazzling truth that dawns on Paul the former persecutor of Christians when, according to the accounts of Paul's conversion in Acts, he is encountered by the risen Lord. The story of this encounter is told three times in the book of Acts, first in the third person (Acts 9:1–9), but then in chapter 22 and again in chapter 26 as a first-person account:

> While I was on my way and approaching Damascus, about noon a great light from heaven suddenly shone about me. I fell to the ground and heard a voice saying to me, "Saul, Saul, why are you persecuting me?" I answered, "Who are you, Lord?" Then he said to me, "I am Jesus of Nazareth whom you are persecuting." Now those who were with me saw the light but did not hear the voice of the one who was speaking to me. I asked, "What am I to do, Lord?" The Lord said to me, "Get up and go to Damascus; there you will be told everything that has been assigned to you to do." Since I could not see because of the brightness of that light, those who were with me took my hand and led me to Damascus. (Acts 22:6–11; cf. 26:12–18)

There is a widespread caution among scholars about taking Luke's reports of Paul's conversion as reliable indicators of what actually happened,[4] but there is a key feature of the three reports in Acts that is unambiguously reflected in Paul's own writings. Slight variations notwithstanding, on each occasion

3. For a brief outline of the diversity of scholarly opinion on this point, see Longenecker, *Studies in Paul*, 2–4.

4. Some scholars, following the lead of John Knox's influential work *Chapters in a Life of Paul*, urge caution about taking the Acts accounts of Paul's conversion at face value, preferring the witness of Paul's own letters. See, e.g., Campbell, *Quest for Paul's Gospel*, 20. The merits of such caution notwithstanding, the point highlighted here—namely, that there was for Paul a moment of realization that Jesus of Nazareth, whose followers he had been persecuting, was indeed the Lord and Messiah—is well attested in Paul's own writings.

of Luke's telling of the story these words are repeated: "I fell to the ground and heard a voice saying to me, 'Saul, Saul, why are you persecuting me?' I answered, 'Who are you, Lord?'" While it may have been Luke himself, as many scholars surmise, who put this question on Paul's lips, Paul's own writings offer clear evidence that in consequence of his encounter with the risen Jesus this is precisely who he then understood Jesus to be: the Lord. We learn elsewhere that Paul became convinced as well that Jesus is Israel's Messiah and that it was the God of Israel who raised him. This recognition of Jesus's true identity transformed Paul from a persecutor of Christ's followers into a passionate proclaimer of the news that Israel's Messiah had come. In virtue of the resurrection, a new theology and "an entirely new approach to life is necessary . . . , one alert to the resurrecting power of Jesus working within history."[5]

Many learned tomes have been written exploring the nature and extent of Paul's transformed understanding of where and how the God of Israel is at work in the world. In what follows I will offer merely a sketch of what I take to be the key features of Paul's theology as developed in the light of the resurrection.

The central elements of the reorientation of Paul's theology are as follows:

- Encounter with the risen Christ gives rise to a radically new understanding of the divine identity (theology).
- That God raised Jesus from the dead means that God has vindicated Jesus and confirmed him as Israel's hoped-for Messiah and thereby the royal Son of God and Lord (Christology).
- Jesus's death was not a sorry end to a misguided mission but a redemptive death for the sins of the world (soteriology).
- The eschatological resurrection of the dead anticipated in Israel's Scriptures has now begun (eschatology).
- The scope of God's creative and redemptive purposes for Israel are now decisively extended to include gentiles as well (missiology).
- The significance of the law, the temple, and the Jewish practice of circumcision need to be reevaluated (ecclesiology).
- Jesus, the living one, calls and enables us through the Spirit to participate in his life of obedient service to the Father (Christian life).[6]

5. Campbell, *Pauline Dogmatics*, 17.
6. I have borrowed extensively here, while modifying some details, from the work of Michael Gorman in *Apostle of the Crucified Lord*, 56–57.

A New Theology

Paul's encounter with the risen Jesus transforms, first of all, his concept of God. The very same God who called Israel to live with God in covenant relationship; who revealed the divine, steadfast love in the lives of Abraham and Sarah, Isaac and Rebecca, Jacob, Leah and Rachel; who led the Israelites out of bondage through Moses and spoke through the prophets—*this God* has now appeared in Jesus, whose followers Paul had been persecuting. Paul's recognition that Jesus had been raised from the dead and that it was the God of Abraham, Isaac, and Jacob who had raised him confirms for Paul the enduring importance of his Jewish heritage. He remains hopeful that the true end of Judaism itself will be realized through salvation in Christ, and he affirms that Israel's gifts and the calling of God are irrevocable (Rom. 11:29). Richard Longenecker observes that Paul speaks of his "conversion" in ways that reflect "a consciousness of never having left his ancestral faith."[7] Similarly, John Barclay, while happy to speak of Paul's experience as a conversion, explains that "Paul did not 'convert' in the sense of changing religion . . . since the God who 'called' him was the same God he had always tried to serve."[8] Far from renouncing his Jewish identity, therefore, Paul's conversion involved instead a radical reconception of where and how the God of Abraham was at work in the world, prompted by the recognition that "God's salvific purposes for both creation in general and humanity in particular are now to be understood as focused in the work and person of Jesus of Nazareth."[9]

The transformation in Paul's understanding of God is everywhere evident in his letters, but consider in particular the following claim from his first letter to the Corinthians: "For us there is one God, the Father, from whom are all things and for whom we exist, and one Lord, Jesus Christ, through whom are all things and through whom we exist" (1 Cor. 8:6). The background of the Jewish Scriptures is again crucial here. Paul, a devout Jew, is likely to have recited twice daily the Shema from Deuteronomy 6:4: "Hear, O Israel: The LORD is our God, the LORD alone." As Douglas Campbell explains,

> First Corinthians 8:6 does something very challenging with this confession. Paul *distributes* the Shema *between* "God the Father" and "the Lord Jesus," all the

7. Longenecker, *Studies in Paul*, 8.
8. Barclay, *Paul*, 7.
9. Longenecker, *Studies in Paul*, 13.

while holding on, somewhat extraordinarily, to the unity of God. There is one divinity, although within this unity, there is someone called God the Father and someone called the Lord Jesus. . . . This move is then emphasized as Paul speaks of Jesus sustaining the creation which is an activity that the Jewish Scriptures reserve for God. . . . God is not reducible to Jesus, but God is not imaginable now without Jesus. Jesus is, as Richard Bauckham puts it carefully, part of the divine identity.[10]

Christology

The second feature worthy of note in 1 Corinthians 8:6 is Paul's identification of Jesus as the Christ. Paul affirms here that Jesus is Israel's Messiah, the fulfillment of Israel's hope that God will dwell with God's people and bring about their final deliverance from sin, from evil, and even from death. The resurrection of Jesus from the dead confirms in Paul's mind Jesus's messianic identity. Richard Longenecker notes a development over time in Paul's use of the titles *Lord*, *Messiah*, and *Son of God*. He argues that while Paul may have understood these terms in a functional way to begin with—as indicating, that is, "the supremacy of Jesus in the divine strategy of redemption"—there is over time a transposition in Paul's use of these terms.[11] Longenecker detects through the course of Paul's writings an increasing use of the term *Christ*, or the compound form *Jesus Christ*, as a proper name.[12] This transposition, along with an emphasis on *Lord* as the associated title, adds an ontological resonance to Paul's understanding of the person of Jesus. The titles speak not only of Jesus's role in the divine economy but also of his divine identity. We will return to the point in chapter 4.

Meanwhile, we may note a second expression of Paul's theological reorientation in the opening salutation of his epistle to the Romans:

> Paul, a servant of Jesus Christ, called to be an apostle, set apart for the gospel of God, which he promised beforehand through his prophets in the holy scriptures, the gospel concerning his Son, who was descended from David according to the flesh and was declared to be Son of God with power according to the spirit of holiness by resurrection from the dead, Jesus Christ our Lord, through whom

10. Campbell, *Pauline Dogmatics*, 14–15, emphasis original.
11. Longenecker, *Studies in Paul*, 15.
12. See Longenecker, *Studies in Paul*, 15–16.

we have received grace and apostleship to bring about the obedience of faith among all the Gentiles for the sake of his name, including yourselves who are called to belong to Jesus Christ. (Rom. 1:1–6)

It is widely agreed that Paul incorporates here, in verses 3–4, a prior liturgical formula, but the formula expresses a theology that Paul now unequivocally endorses: Jesus Christ, who is descended from David according to the flesh, has been declared to be Son of God with power according to the spirit of holiness *by resurrection from the dead*, and is *our Lord*.

Soteriology

Following his recognition that God raised the crucified Jesus from the dead, Paul comes to regard "the message about the cross" no longer as foolishness but as "the power of God" to those "who are being saved" (1 Cor. 1:18). The ignominy of death by crucifixion, "a stumbling block to Jews"—presumably including Paul himself during his career as a persecutor of Christians—"and foolishness to Gentiles" (1 Cor. 1:23), reveals to the eyes of faith the righteousness of God (see Rom. 1:16–17). In the words of Jonathan Linebaugh, "'The righteousness of God' is that which 'has been made visible' (φανερόω) in the event Paul calls 'the redemption that is in Jesus Christ' (Rom. 3:21a, 24) and 'continues to be unveiled' (ἀποκαλύπτω) in the proclamation of the same (Rom. 1:16–17)."[13]

This disclosure through the cross of God's righteousness is arguably the beating heart of Paul's whole theology. It is the foundation of the gospel of grace that Paul proclaims in Romans 3:21–26 whereby those who have faith in Jesus "are now justified by [God's] grace as a gift, through the redemption that is in Christ Jesus, whom God put forward as a sacrifice of atonement by his blood" (3:24–25). The righteousness of God (δικαιοσύνη) is demonstrated in the cross of Christ. Through his sacrifice, the sinner is justified.

Precisely how we are to understand this justifying judgment of God has been a matter of continuing debate in the church. However, Paul does make some important claims in this regard. First, this disclosure of the righteousness of God takes place "apart from the law" (Rom. 3:21). Again, in Romans 3:28:

13. Linebaugh, *Word of the Cross*, 9.

"For we hold that a person is justified by faith apart from works prescribed by the law." The righteousness of God, Paul insists, is not a matter of conformity to the law. There is a strong human tendency to suppose that we get what we deserve in life, whether that be punishment for wrongdoing or reward for good works. But that is not the way God works with us, according to Paul. Salvation comes "apart from the law"—apart, that is, from any performative merit of our own. Law-defined worth is explicitly excluded as the grounds of justification, which is accomplished instead as an unmerited gift of grace. The justification and the righteousness with which God is concerned is not founded on any moral performance or on the meritorious behavior of the individual. That is just as well, for as Paul insists, "all have sinned and fall short of the glory of God" (Rom. 3:23). The justification of the sinner is founded, rather, on the unwavering and costly love of God and is directed toward the restoration of right relationship. It is directed toward the overcoming of enmity and the establishment of peace: "Therefore, since we are justified by faith, we have peace with God through our Lord Jesus Christ" (Rom. 5:1).

The second feature of this justifying righteousness of God is that it is accomplished through faith. But whose faith? This too has been a question much debated in the church. The Greek phrase in Romans 3:22, "δικαιοσύνη δὲ θεοῦ διὰ πίστεως Ἰησοῦ Χριστοῦ," may be legitimately translated as "the righteousness of God through faith *in* Jesus Christ" or, equally legitimately, as "the righteousness of God through the faith *of* Jesus Christ." There are no lexical or grammatical means to determine which rendering of the Greek is to be preferred here. Good arguments have been offered in favor of both options.[14] For theological reasons, I am attracted to the second reading, which attributes the justification of sinners and their reconciliation with God to the faith *of* Christ. Such a reading accords more readily with the overwhelming emphasis Paul places on Christ's saving work on our behalf "while we were yet sinners" (Rom. 5:8) and while indeed we were "dead in our sins" (Eph. 2:1) and unable to do anything for ourselves. Our work in the drama of salvation, initially at least, is simply the offering of our grateful "Amen" to what has been accomplished for us. Christian life consists in the daily offering of this Amen, which is at the same time an expression of the prayer that we will be enabled by the Spirit to share in the resurrection life of our

---

14. A compendium of such arguments is presented in Bird and Sprinkle, *Faith of Jesus Christ.*

Lord as he undertakes the work of bringing in the kingdom of God on earth as it is in heaven.

The subjective genitive rendering of "πίστεως Ἰησοῦ"—that is, "the faith *of* Christ"—is supported, in my view, by the account of God's saving work found in Ephesians 2:4–10:

> But God, who is rich in mercy, out of the great love with which he loved us even when we were dead through our trespasses, made us alive together with Christ—by grace you have been saved—and raised us up with him and seated us with him in the heavenly places in Christ Jesus, so that in the ages to come he might show the immeasurable riches of his grace in kindness towards us in Christ Jesus. For by grace you have been saved through faith, and this is not your own doing; it is the gift of God—not the result of works, so that no one may boast. For we are what he has made us, created in Christ Jesus for good works, which God prepared beforehand to be our way of life.

We are what Christ has made us; it is not our doing! Our responsive act of praise to this unmerited act of grace is to live within the "way of life" that God has prepared for us, and so also in accordance with our true identity as beloved children of God.

We come to a third aspect of the soteriology summarily outlined in Romans 3:21–26: sinners are justified by God's grace as a gift "through the redemption [ἀπολυτρώσεως] that is in Christ Jesus, whom God put forward as a sacrifice of atonement by his blood, effective through faith" (3:24–25). The term ἀπολυτρώσεως (from ἀπολύτρωσις), translated here as "redemption," refers to a release from some kind of bondage or enslavement. The preceding verse indicates that the redemption accomplished through Christ involves release from sin and from the state of falling short of the glory of God. In accordance with this Pauline theology, the state of living in sin is described in Ephesians and Colossians as death.[15] The ἀπολύτρωσις ultimately accomplished in Jesus, therefore, is resurrection—the final overcoming of death and entry into new life.

---

15. See Eph. 2:1 and Col. 2:13. Scholars have commonly argued that these two letters are written by followers of Paul rather than by Paul himself. They reflect Paul's own theology in many respects while also including some distinctive theological features and some stylistic differences from those letters regarded as having come directly from Paul's own hand. A brief summary account of these assessments can be found in Barclay, *Paul*, 18–19.

Eschatology

The resurrection of Jesus from the dead is an event understood by Paul as the inauguration of a new age. Paul reflects here the expectation in Second Temple Judaism "that God would raise the dead in order both to vindicate and to punish human behavior."[16] As Bruce Chilton explains, the eventual vindication of Israel in particular was associated with the creation of new heavens and a new earth and the coming reign of God (see, e.g., Isa. 65:17–19).[17] The giving of new life extended from the resurrection of the dead to the restoration of Israel and the renewal of creation as a whole in new heavens and a new earth. In Ezekiel 37:12 the Lord declares, "I am going to open your graves, and bring you up from your graves, O my people; and I will bring you back to the land of Israel." Wolfhart Pannenberg asserts that the resurrection of Jesus from the dead was understood against this background of eschatological hope. "For Jesus' Jewish contemporaries, insofar as they shared the apocalyptic expectation, the occurrence of the resurrection did not first need to be interpreted, but for them it spoke meaningfully in itself: If such a thing had happened, one could no longer doubt what it meant. . . . The end of the world had begun."[18] N. T. Wright likewise contends that the resurrection was very likely understood as an eschatological event, that "it was the sort of event that second-Temple Jews would see in terms of the apocalyptic climax of their own history."[19]

Against this background, the significance of Jesus's resurrection from the dead extends well beyond Jesus's own being and identity. Thus Paul explains to the Christians in Rome, "Just as Christ was raised from the dead by the glory of the Father, so we too might walk in newness of life. For if we have been united with him in a death like his, we will certainly be united with him in a resurrection like his" (Rom. 6:4–5). In Romans 8:29 Paul speaks of Jesus as "the firstborn within a large family," and in 1 Corinthians 15:20 we read that "Christ has been raised from the dead, the first fruits of those who have died." The idea that Jesus's resurrection is the condition and precursor of resurrection life for others is also taken up elsewhere in the New Testament. Colossians, a letter attributed to but probably not written by Paul, says of Jesus, "He is the beginning, the firstborn from the dead" (1:18). The same

---

16. Chilton, *Resurrection Logic*, 30.
17. Chilton, *Resurrection Logic*, 38.
18. Pannenberg, *Jesus—God and Man*, 67. Cf. Wright, *Resurrection of the Son of God*, 272.
19. Wright, *Resurrection of the Son of God*, 26.

designation for Jesus appears in Revelation 1:5: "firstborn of the dead." Matthew's report, echoing Ezekiel 37:13, of the bodies of saints being raised when Jesus died and emerging from their tombs following his resurrection (Matt. 27:52–53) is surely an imaginative representation of this eschatological hope.

The hope generated by the resurrection of Jesus from the dead is not limited to humanity alone. The transformation and renewal brought about through Jesus's resurrection is cosmic in scope: "The creation itself will be set free from its bondage to decay and will attain the freedom of the glory of the children of God" (Rom. 8:21). As Ernst Käsemann observes, "Hope . . . reaches beyond believers to creation as a whole."[20] The biblical hope for a new heavens and a new earth, considered here by Paul to be bound up with the revealing and the glory of the children of God, looks forward undoubtedly to a future realization of God's purposes for creation as a whole, but Paul is convinced that God's work of new creation has already begun. Michael Gorman explains: "For Paul that new (meaning 'renewed') creation is occurring now, though of course it is still incomplete and will be finished only in the future. The proof that the new creation is under way is the existence of a community of reconciled people, Jews and Gentiles, living in covenantal relationship with God in Christ by the power of the Spirit (cf. Gal. 6:15)."[21]

The present reality of the new creation that will be brought to fulfillment in the future is stressed in 2 Corinthians 5:17: "So if anyone is in Christ, there is a new creation: everything old has passed away; see, everything has become new!" Douglas Campbell sees further evidence for the claim that the new creation has begun in Galatians 3:28: "There is no longer Jew or Greek, there is no longer slave or free, there is no longer male and female; for all of you are one in Christ Jesus." According to Campbell, "this wording again affirms that an entry into the age to come has taken place in some sense right here and now. Christians have already been resurrected."[22]

Missiology

The cosmic scope of the new creation recognized by Paul gives rise to a missiology that is also cosmic in scope. What this means especially is that the

---

20. Käsemann, *Romans*, 234.
21. Gorman, *Apostle of the Crucified Lord*, 129.
22. Campbell, *Pauline Dogmatics*, 106.

gospel given first to the Jews (Rom. 1:16) is to be proclaimed to gentiles as well. Paul sees in the life, death, and resurrection of Jesus the fulfillment of the divine promise that through Abraham's seed all the families of the earth will be blessed (Gen. 12:3; 28:14). It is "in Christ Jesus," Paul says, that "the blessing of Abraham might come to the Gentiles" (Gal. 3:14). Called by God and enabled by divine grace, Paul therefore becomes "a minister of Christ Jesus to the Gentiles" (Rom. 15:16; cf. Gal. 1:15–16) and declares to them, "If you belong to Christ, then you are Abraham's offspring, heirs according to the promise" (Gal. 3:29).

There is a persistent logic running through Paul's theology that confounds the wisdom of the wise and turns on its head Paul's own prior estimations of God's saving work in the world. The new and abundant life that is God's gift to the creature is not predicated, as was supposed, on biological descent from Abraham, or on observance of the law, or on some esoteric wisdom or knowledge that might be attained. According to the gospel Paul proclaims, there is no merit worthy of mention in any of the recipients of divine grace. The people who are given new life, who are justified and thus set free from sin and death, are precisely the ungodly. They are those, "both Jews and Greeks"—i.e., all people—who are "under the power of sin" (Rom. 3:9). "As it is written: 'There is no one who is righteous, not even one; there is no one who has understanding, there is no one who seeks God'" (3:10–11).[23] Paul hammers home the point: "For there is no distinction, since all have sinned and fall short of the glory of God" (3:22–23). But then comes the astonishing reversal of the logic of just deserts: "They are now justified by his grace as a gift, through the redemption that is in Christ Jesus" (3:24).

Within the usual conception of what justice demands, represented by the balanced scales of Lady Justice (*Iustitia*), this makes no sense. Jonathan Linebaugh explains: "In a shocking display of forensic schizophrenia, the judge identifies sinners as sinners (3:23) and then immediately overturns this accurate verdict with the seemingly unjust word of justification (3:24)."[24] The God who raises the dead, however, works according to an entirely different logic than that which supposes justice is achieved when the scales are balanced and offenders have received their "just" deserts. It is the same logic by

---

23. There is no single text from Israel's Scriptures that says precisely what Paul says here, but Robert Jewett explains: "It is widely accepted today that a carefully constructed catena of LXX quotations was used in 3:10–18." Jewett, *Romans*, 259.

24. Linebaugh, *Word of the Cross*, 140.

which the father in Jesus's parable welcomes home the wayward prodigal and treats him as a beloved child. The God "who justifies the ungodly" (Rom. 4:5) and calls them righteous is the God "who gives life to the dead and calls into existence the things that do not exist" (4:17). Given that "all" are included in this drama of salvation, for none are righteous on their own account, Paul recognizes that this gospel ought to be proclaimed to Jew and gentile alike.

The book of Acts records that this missiological imperative was not welcomed by some of the Jews in Jerusalem. While "the brothers welcomed [Paul and his companions] warmly" and while "James and all the elders" praised God when they heard of his mission to the gentiles (Acts 21:17–20), the news of Paul's expansive proclamation "to all the world" (22:15) was met with hostility in the temple. "The Jews from Asia, who had seen him in the temple, stirred up the whole crowd. They seized him, shouting, 'Fellow Israelites, help! This is the man who is teaching everyone everywhere against our people, our law, and this place; more than that, *he has actually brought Greeks into the temple and has defiled this holy place*'" (21:27–28, emphasis added). Despite the initial outrage among the crowd, Paul was given an opportunity to explain himself. When they heard Paul addressing them in Hebrew they quieted (22:2), but their ire was rekindled when Paul declared that God had sent him to the gentiles. "Up to this point they listened to him, but then they shouted, 'Away with such a fellow from the earth! For he should not be allowed to live'" (22:22).

There is, unfortunately, a common tendency among religious people, here demonstrated by Paul's audience in Jerusalem, to restrict God's favor to people of their own kind.[25] It is evident in policies of racial segregation the world over. It is evident, to take an example from my own context, in the insistence of Samuel Marsden, the first Christian missionary to the Indigenous people of Aotearoa New Zealand, that Māori must first be civilized—made more like the English!—before they could be "Christianized."[26] It is evident too in the unofficial but no less pernicious inhospitality of churches to people who are "different" in virtue of their ethnicity, gender, social status, sexual

25. I lament this fault in religious people here not because they are uniquely guilty of it. Tribalism, along with the resultant exclusion of others, is a widespread human tendency. It is also one of the most damaging manifestations of human sin.

26. Marsden wrote in a letter to Rev. Josiah Pratt, "The attention of the Heathens can only be gained and their vagrant Habits corrected, by the Arts. Till their attention is gained, and moral and industrious Habits are induced, little or no progress can be made in teaching them the Gospel." Quoted in Salmond, *Between Worlds*, 407.

identity, and so on. But, as Paul discovered through his encounter with the risen Christ, exclusion and segregation are practices that belong to the realm of sin and death. While still a work in progress—painfully slow progress at times—the sins of exclusion and segregation ought to and finally will be overcome through inclusion in the community of the risen Christ in whom there is no longer Jew or Greek, slave or free, male or female, for all are one (Gal. 3:28). The missionary imperative to proclaim the gospel is therefore extended "to all the world" (Acts 22:15).

Ecclesiology

The inclusion of gentiles among the people of God required a reevaluation of the role of certain practices that preserved in Jewish minds their status as God's chosen people. The people of God had hitherto been distinguished by their observance of the law—or at least by their aspiration to do so—by participation in the rituals of worship and sacrifice at the temple, and, for males, by circumcision. Paul, however, "trenchantly resisted the comprehensive imposition of Jewish practices on his converts."[27] Indeed, "many important Jewish practices were absent from Paul's communities of converts altogether."[28] That made some of Paul's fellow Jews, who were also followers of Christ, very uncomfortable indeed. At a council held in Jerusalem to consider the matter, some insisted that it was necessary for gentiles who became followers of Christ "to be circumcised and ordered to keep the law of Moses" (Acts 15:5). After lengthy debate, however, first Peter and then James offered support for Paul's contention that no obligation to observe Jewish practices should be imposed on the gentile Christians.

What then were to be the distinctive marks of the community of Christ followers? James proposes, "We should write to [the gentiles] to abstain only from things polluted by idols and from fornication and from whatever has been strangled and from blood" (Acts 15:20; cf. 15:29). Only one of those recommendations—abstinence from fornication—survived Paul's scrutiny, for he later argues in 1 Corinthians 8 that there is no intrinsic harm in eating meat that has been sacrificed to idols, which have no real existence and so no power to defile. What does matter, however, is that Christians should not act

27. Campbell, *Pauline Dogmatics*, 482.
28. Campbell, *Pauline Dogmatics*, 479.

in a manner that would cause any weaker members of the church to stumble. If eating food sacrificed to idols might trouble the conscience of another, then it would be best to abstain out of care for the weaker member (1 Cor. 8:1–13; see also Rom. 14:13–15). The behavior Paul commends, then, is loving care for one another. That accords with the teaching of Jesus himself, who tells the disciples, "Just as I have loved you, you also should love one another. By this everyone will know that you are my disciples, if you have love for one another" (John 13:34–35).

That same principle of loving care for others is also apparent in Paul's account of what had been agreed with the leaders of the church in Jerusalem: "When James and Cephas and John, who were acknowledged pillars, recognized the grace that had been given to me, they gave to Barnabas and me the right hand of fellowship, agreeing that we should go to the Gentiles and they to the circumcised. They asked only one thing, that we remember the poor, which was actually what I was eager to do" (Gal. 2:9–10).

Paul's eagerness was no idle boast. Several more times in his letters he stresses the importance of the collection (see 1 Cor. 16:1–4; 2 Cor. 8:1–9:15; Rom. 15:25–31).[29] Care for the poor, and the vulnerable and marginalized we might add, does not feature as one of the marks of the church classically identified in the Nicene Creed, but given the emphasis placed on such care not only in Paul's correspondence but elsewhere in Scripture too, particularly in the teaching and example of Jesus,[30] a strong case can be made that the church that does not care for the poor falls short of its calling to follow in the way of Christ. Certainly Martin Luther thought that hospitality to the poor and the stranger had the status of an essential mark of the church. Leo Sánchez explains:

> By asserting that "there is hospitality wherever the church is" (*Est autem hospitalitas, ubicunque Ecclesia est*) (LW 3:178; WA 43:2.29–30), Luther sees the virtue of hospitality as a mark of the church, "so that those who want to be true members of the church" (*Qui igitur Ecclesia membra vera esse cupiunt*) remember and are "encouraged" to practice it. Since in the Sermon on the

29. For a fuller account of Paul's commitment to the collection, see Duff, *Moses in Corinth*, 76–92.

30. See also the repeated concern expressed in the prophets for the widow, the orphan, and the stranger, and the immediate recognition by the followers of Jesus after the day of Pentecost that they should "sell their possessions and goods and distribute the proceeds to all, as any had need" (Acts 2:45).

Mount, the Lord commanded his disciples to "give to him who begs from you" (Mt. 5:42), the church possesses "a common treasury" through which members care for each other spiritually "not only by teaching" but also bodily "by showing kindness and giving assistance." Such care makes the church a place of "refreshment" (*refectionem*) for the weary (LW 3:178).[31]

Paul's insistence in Galatians 2:9–10 that the sole instruction given by the leaders of the church in Jerusalem as he undertakes his mission to the gentiles was to "remember the poor" is set within a broader argument, as we have seen, in which Paul resists the imposition of Jewish practices on the gentile believers. Such imposition amounts in fact to a perversion of the gospel (see Gal. 1:7; 6:12–15). Getting the gospel straight thus becomes for Paul an essential feature of the church. In the course of his rebuke to the churches of Galatia for so quickly turning to a different gospel (Gal. 1:6), Paul reiterates what the true gospel amounts to. The first such reiteration comes in Galatians 2:16, where Paul says, "Yet we know that a person is justified not by the works of the law but through faith in Jesus Christ [or *the faith of Jesus Christ*]. And we have come to believe in Christ Jesus, so that we might be justified by faith in Christ [or *the faith of Christ*], and not by doing the works of the law, because no one will be justified by the works of the law."[32]

Justification through faith belongs, Paul insists, to the heart of the gospel; whether it is *faith in Christ* or *the faith of Christ* is an important question (touched on above), but it is one that can be set aside for now. If we suppose that justification is the fruit of our own good works, then, in Paul's view, we are reverting to another gospel. This point too was stressed by Luther and the other Protestant Reformers. Justification, they argued, is the article by which the church stands or falls.[33] For Paul—lest we appear to have drifted from the central theme of this book—the resurrection of Christ is the decisive justifying act of God: "It will be reckoned to us [as righteousness] who believe in him who raised Jesus our Lord from the dead, who was handed

---

31. Sánchez, "The Church Is the House of Abraham," 7. The references to LW are to *Luther's Works*, and references to WA are to *D. Martin Luthers Werke*.

32. The two bracketed insertions appear as alternative readings in the NRSV.

33. This phrase is often attributed to Luther, but it doesn't appear in quite this form anywhere in Luther's works. Luther himself does say, however, "*quia isto articulo stante stat Ecclesia, ruente ruit Ecclesia*" (because if this article [of justification] stands, the church stands; if this article collapses, the church collapses). WA 40/3.352.3.

over to death for our trespasses *and was raised for our justification*" (Rom. 4:24–25, emphasis added). It is the resurrection of the one who died while bearing the burden of human sin that is the decisive confirmation of God's gracious judgment that the sinner will be justified, death will be overcome, and the creature shall have life in abundance.

Paul's concern that this gospel be rightly preached was another feature of his epistle to the Galatians that was taken up in the Reformed confessions, as was Paul's concern expressed in his letter to the Corinthians about their abuse of the Lord's Supper (see 1 Cor. 11:17–26). The Belgic Confession, for instance, affirms that "the true church can be recognized if it has the following marks: The church engages in the pure preaching of the gospel; it makes use of the pure administration of the sacraments as Christ instituted them."[34] A third mark noted by the Reformed confessions is the practice of church discipline, a concern that can be found also in Paul, notably in 1 Corinthians 5:1–5.

One last feature of the church is worthy of mention in this brief survey of Paul's ecclesiology.[35] It appears in his discussion of the church as the body of Christ. The church is a body made up of many members all drawn by the same Spirit and each with a contribution to make to the community as a whole. Although Paul identifies various roles within the church, he is radically egalitarian in his estimation of the worth of each person and of the contribution that each makes. None are dispensable, and all have need of one another: "To each is given the manifestation of the Spirit for the common good" (1 Cor. 12:7). Accordingly, none may say to any other "I have no need of you" (12:21). Confirming this irreducibly communal nature of Christian existence in the body of Christ, Paul explains further that "if one member suffers, all suffer together with it; if one member is honored, all rejoice together with it" (12:26). New life in communion with Christ draws us into communion with one another, in which context, marked still by suffering and bearing still the wounds of crucifixion, we are taught by the Spirit the practices and the life of the resurrected Son.[36]

---

34. Belgic Confession, Article 29. A similar insistence on the "lawful and sincere preaching of the Word of God" and participation "in the sacraments instituted by Christ, and delivered unto us by his apostles, using them in no other way than as they received them from the Lord" appears in chapter 17 of the Second Helvetic Confession.

35. For an extensive and thorough study, see Thompson, *Church according to Paul*.

36. I take the point from Knight, *Eschatological Economy*, 136.

Christian Life

The practices of resurrection life are being learned by the church in the midst of a world that is still scarred by sin and death. The overcoming of death, the work of transformation, healing, and renewal, is a work still in progress, for each of us personally and for all of us corporately. Paul is well aware of the continuing struggle against sin and death; the pull of "the flesh," as Paul calls it, toward death and decay remains a powerful influence in our world and in each of our own lives. We are therefore called to a cruciform existence, an existence in which we die to the flesh in order that we might be raised to new life by the Spirit of Christ. It should be noted that this meta-phorical reference to the flesh does not entail for Paul any disparagement of the material world, which is, of course, the good creation of God. Paul does not subscribe to the Gnostic classification of matter as bad and spirit as good. Rather, his repeated contrast between flesh and spirit serves to des-ignate two alternative ways of life.[37] References to the spirit designate a life enlivened by the Spirit of Christ, whereas life in the flesh refers to a life lived apart from that life-giving Spirit. Such a life, in Paul's view, is no life at all; it is death.

The cruciform existence to which Christians are called is characterized both by dying to sin (see Rom. 6:1–11) and by loving and self-giving service to others. Bruce Longenecker explains that this vision of cruciform existence is repeatedly invoked by Paul as the pattern for Christian life in all manner of situations: "In Romans 12–15 his vision of cruciform identity informs the matter of Jewish Christian and Gentile Christian relations; in 1 Corinthians 8–10, it animates his advice concerning food sacrificed to idols (especially chapter 9); in 1 Corinthians 11, it functions to correct abuses of the Lord's Supper (especially 11.23–26); in 1 Corinthians 12–14, Paul allows it to instruct on the matter of spiritual gifts (especially chapter 13); in Philippians, it ap-pears at the heart of his remarks concerning Christian corporate identity (2.6–11)."[38]

This cruciform life, this life of self-giving love, paradoxical though it may appear, is precisely the pattern of resurrection life. Dying to self and giving ourselves for the sake of others is the mode of our participation, enabled by the Spirit, in the life of the risen Christ. This Pauline account of life transformed

---

37. See Barclay, *Obeying the Truth*, chap. 6.
38. Longenecker, *Triumph of Abraham's God*, 187.

and made new reflects the instruction of Jesus that "those who want to save their life will lose it, and those who lose their life for my sake, and for the sake of the gospel, will save it" (Mark 8:35).

Richard Hays explains that Paul's moral vision of life made new is set within an apocalyptic framework: "The death and resurrection of Jesus was an apocalyptic event that signaled the end of the old age and portended the beginning of the new. . . . The church is to find its identity and vocation by recognizing its role within the cosmic drama of God's reconciliation of the world to himself."[39] Hays cites 2 Corinthians 5:14–18 as a representative articulation of Paul's vision:

> We are convinced that one has died for all; therefore all have died. And he died for all, so that those who live might live no longer for themselves, but for him who died and was raised for them. From now on, therefore, we regard no one from a human point of view; even though we once knew Christ from a human point of view, we know him no longer in that way. So if anyone is in Christ, there is a new creation: everything old has passed away; see, everything has become new! All this is from God, who reconciled us to himself through Christ, and has given us the ministry of reconciliation.

Yet, consistent with the point made earlier that the transformation from old life to new remains a work in progress, Hays also points out that while the church exists at the point of transition from the old age to the new, "it must also *wait* for the consummation of its hope. Salvation will be fully accomplished only at the parousia, the coming of the Lord Jesus Christ in glory"; meanwhile, "the 'already' and the 'not yet' of redemption exist simultaneously in dialectical tension."[40] We exist in the tension between the old order that is passing away and the new order of a creation redeemed and perfected and reconciled at last to the God who brought it into being. Those attentive to the biblical narrative of creation, redemption, and new creation feel the pull in both directions.

Paul knows this tension (see Rom. 7:14–25), but he expects to see, nevertheless, the signs of new life in the churches to whom he writes. To the church in Rome he writes, "Do not be conformed to this world, but be transformed by the renewing of your minds, so that you may discern what is the will of

---

39. Hays, *Moral Vision of the New Testament*, 19.
40. Hays, *Moral Vision of the New Testament*, 20–21.

God—what is good and acceptable and perfect" (Rom. 12:2). He then goes on to describe in specific detail what such a transformation will look like:

> Let love be genuine; hate what is evil, hold fast to what is good; love one another with mutual affection; outdo one another in showing honor. Do not lag in zeal, be ardent in spirit, serve the Lord. Rejoice in hope, be patient in suffering, persevere in prayer. Contribute to the needs of the saints; extend hospitality to strangers. Bless those who persecute you; bless and do not curse them. Rejoice with those who rejoice, weep with those who weep. Live in harmony with one another; do not be haughty, but associate with the lowly; do not claim to be wiser than you are. Do not repay anyone evil for evil, but take thought for what is noble in the sight of all. (Rom. 12:9–17)

To the Galatians, Paul commends life in the Spirit, the fruits of which are "love, joy, peace, patience, kindness, generosity, faithfulness, gentleness, and self-control" (Gal. 5:22–23). To the Philippians he writes, "If then there is any encouragement in Christ, any consolation from love, any sharing in the Spirit, any compassion and sympathy, make my joy complete: be of the same mind, having the same love, being in full accord and of one mind. Do nothing from selfish ambition or conceit, but in humility regard others as better than yourselves. Let each of you look not to your own interests, but to the interests of others" (Phil. 2:1–4).

The descriptions of life transformed on account of the resurrection of Jesus from the dead flow readily from Paul's pen. And yet, as we have said, such transformation is a work in progress. It is not completed yet. Thus, in 1 Thessalonians 3:12–13 Paul's account of the new life takes the form of a prayer: "And may the Lord make you increase and abound in love for one another and for all, just as we abound in love for you. And may he so strengthen your hearts in holiness that you may be blameless before our God and Father at the coming of our Lord Jesus with all his saints."

This is a good point on which to conclude our survey of Paul's conviction that a new age has dawned on account of the resurrection of Jesus from the dead. Just as it was God who raised Jesus from the dead, thus ushering in the new age, so too it is the Lord who will enable us to increase and abound in love, who will strengthen our hearts in holiness, and who will render us blameless at the coming of Christ. Our task as believers is to entrust ourselves to this life-giving power of God.

4

This Jesus Whom
You Crucified

We have considered in the preceding chapter the radical shift in Paul's theology that came about through his encounter with the risen Jesus, including a change to his understanding of who Jesus is. Paul came to recognize Jesus as Lord and Messiah. My purpose in this chapter is to explore further, beyond Paul's writings, the christological claims that flow from the resurrection of Jesus from the dead. But first, let us take a step back, to the crucifixion. The crucifixion was itself a verdict on Jesus's identity. Jesus was, according to those who orchestrated his death, a blasphemer, a pretender to the title *King of the Jews*, a criminal, and a false Messiah. His crucifixion settled, it was supposed, the question of his identity. But then he was raised from death, and that raising called into question the verdict declared by those who sentenced him to death. Those to whom Jesus appeared as the risen one were compelled to reassess who this Jesus is.

Thomas's Confession

We may begin with Thomas. The story in John's Gospel of Thomas's encounter with the risen Jesus and his subsequent christological confession is very

simply told. The disciple Thomas, whose first response to the announcement
that others had seen the risen Lord was disbelief, comes face-to-face with the
risen Jesus himself and immediately confesses, "My Lord and my God!" (John
20:28). John presents Thomas's confession as a straightforward conclusion
drawn from the evidence he now sees. Or so it seems.

But the matter is not so simple. Centuries later, G. E. Lessing pointed out
that there is no straightforward logical connection between the raising of
Jesus from the dead and the Christian tradition's creedal claims about Jesus's
identity. "If on historical grounds," Lessing asks, "I have no objection to the
statement that this Christ himself rose from the dead, must I therefore accept
it as true that this risen Christ was the Son of God?"[1] Lessing continues:

> That the Christ, against whose resurrection I can raise no important historical
> objection, therefore declared himself to be the Son of God; that his disciples
> therefore believed him to be such; this I gladly believe from my heart. For these
> truths, as truths of one and the same class, follow quite naturally on one another.
>
> But to jump with that historical truth to a quite different class of truths,
> and to demand of me that I should form all my metaphysical and moral ideas
> accordingly; to expect me to alter all my fundamental ideas of the nature of the
> Godhead because I cannot set any credible testimony against the resurrection
> of Christ: if that is not a μετάβασις εἰς ἄλλο γένος then I do not know what
> Aristotle meant by that phrase.[2]

The Aristotelian phrase "μετάβασις εἰς ἄλλο γένος" means "transformation
into another genus." Lessing contends that we cannot move via a process of
logical inference from historical claims to metaphysical ones. The claim that
the disciples believed that Jesus was the Son of God or even that Jesus declared
himself to be the Son of God are historical claims. So too is the claim, Lessing concedes, that Christ has been raised from the dead. But none of these
historical truths, if we accept them as such, provide a logical proof that Jesus
is indeed the Son of God. They merely show that the disciples believed that
to be the case. Despite Wolfhart Pannenberg's efforts to demonstrate the
contrary, the resurrection, should we accept that it happened, does not lead
by way of straightforward logical inference to the conclusion that Jesus is the
Son of God and second person of the Trinity.

---

1. Lessing, "On the Proof of Spirit and of Power," 54.
2. Lessing, "On the Proof of Spirit and of Power," 54.

John is not inattentive to the epistemic problem that Lessing identifies here. I suspect that he would accept Lessing's point that Thomas's christological confession is not a matter of logical inference. John recognizes, after all, that the Spirit is involved in our learning the truth about Jesus (John 16:12–15). He recognizes too that the confession of Jesus as Lord is justified even for those who "have not seen and yet have come to believe" (20:29). John is not epistemologically naive. Rather, in presenting the story of Thomas's confession as simply as he does, John reveals, I suggest, that he is well aware of the epistemic complexities of the situation. By making no attempt to provide any justification for or logical explanation of Thomas's response, John rejects the premise of Lessing's skepticism—namely, that all our claims to know must pass the test of deductive reasoning whereby a conclusion (e.g., Jesus is Lord and God) follows necessarily from the premise (Jesus has been raised from the dead). The satisfaction of Thomas's insistence on empirical evidence that Jesus was risen does not render his response to that evidence any less a matter of faith. But faith arises in consequence of God's self-disclosure and active agency in the transformation of hearts and minds. Thomas is subject to the same conditions of understanding already indicated in Jesus's promise that "the Spirit . . . will guide you into all the truth" (John 16:13).

The same point is made by Paul when he affirms that "no one can say 'Jesus is Lord' except by the Holy Spirit" (1 Cor. 12:3; see also Eph. 1:17). Ingolf Dalferth correctly observes that "faith in the resurrection message admittedly is produced not without human proclamation, though also not by it (Rom. 10:14–18), but only by the δύναμις θεοῦ [power of God] (Rom. 1:16), which constitutes the content, realization, and causal ground of the message."[3] And further, "Only those whom God himself encounters through Jesus are persuaded of the truth of the resurrection message."[4] We must hold fast to this epistemological principle in all our further exploration of how the recognition that Jesus has been raised from the dead has led the Christian church to confess him as Lord and Savior and second person of the Godhead.

Let us return then to the christological confession itself. Thomas confesses that Jesus is "my Lord and my God." This is an instructive model of what christological confession entails: it is self-involving. Thomas confesses that Jesus is "*my* Lord and *my* God." This does not mean that Thomas's confession is a *merely* subjective judgment. Rather, the objective reality here recognized

3. Dalferth, *Crucified and Resurrected*, 63.
4. Dalferth, *Crucified and Resurrected*, 64.

by Thomas implicates the subject. Thomas is not left unchanged by this moment of recognition. He is transformed by a lordship newly recognized and
accepted and by an understanding of God centered now on relationship with
the risen Christ. That too is a principle that we must continue to be mindful
of as we pursue the explorations of this chapter.

The pattern we have seen in Paul and now in Thomas of the resurrection
prompting a new understanding of the identity of Jesus is repeated often
through the course of the New Testament witness. We will take one more
biblical example before delving into the development of Christology beyond
the canonical texts.

Peter's Proclamation

In a sermon delivered to the gathered crowd on the day of Pentecost, the
apostle Peter proclaims that the risen Jesus is Lord and Messiah: "This Jesus
God raised up, and of that all of us are witnesses. . . . Therefore let the entire
house of Israel know with certainty that God has made him both Lord and
Messiah, this Jesus whom you crucified" (Acts 2:32, 36). Peter is at pains to
point out that this conclusion fits with the biblical story of God's prior engagement with Israel. It fits, Peter contends, using some rather creative biblical
interpretation, with David's anticipation of a coming Messiah who would
not be abandoned to Hades and whose flesh would not experience corruption
(Acts 2:15, citing Ps. 16). The Scriptures attest and the resurrection confirms,
according to the logic of Peter's argument, that Jesus is indeed the Messiah
who succeeds and is superior to David.

Note that we are not abandoning here our previous claim that the identity
of Jesus is scarcely a matter of straightforward logical deduction from the
fact of his resurrection. Peter's proclamation takes place in the context of the
Pentecost, and Peter himself makes clear that Jesus is the agent of his own
self-disclosure, and it is he who in the power of the Spirit "pours out this that
you both see and hear" (Acts 2:33). Divine agency in the process of coming to
believe remains indispensable. Note too that the denial of a straightforward
deductive relation between Jesus's resurrection and his divine identity does
not mean that there is no objective relation between the action of God in
raising Jesus from the dead and his identity as the Son of God. The point is
simply an epistemic one: our apprehension of the objective relation between

resurrection and Jesus's identity depends on divine illumination. God is involved in our recognition that Jesus is Messiah and Lord.

The epistemological point with which I am here concerned is articulated well by John Webster:

> He cannot be approached as if he were an elusive figure, absent from us, locked in transcendence or buried in the past, and only to be discovered through the exercise of human ingenuity. Christology cannot creep up on him and catch him unawares. Nor is it at liberty to decide that his self-presence is so indefinite or fogged over by the distortions and incapacities of his human witnesses that theology must run its own independent checks in order to reassure itself that he really is able to present himself. All such strategies, whether in biblical scholarship or philosophical and dogmatic theology, are in the end methodologically sophisticated forms of infidelity. Their assumption is that he is not present unless demonstrably present—present, that is, to undisturbed and unconverted reason. But to such demonstration he will not yield the mystery of his person.[5]

Christ is known, therefore, in virtue of his presence with us as the risen one.

It does not matter much for our present purposes whether the sermon in Acts 2:14–36 is an accurate recording of a sermon delivered by Peter himself on the day of Pentecost or whether it is largely the work of "Luke," the purported author of Luke-Acts.[6] The key point is that the sermon presents for our consideration the relation between Jesus's resurrection and his identity.

Consideration of the claim made in Peter's sermon that God has made Jesus both Lord and Messiah confronts us immediately with a question: Did the resurrection confirm or establish Jesus's identity as Lord and Messiah? In other words, were these titles (and the identity they designate) conferred on him by God at the time of the resurrection, or did the resurrection confirm that Jesus was indeed Lord and Messiah and had been throughout his ministry? The question arises because of the Greek construction: "Therefore let the entire house of Israel know with certainty that God *has made* [ἐποίησεν ὁ θεός] him both Lord and Messiah, this Jesus whom you crucified" (Acts 2:36). The word ἐποίησεν (has made) implies, according to C. K. Barrett, "that there

---

5. Webster, "Prolegomena to Christology," 137–38.
6. The claim that Luke was the author of both Luke's Gospel and the book of Acts has come down to us from the patristic era. It appeared earliest in the writings of Irenaeus from the late second century. The tradition of Lukan authorship is widely accepted, although there is considerable debate about whether the author Luke is the same Luke referred to in Colossians 4:14.

was once a time when the crucified Jesus was not κύριος [Lord] and χριστὸς [Christ], and the questions arise when he was appointed to these positions, and exactly what positions the terms denote."[7] Bruce Chilton suggests that "the speech in Acts portrays God as *making* Jesus both Lord (*kurios*) and Anointed (*christos*) by means of the resurrection."[8] Barrett himself contends that the surrounding verses "strongly suggest that the appointment took place when God raised up and thereby vindicated Jesus."[9] He does indicate, however, that although it "is not the most natural way of taking the words used," one could take the verse to mean, "Resurrection and ascension prove that God had, before his public ministry, appointed Jesus to these offices."[10]

While we may hesitate at the use of the term *prove*, this less natural way of reading Peter's words aligns with the standard position of orthodox Christian faith as represented in the church's creedal tradition. It is no surprise then that the interpretation of this verse has been frequently debated.[11] Justification for the less natural reading has been offered by a number of scholars, notably in recent years by Kavin Rowe.[12] Rowe acknowledges that the suggestion in Peter's claim that God *has made* Jesus both Lord and Messiah by means of the resurrection is a startling one:

> The initial surprise at Peter's statement comes with good reason, for it certainly seems clear enough from the very beginning of the story in [Luke's] Gospel that Jesus is already Lord and Christ. Indeed, even while still in Mary's womb, Jesus is referred to as ὁ κύριος in Elizabeth's address to Mary: καὶ πόθεν μοι τοῦτο ἵνα ἔλθῃ ἡ μήτηρ τοῦ κυρίου μου πρὸς ἐμέ (1.43). Moreover, the angels announce to the shepherds that Jesus—still only an infant in the story-line—is already κύριος and χριστός: "today is born to you in the city of David a Savior, who is χριστὸς κύριος" (2.11). Prima facie, then, Peter's statement in Acts 2.36 seems to exist in serious tension with the christological claims of Luke's Gospel.[13]

7. Barrett, *Acts of the Apostles*, 151.
8. Chilton, *Resurrection Logic*, 113.
9. Barrett, *Acts of the Apostles*, 151.
10. Barrett, *Acts of the Apostles*, 151.
11. The interpretation of Acts 2:36 was one of the flashpoints in early patristic debates during the development of the church's creedal Christology. For an overview of the classical contestation surrounding the interpretation of Acts 2:36 and its reemergence in the modern era, see Rowe, "Acts 2.36 and the Continuity of Lukan Christology," 38–41.
12. See the aforementioned article: Rowe, "Acts 2.36 and the Continuity of Lukan Christology." For some other examples, see Conzelmann, *Acts of the Apostles*, 21; Schnabel, *Acts*, 151; Neil, *Acts of the Apostles*, 78; and Pervo, *Acts*, 84n87.
13. Rowe, "Acts 2.36 and the Continuity of Lukan Christology," 37.

Rowe goes on to argue, however, that when Acts 2:36 is understood within its wider narrative context, that of Luke-Acts as a whole, it "fits well with the christological logic of the wider Lukan narrative."[14] Central to Rowe's argument is that "for Luke, there was no moment at which Jesus was not κύριος"; indeed, "Jesus is already named κύριος while still in the womb (Luke 1.43)."[15] And further, "Luke is at pains throughout the entire Gospel to narrate Jesus' identity as ὁ κύριος upon the earth."[16]

What then is Peter suggesting with his claim following the resurrection that "God has made him both Lord and Messiah"? I think a clue is given in the words preceding this christological claim: "let the entire house of Israel know with certainty" (Acts 2:36). The resurrection of Jesus from the dead, Peter seems to be suggesting, should leave the house of Israel in no doubt of who Jesus truly is. That God has *made* him both Lord and Messiah does not indicate that there was a time when Jesus was neither of these things, but emphasizes instead that Jesus's identity is established by God. This is especially important, Rowe argues, because his identity as Lord and Messiah "was threatened by his rejection and crucifixion but reaffirmed by his resurrection. Such a reading does not diminish the force of ποιεῖν but rather takes seriously ὁ θεὸς as its subject. In this way the emphasis is placed upon God's continuous action in the life of Jesus despite human violence, rejection, and death."[17] Rowe further explains that "the 'making' of which Acts 2.36 speaks does not refer, therefore, to an ontological transformation in the identity of Jesus or his status (from not κύριος to κύριος) but to an epistemological shift in the perception of the human community."[18] Frank Matera, whom Rowe cites, makes the same point: Acts 2:36 "should be read in light of the angel's announcement to the shepherds that a savior has been born who is Messiah and Lord (Luke 2.11). Since the resurrection is the moment when God enthrones his Son, Israel should now know who Jesus *always* was."[19]

Thomas's confession and Peter's sermon are further instances of the theological claim we have seen in the Pauline correspondence and that pervades the whole of the New Testament. We speak truly of Jesus only when we speak

14. Rowe, "Acts 2.36 and the Continuity of Lukan Christology," 45.
15. Rowe, "Acts 2.36 and the Continuity of Lukan Christology," 51.
16. Rowe, "Acts 2.36 and the Continuity of Lukan Christology," 51. Rowe supplies abundant textual evidence for this claim and further develops the point in his book *Early Narrative Christology*.
17. Rowe, "Acts 2.36 and the Continuity of Lukan Christology," 54.
18. Rowe, "Acts 2.36 and the Continuity of Lukan Christology," 55.
19. Matera, *New Testament Christology*, 268n44. Emphasis original.

of him in relation to God. The converse is also true: we speak truly of God only when we speak of God in relation to Jesus. Furthermore, our speaking truly is enabled, as we insisted earlier, by the power and guidance of the Holy Spirit. Though not yet fully developed, the New Testament's insistence on these three points provides the basis for the doctrine of the Trinity. Here again the resurrection confirms what has always been the case. As John Webster puts it, "The resurrection is the temporal enactment of the eternal relation of Father and Son."[20] Or as John's Gospel formulates it, "For just as the Father has life in himself, so he has granted the Son also to have life in himself" (John 5:26). Webster continues, "[Jesus's] resurrection is the elucidation and confirmation of his antecedent deity, by virtue of which he is the one he is. From the standpoint of the resurrection, Jesus' entire temporal career is to be understood as the dwelling among us of the grace, truth and glory of God's own life. His earthly history is thus stretched between its eternal basis on the Word ('in him was life': Jn 1.4) and its consummation at the resurrection in which that eternal basis becomes manifest."[21]

Under the impact of their experience of the risen Christ, and their consequent apprehension of all that they had experienced of his life and ministry among them, the first followers of Jesus felt compelled to confess that "in Christ God was reconciling the world to himself" (2 Cor. 5:19). This conviction, articulated here by Paul, inspired the narrative recollections of Jesus's life and teachings by the four Gospel writers, each of whom in their respective ways saw that the work Jesus does and the kingdom he proclaims are inseparably bound up with his identity as the one in whom God fulfills the divine promise to dwell with God's people. There are four crucial aspects, however, to this basic affirmation of Jesus's identity. As Ingolf Dalferth points out, the question of Jesus's identity must be answered on four different levels: the historical, the eschatological, the soteriological, and the trinitarian.[22]

The Historical Level

To speak of the one who was crucified and now lives is to speak historically of Jesus of Nazareth, who was born in the time of King Herod, lived in

---

20. Webster, "Resurrection and Scripture," 139.
21. Webster, "Resurrection and Scripture," 139.
22. Dalferth, *Crucified and Resurrected*, 85.

Palestine, taught in the towns and cities of Galilee and Judea, gathered a group of followers about him, was crucified under Pontius Pilate, but then appeared to his followers after being raised from death. Careful attentiveness to the historical reality of Jesus of Nazareth—including all the particulars of Jesus's life and ministry seen in their historical context—is essential, therefore, to a theological account of who Jesus is. Contrary to N. T. Wright's erroneous assertions that theologians commonly "dismiss with scorn" the need for such attentiveness,[23] the theologians Wright appears to have in view have instead argued that the historical reality of Jesus of Nazareth is of the utmost importance. The point at issue is whether the true Jesus of history can be discovered only by setting aside the church's faith that God has raised Jesus from the dead, or whether instead the historical Jesus appears most distinctly precisely in the light of that faith. Thus, for example, T. F. Torrance affirms that "it is indeed the resurrection that really discloses and gives access to the *historical* Jesus, for it enables us . . . to understand him in terms of his own intrinsic *logos*, and appreciate him in the light of his own inherent truth."[24] Historical discourse about Jesus's identity is essential inasmuch as the subject of that discourse is the historical figure of Jesus of Nazareth, but it is a historical discourse informed by theology.[25]

Put simply, it is of the utmost theological importance that the one who was raised from the grave was the same one who proclaimed the coming kingdom of God and taught around the region of Galilee and beyond, who healed the sick and consorted with sinners, who was brought to trial by the religious authorities of his day, and who was crucified under Pontius Pilate. All of these features of Jesus's life are accessible in some degree to historical inquiry and inform our understanding of who Jesus is, but that they constitute together the outworking of the divine economy through which God is bringing to completion God's creative and redemptive purposes for the world can be known only in light of the resurrection of Jesus from the dead and under the guidance of the Holy Spirit (cf. John 16:13). Only in this light is it possible to discern what was really going on in Jesus's earthly career. Theological categories are not adjunct but essential to any adequate proclamation of what happened.

23. Wright makes this and similar accusations multiple times in his 2018 Gifford Lectures, subsequently published as Wright, *History and Eschatology*. The phrase quoted here is found on p. 117.

24. Torrance, *Christian Doctrine of God*, 47.

25. We will say more about the relation between theology and history in chap. 6, below.

The Eschatological Level

Just as historical discourse is essential to a proper description of Jesus's identity, so too is eschatological discourse. In answering the question "Who is Jesus?," we must speak eschatologically of the one who was raised from death and appeared to many in the days following his death and resurrection. To speak thus is not to depart, however, from the realm of historical speech. It is to confess, rather, that in the raising of Jesus from the dead the eschatological reality of God's final victory over sin and death is manifest in history. The tomb is empty and the disciples are able to see and hear and touch the same Jesus, though in a reconstituted body, whom they had accompanied through the course of his ministry, who died and was buried, but who has now been made alive.

The messianic title given to Jesus—he is the hoped-for Messiah of Israel—indicates further that in Jesus the eschatological fulfillment of God's purposes for the world is beginning to take shape within the terrain of human history. "The eschatological kingdom *has already* dawned and no longer needs to be merely hoped for and expected."[26] The signs of this dawn were evident throughout the course of Jesus's ministry, as is confirmed by the delegation of John the Baptist's disciples, who inquire of Jesus whether he is the one to come or whether they should wait for another. "Jesus answered them, 'Go and tell John what you hear and see: the blind receive their sight, the lame walk, the lepers are cleansed, the deaf hear, the dead are raised [ἐγείρονται; from ἐγείρω], and the poor have good news brought to them'" (Matt. 11:4–5; cf. Luke 7:22). T. F. Torrance points out that ἐγείρω, one of two favored terms for resurrection in the New Testament, is used also to speak of the raising up of the sick, thus indicating that "the miraculous acts of healing are regarded as falling within the orbit of resurrection, and as belonging to the creative and re-creative activity of God in incarnation and resurrection. In these miracles the resurrection is already evidencing itself beforehand in signs and wonders."[27] The liberation from various kinds of bondage into new and abundant life is the work that God has been engaged in throughout Israel's history, and it confirms—so Jesus indicates to John's disciples—that he is indeed God's promised Messiah, "the one who is to come" (Matt. 11:3). The resurrection of Jesus from the dead provides decisive confirmation of this reality.

26. Dalferth, *Crucified and Resurrected*, 126.
27. Torrance, *Atonement*, 205.

The Soteriological Level

This claim introduces the third mode of discourse necessary to any adequate account of Jesus's identity: the soteriological. The soteriological dimension of Jesus's identity is summed up in the confession that he is the Savior, the one in and through whom the triune God effects the work of salvation and redemption.[28] This confession of the unity of his person and work was one of the points at issue in the christological debates of the fourth century. Arius, the presbyter from Alexandria whose account of Jesus's identity prompted the debates that led to the ecumenical Council of Nicaea in 325, apparently was able to affirm that Jesus was the redeemer. However, he gave an account of Jesus's identity as one who is other and less than God; and that, in the eyes of his opponents, undermined his soteriological claim.[29] Athanasius, the leading opponent of Arius's views, contended that the work of salvation could be accomplished by God alone and that Jesus could not properly be called Savior if he were not himself divine.

> We also, by God's grace, briefly indicated that the Word of the Father is Himself divine, that all things that are owe their being to His will and power, and that it is through Him that the Father gives order to the creation, by Him that all things are moved, and through Him that they receive their being. . . . He has been manifested in a human body for this reason only, out of the love and goodness of His Father, for the salvation of us men. We will begin, then, with the creation of the world and with God its Maker, for the first fact that you must grasp is this: *the renewal of creation has been wrought by the Self-same Word Who made it in the beginning.* There is thus no inconsistency between creation and salvation for the One Father has employed the same Agent for

---

28. See, e.g., Titus 2:11–14.

29. It is a matter of debate whether we have sufficient extant material from Arius himself to reconstruct his soteriology. Robert E. Gregg and Dennis E. Groh have argued, however, that "the conflict between Alexandrian orthodoxy and early Arianism is at base a clash between two soteriological programmes. . . . Salvation, for orthodoxy, is effected by the Son's essential identity with the Father. . . . Salvation for Arianism is effected by the Son's identity with the creatures." Gregg and Groh, "Centrality of Soteriology in Early Arianism," 262. However, Rowan Williams contends, correctly in my view, that there is no exposition of a soteriology in Arius's own extant writings that would go along with his doctrine of God. Yet Athanasius, as we will see, considered it necessary to stress that the logic of salvation would certainly be undermined should we fail, as Arius does, to uphold the identity in one being of the Father and the Son. Soteriology was evidently a point at issue in the Arian debate, even though we do not have access to Arius's own exposition of the doctrine of salvation. For Williams's discussion of the matter, see Williams, *Arius,* 257.

both works, effecting the salvation of the world through the same Word Who made it in the beginning.[30]

On account of sin, Athanasius argues, human beings have distorted the image of God in which they are made. They are not capable themselves of restoring the image. "How could this be done," Athanasius asks, "save by the coming of the very Image Himself, our Savior Jesus Christ? Men could not have done it, for they are only made after the Image; nor could angels have done it, for they are not the images of God. The Word of God came in His own Person, because it was He alone, the Image of the Father Who could recreate man made after the Image."[31] That salvation is the work of God alone is a point supported by the prophet Isaiah: "For I am the LORD your God, the Holy One of Israel, your Savior. . . . I, I am the LORD, and besides me there is no savior" (Isa. 43:3, 11).

This saving work of Christ is completed through the resurrection, which is a passing from death to life, a re-creation of that humanity which had fallen into the bondage of sin and death. In death, Christ united himself with our weakness and humiliation, took upon himself the dreadful consequences of our sinful defiance of God, and bore the condemnation of that defiance. But he did so precisely in order to show that "neither death, nor life, nor angels, nor rulers, nor things present, nor things to come, nor powers, nor height, nor depth, nor anything else in all creation, will be able to separate us from the love of God in Christ Jesus our Lord" (Rom. 8:38–39). Not even sin and death can separate us from the love of God because the divine Son of God himself makes his way to the far country, to the place where defiance of the Father's love reaches its desperate end in utter degradation and despair. The place of crucifixion is aptly named *Calvariae locus*, Golgotha—the place of the skull. The Son of God descends to this place in order to bring the prodigal home. The creedal confession that he "descended into hell" makes this point at least, that there is no place of degradation and despair that is finally beyond the searching and redemptive love of God.

Resurrection, we might say, is the firstfruits of a harvest that will be completed with the homecoming of prodigal humanity, who chose to wander far

---

30. Athanasius, *On the Incarnation* 1.1. Emphasis original. Athanasius does not mention Arius by name in *On the Incarnation*, but it is clear that he has Arian theology in his sights.
31. Athanasius, *On the Incarnation* 3.13.

away from the giver and sustainer of all life and found itself in an alien and inhospitable land. The allusions to Jesus's parable of the prodigal son here echo the primordial story of humanity's defiance of God, in consequence of which they were sent forth from the garden of Eden (Gen. 2:23). The estrangement from God escalates further when, having murdered his brother, "Cain went away from the presence of the LORD" (4:16). And yet, as it was for Cain's parents, the recipients of garments to cover their own nakedness and shame (3:21), and as it was for Cain himself, who received a mark of protection on his forehead (4:15), so it is for fallen humanity as a whole: it is the Lord who acts to protect and save those creatures who want to live life on their own terms and in defiance of the giver of life, only to discover that life on their own terms is no life at all.

We must emphasize here a further aspect of Jesus's identity that is likewise confirmed by the resurrection. He is the new Adam, the one in whom our true humanity is restored and made new (Rom. 5:12–21; 1 Cor. 15:45–49). But this restoration depends on Christ's thoroughgoing identification with our humanity. The Son of God and second person of the Trinity takes on our identity, even our fallen identity, so that he might rescue it from death. "Though he was in the form of God, . . . [he] emptied himself, taking the form of a slave, being born in human likeness. And being found in human form, he humbled himself and became obedient to the point of death" (Phil. 2:6–8).

Had Jesus not died but ascended to the Father without passing through death, it would have been possible to imagine that Jesus was not truly human. This is indeed what was imagined by some early believers who were influenced by Gnostic habits of mind and so sought to protect God from identification with our humanity in all its material weakness and vulnerability. They worshiped a docetic Christ who only appeared to be human, whose divine soul left the body of Jesus prior to his crucifixion, and who was therefore spared the pain of crucifixion and the corruption of death. But a disembodied soul that does not suffer death but returns directly to life with the Father offers humanity no salvation. For we are embodied creatures. If we are to be restored to life in reconciled relationship with God, that must include the indivisible totality of our human being. It is for that reason that the eternal Word of God became flesh and assumed our human nature in its entirety. Without that full assumption of our humanity, the resurrection of Jesus offers no hope for humankind and no redemption from sin and death. As Gregory Nazianzus famously declared,

"For that which He has not assumed He has not healed."[32] Because the Son of God has assumed our full humanity and is justly called the second Adam, Paul is confident that just as Christ was raised from the dead by the glory of the Father, so we too who have been buried with him by baptism into death might walk in newness of life (see Rom. 6:4). As Colin Gunton thus puts it, "The dogmatic significance [of the resurrection] is as much tied up with Jesus's humanity as with his divinity. As the first-born from the dead, he represents as human the destiny of those who will later die in him as the extended parallel between him and the believer in 1 Corinthians 15 makes clear."[33]

The resurrection of Jesus from the dead both reveals and confirms his identity as truly human and truly divine, as is confessed in the creedal tradition of the church. This is not an interpretation of the event of the resurrection imposed from without but is inherent in the resurrection itself and is recognized through faith under the guidance of the Spirit. In death and resurrection, the divine Son of God takes on our fallen and lost humanity, seeks us out in the valley of death, and drains the bitter cup of alienation from God, all in order to heal our broken humanity and restore it to fullness of life in communion with God. This drama of redemption and reconciliation is aptly summed up in the preamble to Karl Barth's great exposition of the subject in his *Church Dogmatics*:

> That Jesus Christ is very God is shown in His way into the far country in which He the Lord became a servant. For in the majesty of the true God it happened that the eternal Son of the eternal Father became obedient by offering and humbling Himself to be the brother of man, to take His place with the transgressor, to judge him by judging Himself and dying in his place. But God the Father raised Him from the dead, and in so doing recognised and gave effect to His death and passion as a satisfaction made for us, as our conversion to God, and therefore as our redemption from death to life.[34]

The Trinitarian Level

The fourth mode of discourse necessary to proper speech about the person of Jesus the Christ is trinitarian. This mode has been latent in all that has been

---

32. Gregory Nazianzus, "To Cledonius the Priest against Apollinarius, Epistle 101."
33. Gunton, *Father, Son and Holy Spirit*, 154.
34. Barth, *Church Dogmatics* IV/1, 157.

said so far. The drama of redemption and new creation played out through the incarnate life of the divine Word—through his death, resurrection, and ascension—is the act of the triune God: Father, Son, and Holy Spirit. Recognition by the first Christians that in speaking of Jesus we must confess him to be not only our brother but also our Lord led to a radical reconception of the God of Abraham, Isaac, and Jacob. The recognition of Jesus as Lord in virtue of the resurrection did not entail the arrival of a new God on the scene, a God other than the God of Israel. But it did prompt recognition of the fact that, as Richard Bauckham has put it, Jesus is included in the unique identity of the One God of Israel. "Jesus, the New Testament writers are saying, belongs inherently to *who God is*."[35] This is a point evident in Peter's speech in Acts 2, to which we have already referred. There are seven instances of the term κύριος (Lord) in Peter's speech, five of which appear in Old Testament quotations. As Ling Cheng has pointed out, the references serve to make clear that "the Pentecostal happening is the fulfilment of God's promises and Jesus is the key to that realisation."[36] Cheng explains further that while κύριος is a term used to refer explicitly to God, in Peter's speech and in the Old Testament texts he cites it is used of God and of the Messiah with whom Jesus is fully identified. Jesus shares the divine name.[37] What is more, it is Jesus who, having received the Spirit from the Father, then pours out that which the crowd has witnessed at Pentecost. He is thus an agent of divine action.

Throughout the course of the Gospel narratives we discover that the full span of Jesus's life and ministry—from his conception in the womb of Mary through to his death, resurrection, and ascension—is rooted in his relation to the one he calls Father and is sustained and empowered by the Spirit. Jesus is who he is, according to the New Testament record, in virtue of his relation to the Father as mediated by the Spirit.[38] The whole story of the gospel is predicated upon this triune relationality. The Son does the work of the Father in the power of the Spirit. The implied unity of Father and Son in the execution of this work was such as to provoke repeated charges of blasphemy from some who perceived Jesus to be assuming prerogatives in word and action that belonged to God alone. He forgave sinners (Matt. 9:2–3; Mark 2:5–6; Luke 5:20–21); he assumed authority over the Sabbath law (Matt. 12:8; Mark

35. Bauckham, *God Crucified*, 45. Emphasis original.
36. Cheng, *Characterisation of God in Acts*, 51.
37. See Cheng, *Characterisation of God in Acts*, 51.
38. I take the point from Gunton, *Father, Son and Holy Spirit*, 161.

3:27–28; Luke 6:5; John 5:18); he referred to himself as the Son of Man seated at the right hand of God (Matt. 26:64; Mark 14:61–64); he placed himself before Abraham (John 8:58–59). These were offenses against the theological sensibilities of the religious authorities of the day and resulted in his being brought to trial before the council of priests and crucified at the hands of the Romans. As noted earlier, the trial and execution were intended to settle the question of Jesus's identity as a blasphemer, for which Levitical law prescribes a penalty of death (Lev. 24:13–16). The presumptuous claim of unity with the Father would be exposed through the just sentence of death as an offense against the holiness and the oneness of God. Or such was the intent.

It is in this context that the raising of Jesus from the dead is properly spoken of as God's vindication of Jesus. The charges of blasphemy are overturned by the resurrection precisely because the Father and the Son truly are one. Their unity is confirmed. Jesus is shown to be the beloved Son in whom God is at work reconciling the world to Godself (2 Cor. 5:19). The Father is shown to be the creator and giver of life. The Spirit, moreover, is shown to be the life that flows between Father and Son and that is poured out on all who through baptism are crucified and raised to new life with him (Rom. 8:9–11).

A further feature of the divine vindication of Jesus through the resurrection is that the entire drama of Jesus's life, death, and resurrection ought now to be recognized both as the definitive disclosure of who God is and as the salvific working out of God's purposes. It is an act through which God simultaneously reveals God's own life to us and enables us to share in it. The point is evident throughout the Gospel narratives but is given explicit expression in Jesus's prayer to the Father in John 17:

> As you, Father, are in me and I am in you, may they also be in us, so that the world may believe that you have sent me. The glory that you have given me I have given them, so that they may be one, as we are one, I in them and you in me, that they may become completely one, so that the world may know that you have sent me and have loved them even as you have loved me. Father, I desire that those also, whom you have given me, may be with me where I am, to see my glory, which you have given me because you loved me before the foundation of the world.
>
> Righteous Father, the world does not know you, but I know you; and these know that you have sent me. I made your name known to them, and I will make it known, so that the love with which you have loved me may be in them, and I in them. (John 17:21–26)

We learn also through the resurrection not only that *God loves*, as had long been recognized (see, e.g., Deut. 7:9; Ps. 86:15), but that *God is love* (1 John 4:8, 16). The unity of Father and Son in the power of the Spirit that cannot be destroyed even by death confirms that love is the content of God's being. This is what it means to say that God is impassible—not that God cannot suffer the agony of crucifixion or genuinely experience the reality of death (Heb. 2:9). It means, rather, that God's being as love is inviolable. The passion of Christ is the decisive manifestation of divine love through which God's impassibility is revealed. For God's love is shown to be steadfast even when mocked, scorned, and rejected by the creatures God's loving hand has made. Even the death of the beloved Son cannot destroy God's being as love, for it is divine love that raises the Son from the grave and wins the final victory over death.

In the death and resurrection of Christ, therefore, we see the Father at work as the one who gives life to the dead and calls into existence that which is not (Rom. 4:17); we see the Son at work as the one who descends to the realm of alienation and death in order to seek and to save those who are held in bondage there (John 5:25); and we see the Spirit at work as the one who raised Jesus from the dead (Rom. 8:11) and who is now at work drawing human beings into the resurrection life of the Son, thus completing their liberation from the bondage of sin and death (Rom. 8:2).

I have argued that the resurrection both confirms and reveals the identity of Jesus as the beloved Son of the Father and second person of the Trinity, but it is important here to reiterate two earlier points: First, the resurrection confirms and reveals the *eternal* relation between Father and Son; it does not establish that relation in some adoptionist fashion.[39] The resurrection is not a retrospective declaration of the Son's divinity but the expression of his eternal participation in the divine life—that is, of his eternal communion with the Father in the power of the Spirit. And second, we must stress again that the agent of this revelation is God. Only God can enable our human apprehension and recognition of the risen one as the beloved Son of God.

39. On the need to guard against the adoptionist view, found all too often among contemporary theologians, see Molnar, *Divine Freedom*, esp. 34–37.

5

Creation Made New

This book began with an exploration of the "evangelical witness"—that is, with the testimony of the Gospel writers to the resurrection of Jesus from the dead. Let us recall once more the testimony of Mary Magdalene, the first consistently attested witness to the reality of the resurrection. I'll take John's version, but as we have seen, Matthew and Luke support the point.

As John has it, "Early on the first day of the week, while it was still dark, Mary Magdalene came to [Jesus's] tomb and saw that the stone had been moved from the tomb. So she ran and went to Simon Peter and the other disciple, the one whom Jesus loved, and said to them, 'They have taken the Lord out of the tomb, and we do not know where they have laid him'" (John 20:1–2). Neither Mary nor the disciples yet know what to think, but as the story unfolds it is Mary who first encounters the risen Lord and returns once more to tell the news: "I have seen the Lord" (20:18). With these words, and the reality to which they bear witness, the world is changed. A new creation dawns. In this chapter, I will explore this theme of new creation. The world is changed because of the resurrection. A process of renovation is underway; a new creation has begun as the world in God's hands is made new and directed to its final end. That is what the resurrection signifies. Choan-Seng Song writes, "Because of the empty tomb, the world no longer lies at the mercy of the power of destruction and decay. On the contrary, the world

81

can be renewed and revitalized as witness to God's victory over the power of death and destruction."[1]

A careful articulation of the point is required here. On the one hand, the resurrection enables us to recognize that the divine work of renovation and the renewal of creation has been underway throughout the course of human history—ever since, that is, the creature first sought to take charge of creation and fashion a life for itself apart from the one who is the giver of life. On the other hand, the resurrection establishes something decisively new. The final victory over the creature's resistance, the victory over sin and death, is accomplished in the midst of history. That does not mean that sin and death do not as yet retain a hold on the creature, but the resurrection makes clear that they have no future. Sin and death belong to a world that is passing away; the renewal of creation has begun.

The Decisive Clue

The long history of God's dealings with Israel, including the career of Jesus of Nazareth, provides much evidence of the divine work of transformation and renewal. But all of this would be, and indeed was for the first disciples, so much puzzling data were it not for the resurrection. That event, the raising of the crucified Jesus, confirms once and for all that the life of the world is sustained and renewed through the faithfulness and the sovereign love of God. Despite appearances sometimes, and despite our sinful resistance, the nature of reality and the final telos of creation is revealed in the one who says "See, I am making all things new" (Rev. 21:5) and whose own resurrection is the confirmation of precisely that fact.

My suggestion that the resurrection is the decisive clue to what is going on in the world is not original, of course. I take it from the New Testament. For instance, we see it in Luke 24 through Jesus's conversation with the disciples on the road to Emmaus who were struggling to make sense of all that had gone on in Jerusalem, including especially the reports of the women who had found the tomb empty and had seen a vision of angels who declared that Jesus was alive (Luke 24:23). Jesus explains to the disciples how all of this fits with and illumines God's dealings with Israel throughout the course of

1. Song, *Compassionate God*, 101–2.

its history. Commenting on Luke 24, N. T. Wright explains that "Easter for Luke is about the meaning of history on the one hand . . . and the task and shape of the church, flowing directly from that history, on the other."[2] Stefan Alkier sees the same theological claim being made in the writings of Paul: "In the light of the cross and resurrection, the faithfulness of the creator God and the reliability of his traditional promises and the cosmological turning of the ages, through God's powerful act of raising the Crucified One, build the hermeneutical system for interpretation [of] the reality of the world."[3]

"See, I am making all things new." These words from Revelation 21 are spoken by the one who sits on the throne, who identifies himself as the Alpha and the Omega, the beginning and the end. They are spoken by the one who calls forth life from the formless void and who directs all things to their final end. In the earlier writings of the New Testament, Jesus of Nazareth, confessed by Christians to be the Messiah, is identified as the one who undertakes this work. We see this claim in the Epistle to the Colossians: "He is the image of the invisible God, the firstborn of all creation; for in him all things in heaven and on earth were created. . . . He himself is before all things, and in him all things hold together" (Col. 1:15–17). And then, alluding to the resurrection, the author continues: "He is the beginning, the firstborn from the dead, so that he might have first place in everything. For in him all the fullness of God was pleased to dwell, and through him God was pleased to reconcile to himself all things, whether on earth or in heaven, by making peace through the blood of his cross" (Col. 1:18–20). The one in and through whom all things were created has come among us and is about the work of new creation—bringing forth new life, not this time from the formless void but from a creation that has been left scarred and disfigured through the ravages of sin and death. Wright observes that this passage from Colossians "places Jesus' resurrection (1.18) in parallel with the creation of the world (1.15), seeing it as the ground and origin of what the creator has now accomplished and is now implementing, namely the reconciliation of all things to him. The very shape of the poem," Wright explains, "insists that Jesus' resurrection, as a one-off event, is an act not of abolition of the original creation but of its fulfilment."[4]

Whether or not Colossians was written by Paul himself, there is no doubt that the verses referred to here replicate a theme that is pervasive in Paul.

2. Wright, *Resurrection of the Son of God*, 649.
3. Alkier, *Reality of the Resurrection*, 15.
4. Wright, *Resurrection of the Son of God*, 239.

Alkier explains that "the theological knowledge of Paul is structured by a great, coherent narrative that extends from the creation of the world to the new creation at the end of the world. This great story forms for Paul the hermeneutical framework for the interpretation of the world, the interpretation of history, and every single event in past history as well as present in future."[5] The resurrection stands at the center of this narrative as the turning point from the old creation, plunged into travail and destined for death, to the new creation, in which all things will be reconciled to God and so attain their true end.

"In the Beginning Was the Word"

We could follow this narrative of the transition from old creation to new much more extensively through Paul's writings, and indeed through much of the New Testament. But as indicated earlier, I want to focus in this chapter especially on the Gospel of John. The very first words of John's Gospel alert us to the fact that the story he is about to tell is a story about creation:[6] "In the beginning was the Word." The echo of Genesis 1 resounds clearly in our ears. The story of Jesus, John wants us to understand, is the continuation, and indeed the fulfillment, of what took place in the beginning when God gave the Word, and there was light. John's story too is the story of creation, but now of creation rescued and renewed. The darkness now to be overcome is not the darkness of a formless void but the darkness of a world scarred and disfigured by sin and death.

The prologue continues by reminding us that in the beginning, and through the divine Word, God brought forth light and life. It is that Word, full of grace and truth, that has come into the world. Those who receive him are given "power to become children of God," children born "not of blood or of the will of the flesh or of the will of man, but of God" (John 1:12–13). John's prologue hereby establishes the conceptual framework and the vocabulary that will enable us to make sense of "the many things that Jesus did" (21:25). "The story about to be narrated is the sequel in the story of God's relationship to

---

5. Alkier, *Reality of the Resurrection*, 8. Alkier cites in support of this view the work of Richard Hays, Ben Witherington III, Eckhart Reinmuth, and Ian Scott.

6. On which, see Brown, "Creation's Renewal," 275–90; and, more extensively, Moore, *Signs of Salvation*.

the world: created, sustained, and re-created by the one, gracious, speaking Word."[7] And just to be sure that we understand aright, we are repeatedly reminded throughout the Gospel that Jesus is doing his Father's work (John 5:16–47; 10:22–39; 14:1–14); it is the work begun in creation, and which is directed toward the flourishing of all that God has made. As Jesus says to a group of Pharisees who were having trouble understanding what he was doing, "I came that they may have life, and have it abundantly" (10:10). And to Nicodemus, another of the Pharisees, Jesus explains that if we are to see the kingdom of God, new birth, or new creation, is required (3:3).

Genesis Again

The Nicodemus narrative is worth investigating further. Nicodemus comes to Jesus "by night," we are told (John 3:1). This detail is not incidental. John means us to recognize a parallel with the state of affairs before the dawn of creation, when, according to Genesis 1:2, "darkness covered the face of the deep." The Johannine echo of Genesis alerts us to the possibility that a new dawn is about to break; light and life are being given again. Nicodemus is intrigued but doesn't yet understand the full import of the work that Jesus is doing. So Jesus explains, "Very truly, I tell you, no one can see the kingdom of God without being born *from above* [ἄνωθεν, which can also be translated 'again']" (John 3:3).

Two things are to be noted here: First, the kingdom of God is another way of speaking about the new creation; both refer to the things of the world, of the creation being rightly ordered again. The diverse terminology—"kingdom of God" and "new creation"—draws attention to different aspects of the new reality established and fulfilled in Christ. Kingdom language stresses God's sovereignty over the new reality and reminds us that God is establishing a new form of community, a new and proper ordering of our life together. The language of new creation helps to make clear both that it is the stuff of creation—of this good, material world—that God is in the process of renewing and that it is not just human souls but all of God's creatures who are gathered into the new reality. The second thing to be noted is that the kingdom of God / the new creation can be seen only by those who have been

---

7. Lee, *Creation, Matter and the Image of God*, 42–43.

"γεννηθῇ ἄνωθεν," which the NRSV translates "born from above" but which might also be translated "born again," or, more literally, "genesis again."

The allusions to Genesis come thick and fast through this dialogue with Nicodemus: in answer to Nicodemus's puzzlement about how he could be born again, Jesus explains a second time: "Very truly, I tell you, no one can enter the kingdom of God without being born of water and Spirit. What is born of the flesh is flesh, and what is born of the Spirit is spirit" (John 3:5–6). Water and spirit are the elements present at the beginning when God stirs creation into being: a wind or spirit from God "swept over the face of the waters. Then God said, 'Let there be light'" (Gen. 1:2–3). Other echoes sound clearly here. Jesus is speaking of baptism, which is a dying and rising with Christ. New life comes, new creation comes, Jesus explains, through death and resurrection. Nicodemus, however, is slow to catch on, so Jesus finally makes it explicit: "Just as Moses lifted up the serpent in the wilderness, so must the Son of Man be lifted up, that whoever believes in him may have eternal life" (John 3:14–15). The words "lifted up" do double, or even triple, duty here: they refer to the cross and to the exaltation of Christ, an exaltation that includes both resurrection and ascension.[8] For John, the cross, the resurrection, and the ascension are all of a piece in showing forth the glory of Christ.[9] To return, however, to the central point: the new birth or new creation, the "genesis again," that Jesus commends to Nicodemus is made possible through the drama of Jesus's own death and resurrection. The promise of new life pertains to Nicodemus himself, but, as the allusions to Genesis 1 make clear, Nicodemus is being invited to take part in nothing less than the renewal of creation itself—the renewal of the cosmos.

We are told at the beginning of the episode that Nicodemus came to Jesus and said to him, "Rabbi, we know that you are a teacher who has come from God; for no one can do these signs that you do apart from the presence of God" (John 3:2). Nicodemus recognizes Jesus's authority on account of the signs that Jesus is doing. There is no doubting the importance of the signs in John's Gospel. We are told, following the turning of water into wine at Cana, that the signs reveal Jesus's glory (2:11), but they serve as well to indicate what Jesus is up to. They reveal, we might say, the nature of his messianic project.

8. It is widely recognized that John's Gospel contains numerous examples of *amphibologia* or double reference. For comment on this, see Moore, *Signs of Salvation*, 9–11.

9. C. K. Barrett makes a similar point. Barrett, *John*, 178–79. See also Brown, *John I–XII*, 145–46.

Unsurprisingly, given the importance of the signs in John's Gospel, much has been written about them. The majority view among commentators is that there are seven signs, though there is some, relatively minor, disagreement about what the seven signs are.[10] While that dispute is not irrelevant to my project, the widespread agreement that there are seven signs is sufficient for my present purpose. These seven signs, some commentators have observed, echo the seven days of creation in Genesis 1 and so are signs of a new creation that Jesus is bringing to fruition.[11] If, as is my own view, the seventh sign, corresponding to the seventh day of creation, is the cross and resurrection, then Jesus's final word from the cross, "It is finished" (John 19:30), signals the completion of his re-creative work.[12] Jesus's dying cry, Martin Hengel observes, "represents the goal of the incarnation of the Logos. On the cross the creator of the world completes his work of the new creation."[13] The new creation has still to be realized in full, but the decisive intervention of Christ in turning creation back toward its final goal has been accomplished once and for all. The point is supported by the frequent refrain in John's Gospel that Jesus has come to complete the Father's work, and the echo again of the Genesis creation narrative in which it is said on the seventh day, "God finished the work that he had done. . . . God rested from all the work that he had done in creation" (Gen. 2:2–3).

Water and Wine

When Nicodemus comes to Jesus, attracted by the signs that Jesus is doing, only one sign has so far been reported in the Gospel: the sign of the water and the wine at the wedding feast in Cana. At face value, the work Jesus does here of turning water into wine averts a social disaster and saves the host from considerable embarrassment, but there is much more to the story than that.

10. For a brief survey of the discussion on this matter, see Crowe, "Chiastic Structure of Seven Signs in the Gospel of John."
11. See, e.g., Painter, "Earth Made Whole," 77; Du Rand, "Creation Motif in the Fourth Gospel," 25; Brown, "Creation's Renewal," 287.
12. The resurrection cannot be left out of the work of new creation, of course, but because John treats the cross and resurrection as a single extended episode, the verdict "it is finished" may apply to the episode as a whole. For a more comprehensive discussion of the cross and resurrection as the seventh sign in John's Gospel and the consummation of Christ's work, see Vistar, *Cross and Resurrection.*
13. Hengel, "Prologue of the Gospel of John," 270.

Three additional and closely related themes also run through the story: the renewal of creation, the repair of humanity's relationship with God, and the passion and resurrection of Christ.

Consider first the calamity that Jesus is called upon to put right: "The wine gave out" (John 2:3). In response to this disaster, "the mother of Jesus said to him, 'They have no wine'" (2:3). This is not the first time in the Bible that we hear of there being no wine, nor the first time that such an event has caused consternation. In Isaiah, we read,

> The earth dries up and withers,
>   the world languishes and withers;
>   the heavens languish together with the earth.
> The earth lies polluted
>   under its inhabitants;
> for they have transgressed laws,
>   violated the statutes,
>   broken the everlasting covenant.
> Therefore a curse devours the earth. . . .
> The wine dries up,
>   the vine languishes,
>   all the merry-hearted sigh. . . .
> No longer do they drink wine with singing;
>   strong drink is bitter to those who drink it.
> The city of chaos is broken down,
>   every house is shut up so that no one can enter.
> There is an outcry in the streets for lack of wine;
>   all joy has reached its eventide;
>   the gladness of the earth is banished.
>
> (Isa. 24:4–11)

Isaiah tells of an ecological disaster, the withering of creation. It is a disaster brought about because the earth's inhabitants "have transgressed laws, violated the statutes, broken the everlasting covenant" (Isa. 24:5). Of particular interest, however, is the prominence given to the drying up of the vine and the lack of wine: "There is an outcry in the streets for lack of wine" (24:11). When Jesus averts social disaster at the wedding in Cana and produces wine of the highest quality for the feast, John would have us recognize that Jesus is about the work of restoring creation, overcoming the disaster of which

Isaiah speaks, and making the earth fruitful once more. This replenishment of creation involves the overcoming of human sinfulness, for as Isaiah observed, the earth lies polluted because humanity has transgressed laws, violated the statutes, and broken the everlasting covenant. It will take the whole of the Gospel for John to work through how those transgressions are overcome, but here at the wedding feast reported in chapter 2, there is already an indication that amends must be made for humanity's pollution of the earth. Jesus instructed that the water be poured into six stone jars used for the Jewish rites of purification. These become the vessels through which the miracle of renewal and replenishment takes place.

An indispensable part of that renewal and restoration is the healing of humanity's relationship with God. That the transformation takes place at a wedding feast is therefore richly suggestive. God's covenant relationship with humanity is commonly referred to in Scripture as a marriage. Here the story works at multiple levels. The turning of water into wine at Cana saves that wedding day, to be sure, but restoring the marriage covenant between God and God's people is the greater work that Jesus is engaged in.

Let us note, finally, the clues John gives us about how that work will be accomplished. When Mary tells Jesus of the lack of wine, clearly expecting him to do something about it, Jesus's response is surprising: "Woman, what concern is that to you and to me? My hour has not yet come" (John 2:4). Again, we see John's story working at multiple levels. The immediate catering disaster can be dealt with, apparently, even if Jesus appears reluctant to begin with, but the renewal of creation and the mending of humanity's covenant relationship with God—we have now moved to the second level of John's story—fills Jesus with foreboding. "My hour has not yet come," Jesus says, knowing that it will come on the cross. Jesus's initial reluctance to perform the work of replenishing the wine reveals his awareness that the journey toward Calvary, and so the greater work of releasing creation from the bondage of death, is about to begin in this "the first of his signs" (2:11).

One further detail of the Cana story, one that foreshadows the crucifixion, is worth pointing out. Fast-forward to John 19:31–34:

> Since it was the day of Preparation, the Jews did not want the bodies left on the cross during the sabbath, especially because that sabbath was a day of great solemnity. So they asked Pilate to have the legs of the crucified men broken and the bodies removed. Then the soldiers came and broke the legs of the first and

of the other who had been crucified with him. But when they came to Jesus and saw that he was already dead, they did not break his legs. Instead, one of the soldiers pierced his side with a spear, and at once blood and water came out.

Blood and water, water and wine. The turning of water into wine is a sign, John tells us. But what is it a sign of? There had been hints clearly enough in the echoes of Isaiah, in the reference to the Jewish rites of purification, in Jesus speaking of "his hour," and in the whole episode taking place at a marriage feast. Here in John 19 is further confirmation: the turning of water into wine is a foreshadowing of Jesus's passion; it is a sign of the work Jesus does in overcoming sin and death and so giving new life not only to humanity but to creation as a whole. Jesus turns the world back to its true purpose in communion with God in order that it might flourish as God intends.

The wedding feast and the wine are widely recognized as images of the messianic age in Jewish tradition. But as Richard Bauckham reminds us, there is also an important connection with the resurrection.[14] Bauckham draws our attention to Isaiah 25.

> On this mountain the LORD of hosts will make for all peoples
>   a feast of rich food, a feast of well-aged wines,
>   of rich food filled with marrow, of well-aged wines strained clear.
> And he will destroy on this mountain
>   the shroud that is cast over all peoples,
>   the sheet that is spread over all nations;
>   he will swallow up death for ever.
> Then the Lord GOD will wipe away the tears from all faces,
>   and the disgrace of his people he will take away from all the earth,
>   for the LORD has spoken.
>
> (Isa. 25:6–8)

The provision of wine is here linked with the overcoming of death. Bauckham suggests that this text from Isaiah "provides a Scriptural basis for connecting the miracle of Cana, the first of Jesus' signs, with the seventh sign, the resurrection of Jesus from the dead."[15]

---

14. Bauckham, *Gospel of Glory*, 182.
15. Bauckham, *Gospel of Glory*, 182.

One last clue supports this linkage. The story of the water turned to wine begins, "On the third day, there was a wedding in Cana in Galilee" (John 2:1). The resonances here are obvious. In turning water into wine "on the third day," in restoring the fruitfulness of creation, Jesus is doing resurrection work. He is giving life to the world and enabling creation to flourish once more. Wine is commonly a symbol of blessing and abundance in the Bible (e.g., Joel 2:24; 3:18; Amos 9:13; Zech. 10:7). In restored covenant relationship with God, we may indeed have wine, but in these carefully crafted portents of Jesus's death and resurrection, John is telling us how we may have it.

Temporal indicators such as "on the third day" are frequently important in John's Gospel. This is also the case in John's reporting of the third and fifth signs, which both take place on the Sabbath. Healing, it turns out, is Sabbath work, for healing is a realization of God's creative intent that the creature should flourish and enjoy abundant life. The healings reveal and confirm what the Sabbath is supposed to be for. The afflicted are healed, set free from their travail, and given new life. This is also what the resurrection enables: the whole of creation, with humanity a part of it, is set free from its bondage to decay, as Paul puts it (Rom. 8:21), and enabled to flourish once more. When some observers of the healings in question object to Jesus's healing on the Sabbath, Jesus responds with the claim, as he often does in John's Gospel, that he is doing the work of his Father (e.g., 5:19). The Sabbath work of healing is the work of the Creator, and it brings creation to its intended goal.

Bread for All

The fourth sign in John's Gospel is the feeding of the five thousand in chapter 6. That feeding is followed by an extended discourse on the bread of life, but between the sign and the discourse we find John's understated account of Jesus walking on the water. The walking on water is not called a sign by John, but it is nevertheless a further instance of Jesus exercising his sovereignty over creation, a theme that is also evident in the feeding of the five thousand.

In the preamble to the feeding of the five thousand, John observes that the Passover was near (John 6:4). It is a passing comment, but the point is clear: the episode John is about to recount is part of the larger story of salvation, of God's continuing deliverance of God's people. We must be sure not to lose sight of the passion of Christ, his forthcoming death and resurrection, in which the drama of divine provision and deliverance comes to a head. Echoes of the grand narrative of Scripture resound throughout John's telling of the feeding story. I will draw attention just to those that bear upon the theme of new creation.

To begin with, notice Jesus's handling of the fruits of creation—five barley loaves and two fish, in this instance. Among humanity's many failures in its stewardship of creation, one of the most egregious, especially in its defiance of God's good purposes for us, is our failure to distribute the fruits of creation so that everyone has enough. When Jesus handles the fruits of creation, however, he sees to it that everyone is satisfied, that everyone has enough. Then, at the conclusion of the meal, he tells his disciples, "Gather up the fragments left over, so that nothing may be lost" (John 6:12). This is what faithful stewardship of creation looks like. Jesus is restoring the divinely intended order of things, an order in which nobody goes hungry and nobody accumulates for themselves more than they need. A just economic order is an important characteristic of a world ordered according to God's good purposes. John is offering us an inaugurated eschatology. The signs Jesus performs are signs of what is to come when all creation will be made new, but this newness is appearing already wherever Christ is at work—through the replenishment of creation and the provision of wine, in the healings, in the equitable distribution of the fruits of creation so that all have enough and are satisfied. These are foretastes of that fullness of life in which not merely our souls, nor even human beings alone, but the whole of creation will be made new.

Between the feeding of the five thousand and the following discourse on the bread of life, there is, as I mentioned earlier, a brief interlude in which John reports Jesus's walking on the water. John's account of this episode is much briefer than the accounts given in Mark 6 and Matthew 14. Discarding all additional detail, John's purpose in telling the story, it seems, is to stress that Jesus is Lord of creation:

> When evening came, his disciples went down to the sea, got into a boat, and started across the lake to Capernaum. It was now dark, and Jesus had not yet come to them. The sea became rough because a strong wind was blowing. When they had rowed about three or four miles, they saw Jesus walking on the sea and coming near the boat, and they were terrified. But he said to them, "It is I; do not be afraid." Then they wanted to take him into the boat, and immediately the boat reached the land toward which they were going. (John 6:16–21)

We note first of all the echo of Genesis 1:2: "The earth was a formless void and darkness covered the face of the deep, while a wind from God swept over the face of the waters." Compare John 6:17: "It was now dark, and Jesus had not yet come to them. The sea became rough because a strong wind was blowing." We are taken back to the primeval chaos, the threatening darkness, and the forbidding face of the deep waters. It is God who overcomes the darkness, who gives light, who separates the seas from the dry land and makes a place where life can emerge and God's creatures may flourish. This work of creation happens again when Jesus walks over the choppy waters, brings order in the midst of chaos, and stills the disciples' fears. Jesus says, "It is I; do not be afraid," and immediately the boat reaches the land. There may be an echo here of Genesis 1:9: "And God said, 'Let the waters under the sky be gathered together in one place and let the dry land appear.'" The land is a place of refuge and of safety suitable for human habitation.

Why does John place this story of Jesus subduing the swirling waters in the midst of a chapter that is otherwise concerned with the giving of bread? Perhaps Psalm 23 offers an answer: "The LORD is my shepherd, I shall not want. He makes me lie down in green pastures; he leads me beside still waters" (Ps. 23:1–2). Indeed, when Jesus is making preparation to feed the five thousand, he says to the disciples, "Make the people sit down" (John 6:10). The word the NRSV here translates as "sit down" is from ἀναπίπτω, which is better translated as "recline." Then John adds, "Now there was a great deal of grass in the place; so they reclined [ἀνέπεσαν], about five thousand in all" (John 6:10, NRSV alt.). By following this story with Jesus walking on the water and calming the disciples' fears, it is possible that John is following the pattern of Psalm 23: "The LORD . . . makes me lie down in green pastures; he leads me beside still waters." Jesus is doing the work of the Lord, the work referred to by the psalmist; he is restoring creation, making it suitable once more for the peaceful dwelling of his creatures.

The Lord of Creation

By now, I hope, the pattern emerging through the course of John's Gospel is clear. Jesus's identity as the one who was with God in the beginning and through whom all things came to be is being revealed and confirmed through the signs that he does. Those signs indicate that he is Lord of creation and is about the business of setting creation again on its trajectory to fullness of life, of making all things new. The creation that has been subjected to disorder is being restored. It will flourish and be a blessing once more. But as John repeatedly reminds us, this work will be brought to completion only through Jesus's death and resurrection.

Among many further allusions to the Old Testament stories of creation in John's Gospel, two more are especially worth noting. We are guided to the first by Irenaeus, who observes that, in the healing of a man born blind (as reported in John 9:1–41), Jesus "shows forth the hand of God . . . which at the beginning had moulded man. . . . For as the Scripture says, he made [man] by a kind of process: 'And the Lord took clay from the earth and formed man.' Wherefore also the Lord spat on the ground and made clay, and smeared it upon the eyes, pointing out the original fashioning [of man], how it was effected, and manifesting the hand of God."[16]

Irenaeus explains at considerably more length that in the healing of the man born blind, as indeed throughout Jesus's ministry, we are seeing the Creator at work. "But He, the very same who formed Adam at the beginning, with whom also the Father spake, [saying], 'Let Us make man after Our image and likeness,' . . . formed visual organs [*visionem*] for him who had been blind."[17] The work being done here, Irenaeus had earlier pointed out, is the work of *regeneration*.[18]

A further allusion to the Genesis story of the creation of humankind appears in John's account of the appearance of the risen Christ to the disciples on the first Easter day (John 20:19–23). John reports that the disciples had hidden away in fear, but Jesus appeared to them and said, "Peace be with you"; then "he breathed [ἐνεφύσησεν] on them and said to them, 'Receive the Holy Spirit'" (20:22). There is a clear echo here of Genesis 2:7: "Then the LORD God formed man from the dust of the ground, *and breathed* [ἐνεφύσησεν, LXX] *into his nostrils the breath of life; and the man became a living being*" (emphasis added). John Marsh comments, "The very same verb used [in John 20:22] for 'breathe' is used in Genesis 2:7 in the Greek translation of the He-

---

16. Irenaeus, *Against Heresies* 5.15.2, in *Ante-Nicene Fathers* 1:543. The square brackets appear in the *ANF* edition.

17. Irenaeus, *Against Heresies* 5.15.4 (*ANF*, 543).

18. *Regeneration* derives from the same root as *genesis*. Irenaeus uses this term in his further exposition of the healing story. See *Against Heresies* 5.15.3. The Latin translation of Irenaeus's original Greek text uses the term *regenerationis*. The extant Greek text, which is available only in fragments, does not include the relevant passage. See Irenaeus, *Libros quinque adversus haereses*.

brew text (Septuagint). So John's gospel ends with an announcement of the new creation, as it also began."[19]

Bodily Resurrection

It is crucial to recognize that the story John tells of new creation—the story supported by the New Testament as a whole—is completely undermined if we suppose, as many have, that the resurrection of Jesus to which the New Testament bears witness is anything other than bodily resurrection. If Jesus is in the business of making all things new, of ushering in the new creation, then it is the stuff of creation as we know it, in all its materiality, that is the object of his redemptive and transformative work. Jesus's healings of the official's son who was close to death, of the lame man at Beth-zatha, and of the man born blind may well have involved spiritual renewal of some kind, but these healings involved also, and crucially, transformations of the impaired bodily matter that caused the various afflictions. The official's son was rescued from the point of physical death; the lame man got up and walked; the man born blind could see as he had never done before. God's work of new creation includes the transformation and renewal of the material world so that it may become what God intends it to be.

Irenaeus's observations about the materiality of Jesus's transformative work are apposite here. Contending against Gnostic assumptions about the impermanence and irredeemability of the material world, Irenaeus insists that "if the flesh were not in a position to be saved, the Word of God would in no wise have become flesh"; and further: "nor would the Lord have summed up these things in Himself, unless He had Himself been made flesh and blood after the way of the original formation [of man], saving in His own person at the end that which had in the beginning perished in Adam."[20] The resurrection of the body, and so the emptiness of Jesus's tomb, constitute the fulfillment of the divine intent to give life to creation—in all its material splendor!

N. T. Wright has shown, convincingly in my view, that whatever we may take resurrection to mean, or however we may try to reinterpret it so as to avoid any supposed offense to modern sensibilities, the New Testament writers quite clearly meant when they said that Jesus had been raised that the body

19. Marsh, *Saint John*, 644.
20. Irenaeus, *Against Heresies* 5.14.1 (ANF, 541).

of Jesus, taken down lifeless from the cross and laid in a tomb, was no longer in that tomb but had been raised to new life.[21] To be sure, the body had been transformed in some way, but it was still the physical body of the one who had been crucified.[22] Margaret Davies likewise stresses that when the Gospel writers speak of resurrection they are referring quite clearly to the resurrection of Jesus's body: "All the Gospels record, with varying details, that women (in John, only Mary Magdalene) found the grave empty. This implies that resurrection was understood to involve bodily transformation. Resurrection was not the survival of Jesus's soul after his physical death but the transformation of his corpse into a new bodily life. It assumes an anthropology which did not separate soul and body, and which conceived post-mortem existence as bodily existence. Moreover, bodily resurrection implies personal, individual survival after death, not the post-mortem survival of an undifferentiated humanity."[23]

Should we wish to take this testimony to the resurrection and make it fit within a secular and naturalistic worldview according to which the dead are not raised, we must be clear that we are not distilling the essence of what the New Testament writers say. We are proclaiming a different reality altogether. Indeed, we are proclaiming a different gospel, a gospel in which the full reality of our material, creaturely existence is excluded from the redemptive and transformative work of God. The ethical, social, and political implications of that Gnostic distortion of the gospel are very grave indeed: disease, poverty, environmental degradation, even the countless victims of violence and war can be passed off as unfortunate but nonetheless temporary inconveniences that have no bearing in the end upon the realization of God's purposes.

The good news of the gospel, however, is that the whole of our created reality is the object of God's creative and redemptive love. The material world is neither an unfortunate product of forces that lie outside the sovereignty of God and from which we need to be liberated (as various Gnosticisms, both ancient and modern, propose) nor a reality impervious to the divine action of redemption and renewal. The created world is instead the terrain within which God is bringing to fulfillment God's loving intention that the creature should have life and have it abundantly. That John begins his Gospel with the proclamation that the eternal Word of God has become flesh and concludes

---

21. See Wright's extensive analysis of the New Testament writings in *Resurrection of the Son of God.*

22. Wright develops his argument at length in *Resurrection of the Son of God*, but for a brief summary of the point see pp. 477–78.

23. Davies, *Matthew*, 233.

by reporting that the risen Christ appeared to his disciples in the flesh is the confirmation of Israel's faith that all creation is declared good by God and is essential to the working out of God's purposes. Commenting on the use of the term σάρξ (flesh) in John's Gospel, Dorothy Lee rightly observes that "flesh here signifies the full materiality of the divine Word, a materiality that is both embodied and spirited." She continues, "God's means of salvation is not by means of a disembodied Spirit but rather through the spirit operative in the incarnation: in this narrative, through the flesh and blood of the Johannine Jesus."[24] Consistent with God's affirmation of the goodness of the material world that is evident in the incarnation, so too in the resurrection it is the material of the created order that is resurrected and made new, both in the case of Jesus and, as God continues God's transformative work, in creation as a whole.

A Work in Progress

I began this chapter with the claim that the resurrection of Jesus is the decisive clue to what is going on in the world; it confirms that sin and death have no final power, that the forces of death have no future, and that God is at work in the world making all things new. That is a claim that can easily be resisted. I understand the warrant for the Jewish claim that if the Messiah has come then the world ought to look more redeemed. Martin Buber, for instance, wrote in 1933, "The church rests on its faith that the Christ has come, and that this is the redemption which God has bestowed on mankind. We, Israel, are not able to believe this. . . . We know more deeply, more truly, that world history has not been turned upside down to its very foundations—that the world is not yet redeemed."[25]

There is no question that the world is not yet as God intends it to be. Sin and death, very obviously, have not yet been brought to an end. To confess, however, that Jesus has been raised from the dead is to express the faith that God's final verdict has been declared. The final verdict, the same as that given in the beginning, is that the creature shall have life.[26] The resurrection reveals that neither death nor the forces of death will have the last word. This reality

24. Lee, *Creation, Matter and the Image of God*, 44, 45.
25. Buber, *Der Jude und sein Judentum*, 562, as quoted by Jürgen Moltmann in *Way of Jesus Christ*, 28.
26. This verdict is the basis of Oliver O'Donovan's profound exploration of Christian ethics in O'Donovan, *Resurrection and Moral Order*.

will not become universally evident until the final enemy is defeated and Jesus "hands over the kingdom to God the Father" (1 Cor. 15:24). To say then that the redeemer has come and has been raised from the dead is not to say that the work of redemption is complete; it is to confess, rather, that the new creation has begun and the old is passing away.

The eschatological reality to which Christian faith bears witness leaves traces, I suggested, upon the fabric of history. The empty tomb was one of those traces; so too are the appearances of Jesus recorded in the Gospels. We may also adduce the marks to which Jesus pointed when questioned by disciples of John the Baptist: "The blind receive their sight, the lame walk, the lepers are cleansed, the deaf hear, the dead are raised, and the poor have good news brought to them" (Matt. 11:5; cf. Luke 7:22).

A few weeks before I wrote this chapter, the church I belong to commissioned one of our members for missionary service. He turned up on our doorstep twelve years ago as a broken man, wrestling with demons and plagued by mental and physical health challenges. In that twelve years he has, by his own testimony, become a new man, and that newness he attributes to the love and the transformative grace of God. This too is one of the traces of new creation that appears in the fabric of history. Or so I believe. I can offer this story only as a testimony. It is not a proof of any particular conclusion. I claim simply—and it is a claim of faith to be sure—that it is the resurrection of Jesus from the dead, his defeat of sin and death, that provides the proper frame of reference within which to understand this little part, indeed all parts, of what is going on in the world.

Participating in the New Creation

In his book *The Resurrection of the Son of God*, N. T. Wright contends that "one cannot say 'Jesus of Nazareth was bodily raised from the dead' [in a way that is minimally self-involving]. If it happened, it matters. The world is a different place from what it would be if it did not happen. The person who makes the statement is committed to living in this different world, this newly envisioned universe of discourse, imagination and action."[27]

The question then to be asked is, What does participation in the reality of new creation look like? At one level, that is a very easy question to answer.

27. Wright, *Resurrection of the Son of God*, 714.

We need simply recall the signs of new creation set out in John's Gospel: the sick are healed; the earth is replenished and enabled to yield good fruit once more; the resources of creation are shared equitably among all who have need, while the surplus is gathered up for use on another day. We gain more clues from the other Gospels: ill-gotten gains are repaid fourfold; workers are paid, at the end of the day, enough to provide for their families; prodigal sons are welcomed home; women victimized by oppressive social conditions are given the dignity and the freedom they deserve; and so on. This is what new creation looks like; this is the nature of the divine economy established on the firm foundation of Jesus's resurrection from the dead. This is the new reality in which we are called to share. We may put it simply, in colloquial terms: the challenge of the gospel is to get with the program. But here's the rub: the cross comes first. Dying comes first. We are to die to the old order, the order that is passing away. Only then may we truly share in the age that is to come. And for that too, we have need of the Spirit's help.

6

Resurrection and History

The claim that "Jesus has been raised from the dead" is a claim about something that is alleged to have happened in space and time. Precisely as such, it left traces in the world that were apprehended by eyewitnesses. It was possible to see, so the Gospel writers claim, features of the world that had been rearranged on account of Jesus having been raised from the dead. The stone had been rolled away from Jesus's grave, the grave itself was empty, and Jesus's grave clothes lay folded on the stone bench on which his body had been laid. Later, through a series of encounters with the risen Jesus, the disciples were able to see him standing on the lakeshore or in a room in which they had gathered, share food with him, and put their fingers in the wounds left in his hands and side. These traces in space and time of Jesus having been raised from the dead appear within the realm of ordinary human experience, and yet they are contingent on an event—the resurrection itself—that lies far beyond the bounds of ordinary human experience and is commonly deemed to be impossible. God's raising of Jesus from the dead, if it happened, defies any naturalistic explanation and is conceivable and hence perceivable only within a theological conception of how reality is constituted.

The traces left by this extraordinary event on the fabric of human history[1] present us with a conundrum. Belief in the resurrection, as presented

---

1. I am using the term *history* here in the first of four senses identified by N. T. Wright to refer to "actual happenings in the real world." There are other senses of this term that will also be invoked at various points in this chapter. Wright pointed out in *New Testament and the People of God* that "the word 'history' is regularly used in two quite different but related

in the New Testament, involves some very particular claims about what has happened in the past and about God's involvement in what has happened. Historians, however, whose work it is to investigate what has happened in the past, are not in the habit of invoking divine agency as a causal factor in their explanations of what has taken place. The problem becomes more pronounced in light of the widespread insistence among contemporary Western historians[2] that divine action simply has no place in the range of causal categories that may be invoked when speaking of what has gone on in the world. Individual historians may offer different reasons for the legitimacy of this exclusion. Some contend simply that God does not exist. If God does not exist, then the concept of divine action clearly has no place in any explanation of what happens, except perhaps when speaking of the "mistaken" beliefs that have often motivated human action. The eminent American historian Richard White provides a relatively recent example of this dogmatic naturalism. He once declared, "I am a historian. I don't believe in transcendence. There is only the everyday."[3]

Others may take a deist view, according to which it is supposed that while God may exist, God does not "interfere" with the everyday workings of the world. God may be the creator who set the world in motion and established the laws of nature, but those laws along with human agency account without remainder for all that happens in the world. All events are of the same order and take place within a closed causal continuum.

A third justification sometimes offered for the exclusion of divine agency when accounting for what goes on in the world is the claim that, while God may exist and engage in some fashion with "actual happenings in the real world," historical scholarship is concerned exclusively with human agency. This view is expressed by the renowned philosopher and historian R. G. Collingwood, who asks, "What kinds of things does history find out? I answer,

---

ways, to refer to (1) actual happenings in the real world and (2) what people write about actual happenings in the real world." See Wright, *New Testament and the People of God*, 81. More recently, Wright has noted two further common uses of the term. "History," Wright explains, may refer as well to "the *task* which historians undertake" and to "the *meaning* they and others discern in events, especially in the sequence of events." Wright, *History and Eschatology*, 79 (emphasis original). See also Wright, "Meanings of History," esp. 5–11.

2. The qualifier "Western" historians is important here, for the insistence that historians adopt a secular historiography from which God is excluded is a peculiar feature of modern Western thought that is not shared by most other cultures.

3. White, *Remembering Ahanagran*, 40.

res gestae: actions of human beings that have been done in the past."[4] That does not mean that no other causal agents are at work in the world, but the study of those other causal agents, should they exist, lies beyond the concern, and the competence, of historical scholarship. So, for instance, study of the causal factors at work in the movement of tectonic plates or in the eruption of volcanoes lies beyond the scope of historical research and is properly undertaken instead by geologists and volcanologists, respectively. If, however, one wishes to study the impact that the eruption of Mount Vesuvius had on the city and people of Pompeii in AD 79, then one is engaged in historical research.[5]

According to these disciplinary demarcations, the study of divine agency, should there be such a thing, is best left to theologians. Historians thus contend, or simply presume, that theological concerns should have no bearing on their work as historians. This attitude is adopted by many biblical scholars as well, who commonly appeal for freedom to engage in their study of the biblical testimony without the distorting influence of theological beliefs about what happened in and through the career of Jesus. Renowned biblical scholar E. P. Sanders, for example, contends, "I have been engaged for some years in the effort to free history and exegesis from the control of theology; that is from being obligated to come to certain conclusions which are predetermined by theological commitment. . . . I aim to be only a historian and an exegete."[6] We may note, first of all, the questionable characterization of theology's engagement with historical scholarship as controlling rather than, say, collaborative; but it is necessary also to interrogate Sanders's assumption that his work as a historian (and biblical exegete) can be undertaken without need of any theology.

We should note, as well, that we are not engaged here in a dispute between purportedly neutral, objective, and critical scholarship, on the one hand, and naive, uncritical subjective biases on the other. We are involved, rather, in a dispute about two incompatible sets of metaphysical beliefs about the nature of reality: one atheistic, and the other theistic. There are cases, of course, where biblical scholars or historians subscribe to the creeds of Christian faith "in their personal life," so to speak, and yet insist on adhering to the

---

4. Collingwood, *Idea of History*, 9.
5. It is worth acknowledging here, as Alan Torrance has reminded me, that one can use the term *history* to refer to what is not human; for example, "geological history."
6. Sanders, *Jesus and Judaism*, 333–34.

atheistic, or at best agnostic, secular historiography of the Western academy when pursuing their scholarly endeavors. I wish to propose in what follows that this contradiction is unnecessary. I will suggest, furthermore, that the resurrection of Jesus from the dead validates and indeed requires a theistic historiography if we are to speak truly of what has taken place. It requires an account of history and of the task of historical inquiry capacious enough to include divine action.

History and the Historian

It is uncontroversial to say that historians are interested in studying the surviving traces of past events and the impact of those events on human affairs. The traces of past events that concern us especially here are the reports found in the Gospels of the New Testament that some women went to Jesus's tomb on the Sunday morning following the crucifixion of Jesus of Nazareth and discovered that his tomb was empty. Historians may readily agree that these reports are a proper subject of historical investigation. The reports are the kind of artifact that legitimately attracts the attention of historians; that is, they are documented claims about something alleged to have happened in the realm of space and time. Furthermore, those reports, along with other supposed corroborating evidence—in particular the reports of Jesus having appeared to a number of people following his death—have had a profound impact on the subsequent course of human history.

It is surely of interest to the historian, and indeed to all who wait eagerly upon their investigations, to consider whether Jesus's tomb was really empty and, if so, what became of the body. As noted earlier, alternative explanations of the various phenomena said to have taken place on Easter morning and during the following days are readily available: (1) The body was stolen, some contended. Less credibly still, others said (2) the body was removed by agents acting on behalf of the religious and political authorities of the day. Some more recent commentators have argued that (3) reports of the resurrection were fabricated by Jesus's followers who were seeking some advantage for themselves. And still others propose that (4) the biblical reports of resurrection are a mythological way of proclaiming a spiritual or theological truth and have nothing to do with the revivification of Jesus's dead body. One further explanation must also be considered, of course. It is that offered by the New Testament writers themselves—namely, that (5) God in fact raised Jesus from the dead.

It should be very clear, given the massive impact that the alleged happenings on Easter morning have had on the course of human history, that it matters a good deal which of these interpretations (or perhaps another, not yet formulated) is true. Precisely here we see the problem: Historians of Sanders's ilk—and he is here merely following the Western academy's standard account of the historian's task—have determined in advance that the fifth of these interpretations is not available to the historian qua historian. Appeal to divine agency, for one of the possible reasons noted above, lies outside the scope of the historian's competence. This a priori stipulation, commonly grounded in a set of metaphysical beliefs about the world, places a severe limitation— indeed, a debilitating limitation—on the range of options available to historians as they seek to explain this episode in human history and its enduring significance for human life. They might advise that the evidence does indeed suggest that the tomb of Jesus was found empty on Easter morning, but their explanatory options are limited to just two. Either they can concede that they simply don't know how the empty tomb came to be so or they can offer some or other variation of the theme evident in the first four options listed above, the common feature of which is that Jesus was not raised from the dead, at least not in the way clearly presented by the writers of the four Gospels.

I have focused here on the reports of the empty tomb. But there is, of course, other evidence for the resurrection that requires consideration, principally the appearance stories and the subsequent history of the Christian movement, especially the readiness of Jesus's followers to lay down their lives in consequence of their conviction that Jesus had been raised. No such corroborating evidence, however, has persuaded the guild of Western historical scholars to reconsider their exclusion of divine agency from the causative factors shaping the course of human history.[7]

Perhaps we have to just accept the prerogative of historians to operate under this constraint, shake the dust from our feet, and look elsewhere in our efforts to comprehend what happened on Easter morning. I confess, however, my reluctance to accept this proposal, for it drives us toward a dualistic conception of the way reality is constituted. The world accessible to the historian's

---

7. I am not suggesting here that this accumulation of evidence constitutes a proof that the resurrection actually happened. More on this below. My point rather is to draw attention to the determined exclusion of one possible explanation for the evidence that is available.

gaze, the world of human habitation and experience, is conceived to be a closed causal continuum. It entails, furthermore, that God is not involved and need not be invoked when seeking to understand what has happened in the course of human history.

We return briefly here to Sanders's inadvertent disclosure of the *control* exercised on his own historical and exegetical work by his prior theological and metaphysical assumptions, most especially on the conclusions he draws about Jesus. "I am," says Sanders, "a liberal, modern, secularized Protestant, brought up in a church dominated by low christology and the social gospel. I am proud of the things that that religious tradition stands for. I am not bold enough, however, to suppose that Jesus came to establish it, or that he died for the sake of its principles."[8] We see here a clear statement of the view that the substance of Christian faith can be articulated without invoking the category of divine action. The corollary is that the events narrated in the Gospels, especially the events of Easter, are also explicable without reference to divine action. Sanders's beliefs about history—particularly the belief that what happens in the world is wholly explicable within the realm of immanent causality, and so without reference to divine action—inevitably shape the judgments he is inclined to make about what has happened in the past. I should point out that Sanders has been singled out here not because I consider him to be especially worthy of critique and others not but, rather, to illustrate the unavoidable entanglement of historical scholarship and the theological, or at least metaphysical, commitments of any given historical scholar.

Historical Method

The best account I have come across of the historical method employed by contemporary Western historians and commonly adopted by those seeking to investigate the career of Jesus is that of Robert L. Webb in "The Historical Enterprise and Historical Jesus Research."[9] Webb explains that the task of historians is to sift through the surviving traces of past events in order to produce an account of his or her understanding of the past event that

8. Sanders, *Jesus and Judaism*, 334.
9. Webb, "Historical Enterprise and Historical Jesus Research," 9–93. I have written elsewhere on Webb's discussion. See Rae, "Theological Interpretation and Historical Criticism," 94–109.

narrates a description and explanation of it.[10] "History focuses its inquiry," Webb contends, echoing R. G. Collingwood's principle that we encountered earlier, "on human actions in specific events in the past."[11] This limitation of scope is of the utmost importance because it begs the question of whether this narrow focus on human actions is sufficient to describe, let alone "explain," what happened on Easter morning. Webb's account of the historian's task may exclude the very category—namely, divine agency—that is essential to any adequate explanation of what happened and so preclude us from understanding what really happened.

Here is the nub of the issue with which we are concerned in this chapter. What methodological resources are needed for us to apprehend what really happened on Easter morning, and what explanatory categories are required if we are to give an adequate account of those events? The question becomes especially acute when Webb later contends, "Historical explanation is particularly concerned with causality: Why did a particular event happen? What factors led to it happening and to it happening the way it did? What impact did this event have on subsequent events?"[12] We must surely ask, in relation to the events of Easter morning, whether it is proper for historians to begin their investigations by bracketing out in advance the possibility that God was involved. It is important to note here that the decision to exclude divine agency from among the causal categories needed for an adequate explanation of what has happened in the past is not a decision that has been justified by the findings of historical inquiry itself. Historical inquiry has not proven the legitimacy of this exclusion. Rather, the exclusion of divine agency from our explanations of past events is an a priori metaphysical commitment.

Despite wishing to restrict the object of historical inquiry to human actions in the past, thereby excluding divine agency, Webb acknowledges that the matter becomes more complex when historians turn their attention to events reported in religious texts like the Bible. As we have noted, such texts typically appeal to divine intervention as a causal explanation.[13] The question thus arises, What are we to make of such interpretations? Webb explains that there are three basic alternatives. The first is the naturalistic approach already discussed above, in which it is supposed that divine intervention must be

10. See Webb, "Historical Enterprise and Historical Jesus Research," 14.
11. Webb, "Historical Enterprise and Historical Jesus Research," 41.
12. Webb, "Historical Enterprise and Historical Jesus Research," 36.
13. See Webb, "Historical Enterprise and Historical Jesus Research," 39.

ruled out because "cause and effect in the space-time universe is understood to operate within a closed continuum."[14] A second approach is described by Webb as the "theistic" approach, which does not naively accept all reports that God has acted in particular ways but is willing to entertain the possibility that God may sometimes be involved as a causal agent in events that are of interest to historians. Webb here confirms the point made above, that the difference between these two approaches is a difference in ontologies. "A naturalistic approach may be (but not necessarily so . . .) associated with a world view that understands the physical, space-time universe to constitute the totality of reality. Whereas a theistic approach . . . arises out of a worldview in which reality includes not only the physical, space-time universe but also a supra-mundane, supernatural world that can and does interact with humans in the physical space-time universe."[15]

These two views are further defined as "ontological naturalistic history," in the first case, and "critical theistic history," in the second case.[16] As Webb points out, these two views are incompatible, and so he proposes a third view, which attempts to find common ground between the first two. Webb calls this view "methodological naturalistic history." The historian adopting this approach accepts that the historian's task is to investigate "causation within the physical space-time universe, but this does not limit the historian's personal ontological worldview, just his or her historical method as a historian."[17] This approach, Webb claims, "offers a methodological definition without imposing an ontological viewpoint on history / reality."

It appears to me, however, that Webb's quest for "common ground" is tilted almost completely to the side of the ontological naturalist. Webb's "mediating" position requires no alteration whatsoever to the method adopted by the ontological naturalist, whereas the critical theistic historian, who may believe that God was in Christ reconciling the world to Godself (to take a representative claim from the New Testament about what was going on in and through the career of Jesus of Nazareth), is required to set that belief aside when doing the historian's work of investigating what took place on Easter morning and during the following days. They are precluded from saying, qua historian, that God did this or that. If it is the case, however, as the

14. Webb, "Historical Enterprise and Historical Jesus Research," 40.
15. Webb, "Historical Enterprise and Historical Jesus Research," 41.
16. Webb, "Historical Enterprise and Historical Jesus Research," 41.
17. Webb, "Historical Enterprise and Historical Jesus Research," 42.

New Testament writers proclaim, that the events of Easter morning—to say nothing at this stage of the rest of Jesus's career—can be explained only with reference to the action of God, then the true nature of what took place will remain out of reach for those historical scholars who are determined not to invoke divine agency when reporting the outcome of their investigations.

It is worth noting here an observation made by Donald Hagner in his contribution to the same volume in which Webb's chapter serves as the introduction. Hagner writes, "The quest of the historical Jesus is a misnomer. It is not a search that can bring us the real Jesus . . . but rather a search that provides what necessarily and finally must remain an artificial construct. The fact remains that the historical method, strictly practiced . . . , is ill-equipped to deal with the uniqueness represented by the story of Jesus."[18] Sarah Coakley likewise observes that the historical approach "*shrinks* what can be said of Jesus to what secular historians regard as appropriate to their task and duty and so necessarily consigns him to the past."[19]

Here then are the key questions we face when speaking of the resurrection of Jesus from the dead: What happened? How do we know? And what explanatory categories are needed in order to speak truthfully of what took place? Put simply, if the biblical testimony concerning God's raising of Jesus from the dead is true, and there seems to be no good reason to exclude that possibility in advance, as methodological naturalism requires us to do, then we need to reconsider the relation between theology and history. The mutual exclusion of one field of inquiry from the other—particularly, the exclusion of divine agency from any adequate account of what took place on Easter morning—is no longer tenable.

Thinking History and Theology Together

Since the beginnings of the so-called Quest of the Historical Jesus in the late eighteenth and early nineteenth century and on through its second and third phases in the twentieth and early twenty-first century, it has commonly been supposed among pursuers of this Quest that the tools of historical inquiry provide the appropriate means for discerning what really happened, or at least what we can be reasonably confident of having happened, during

18. Hagner, "Jesus and the Synoptic Sabbath Controversies," 254.
19. Coakley, "Identity of the Risen Jesus," 306. Emphasis original.

the course of Jesus's career. It was further assumed, in the first phase of the Quest at least, that the tools of historical inquiry, when consistently applied, could provide a truly objective portrait of the real Jesus stripped bare of the unwarranted accretions of theological dogma. As we have moved through the second and third phases of the Quest, we have become increasingly aware that objectivity is not as easily achieved as was initially thought. This became very apparent as the first Quest ran out of steam toward the end of the nineteenth century. The strenuous efforts of the historical-critical scholars had produced no unanimity about how Jesus was to be properly understood. William Lane Craig echoes the views of many commentators in his observation concerning the Questers: "Apparently unaware of the personal element they all brought to their research, each writer reconstructed a historical Jesus after his own image. There was Strauss's Hegelian Jesus, Renan's sentimental Jesus, Bauer's non-existent Jesus, Ritschl's liberal Jesus, and so forth. To paraphrase George Tyrrell, each one looked down the long well of history and saw his own face reflected at the bottom."[20]

This same observation was also made by Albert Schweitzer, whose 1906 book, translated into English as *The Quest of the Historical Jesus*, effectively brought the first Quest to an end. Schweitzer wrote that "it was not only each epoch that found its reflection in Jesus; each individual created him in accordance with his own character."[21] So much for the promise that historical scholarship, "freed from the control of theology" (to recall E. P. Sanders's estimation of what is needed), would deliver the real Jesus into our hands. The problem, as we have seen above, is that no judgments about what happens in the world, including those of historical scholars, take place in a conceptual vacuum. Our perceptions of reality are profoundly shaped by our conceptual frameworks, or by what Peter L. Berger famously called "plausibility structures."[22] That is to say, our beliefs about the nature of reality, about the way the world works, about what is or is not possible within the terrain of

---

20. Craig, *Reasonable Faith*, 218. The paraphrase of George Tyrrell is drawn from Tyrrell, *Christianity at the Crossroads*, in which, commenting on Adolf von Harnack's *Wesen des Christentums*, Tyrrell remarks, "The Christ that Harnack sees, looking back through nineteen centuries of Catholic darkness, is only the reflection of a Liberal Protestant face, seen at the bottom of a deep well" (p. 44). Among many scholars who have said much the same thing as Craig about the diversity of portraits produced in the first Quest, see Wright, *Jesus and the Victory of God*, chap. 1; and Carleton Paget, "Quests for the Historical Jesus," 145.

21. Schweitzer, *Quest of the Historical Jesus*, 4.

22. Berger, *Sacred Canopy*, 45–47.

human history, and indeed about God—to name just a few especially relevant components of such plausibility structures—shape the way we perceive and assess what is reported to have happened in the past. This is widely recognized now among historians, and by biblical and theological scholars, but despite the efforts of some,[23] the implications of this have not yet been fully brought to bear upon the scholarly reading of the biblical narratives, especially upon the reading of those narratives that proclaim the resurrection of Jesus from the dead.

In what follows, I will attempt to show that it is the resurrection itself that establishes the need for a new approach to the reading of the biblical narratives concerning the resurrection. That sounds somewhat circular, but it is no more so than the methodological naturalist's presumption that we must set aside the category of divine agency when investigating the biblical proclamation that God has raised Jesus from the dead. It is in the nature of plausibility structures that the modes of inquiry and the kinds of explanation that may be invoked in any study of the past are determined by the plausibility structure that the inquirer inhabits. In pursuing their investigations, particular inquirers may find that certain features of the reality they are investigating cannot easily be accommodated within the plausibility structure within which they are operating. They are, to recall again Thomas Kuhn's terminology, "anomalies" or "novelties of fact."[24] Such was the case, Kuhn explains, when Copernicus and others began to observe that the behaviors of the planets did not fit the Ptolemaic, or geocentric, model of the universe that had served well and been taken for granted hitherto.[25] Observance of the anomalies led to what we now call the Copernican revolution, in which it was proposed that our conception of the structure of the then known universe be revised from a geocentric to a heliocentric model. Kuhn further explains that a conceptual revolution of this nature that may happen from time to time, if only very occasionally, in any field of inquiry, involves "a reconstruction of the field from new fundamentals, a reconstruction that changes some of the field's most elementary generalizations as well as many of its paradigm methods and applications."[26]

23. See, e.g., Evans, *The Historical Christ and the Jesus of Faith*; Adams, *The Reality of God and Historical Method*; and Heringer, *Uniting History and Theology*.

24. See Kuhn, *Structure of Scientific Revolutions*, 52–53.

25. Kuhn, *Structure of Scientific Revolutions*, 68–69.

26. Kuhn, *Structure of Scientific Revolutions*, 85.

Suppose, for the sake of the present argument, that the historical method widely preferred by contemporary historians stands in need of reconstruction, the kind of reconstruction that "changes some of the field's most elementary generalizations as well as many of its paradigm methods and applications." The need for such reconstruction might be prompted, let us further suppose, by some anomalous event that cannot be accommodated within the reigning paradigm. Such an event might be one that defies explanation within the continuum of natural causes, appeal to which has proven to be sufficient when explaining much else that has happened through the course of human history. It matters not for the sake of this thought experiment whether the historian is an ontological or merely a methodological naturalist when they encounter the imagined anomalous event, for both are committed as historians to the same methodological paradigm. Now, can we imagine further that it really did happen that in the days following Jesus's crucifixion and burial the tomb in which he was laid was found to be empty and that he later appeared on several occasions to a number of people who testified with utter conviction to the authenticity of their encounter with the same Jesus whose death they had witnessed just days earlier?

Let us note to begin with that if such a thing happened it would be anomalous, according to our well-formed and hitherto well-justified expectations of what goes on in the world. Those expectations don't include the possibility that a man who was dead and buried should leave his tomb and be found wandering about among his former friends. Choan-Seng Song rightly observes that "the process that led to the cross was in a sense comprehensible, but the empty tomb destroyed the logic of life and death, contradicted the law of nature, and disrupted the continuity of historical experience."[27]

Two, or perhaps three, possibilities lie open to the methodological naturalist who comes upon reports of such a thing having happened. The first is to redouble the effort to find naturalistic explanations for the empty tomb and the appearance stories, included among which will be the dismissal of such stories as fabrications or as mythological renderings of some natural reality. This has been a common approach in the face of the resurrection narratives in the Gospels and is the project favored by the ontological naturalist. The second possibility is to recognize that the reported event, if it really happened, will require a rather substantial modification to the plausibility structure

27. Song, *Compassionate God*, 100.

and methodological paradigm that have served well in most other cases but have been found wanting in this one. The third possibility facing the committed methodological naturalist is simply to say, "I cannot be sure of what happened in this case or whether the available reports are true." That is an honorable path to take, but it is important to note that such a person is really saying, "I am not willing at this point to commit myself to either option one or two." Options one and two are the only options, however, that can offer any resolution to the question of what really happened on Easter day. Ontological naturalists, perhaps rightly, remain committed to the view that God cannot be involved, but in doing so they run the risk of failing to apprehend what really happened. Conversely, open-minded historians—those willing to entertain the possibility that the most elementary generalizations, as well as many of the paradigm methods and applications of historical scholarship, may need to be reconstructed in light of what appears to have happened on Easter morning—may open themselves up to the possibility of an explanation that includes the statement "God raised Jesus from the dead."

Some further observations are apposite at this juncture. In my imagined scenario of a historian entertaining the possibility that the methodological commitments and conceptual frameworks of her discipline might need to be reconstructed, her entertainment of that possibility is prompted by an event, or by reports of an event, that cannot be accommodated within the conceptual framework that historians have taken as normative, at least during the past two hundred years. As stressed repeatedly above, that conceptual framework has among its central principles that God is not involved in what goes on in the realm of space and time, or that divine agency is a category that must be set aside when explaining, qua historian, what has happened in the past. Confronted with reports of the resurrection, however, the open-minded historian is one who is willing to entertain the possibility that the anomalous nature of this event is such that a reconstruction of the field of historical inquiry may be needed.

This feature of the scenario I am imagining is no different in one crucial respect to what happened in the case of Copernicus. Recognition of the need for a reconstruction of the field comes through encounter with the anomaly itself. It is prompted by what we might call revelation, by the revelation of some feature or other of reality that is not explicable within the previously operative paradigm. The adoption of a new paradigm, should that be deemed appropriate, follows a posteriori rather than being imposed a priori on the reality with which Copernicus in his time was concerned, or on the reality of the resurrection with which our imagined historian is concerned.

It is important to emphasize here that according to the New Testament reports, belief in the resurrection did not emerge because those named as witnesses were committed to a view of reality that could readily accommodate the resurrection. Quite the contrary: the reports of Mary and her companions rushing from the tomb to declare that Jesus had been raised met with confusion and disbelief among those who had been closest to Jesus during his ministry. Likewise, the disciples said to have encountered Jesus on the road to Emmaus were unable to recognize him, precisely because their prior theological and conceptual frameworks were not able to accommodate the possibility that a dead man had been raised. It was their encounters with the risen Jesus himself that brought about the radical transformation of their understanding of what is possible in the realm of space and time.

The importance of the point just made cannot be overestimated. The resurrection itself brings about a revolution in our understanding of the nature of reality. It confirms that the world is not after all a closed causal continuum impervious to divine action. If it is true, furthermore, that God has raised Jesus from the dead, then it will have to be admitted that the methodological naturalism favored by modern Western historians, just insofar as it limits itself to the investigation of natural causes and human action, will not be able to give an adequate account of what really happened. As it was with the two disciples whose eyes were kept from seeing Jesus as they talked with him on the road to Emmaus, we must say, if God really did raise Jesus from the dead, that the eyes of the methodological naturalist will be kept from seeing the true nature of what has taken place.

We must be clear at this point: if God really did raise Jesus from the dead, then the failure of the methodological naturalist, and even more so of the ontological naturalist, to see what happened is a function not of some self-evident truth about the nature of things but of a *mistaken* set of beliefs about the nature of reality. The methodological naturalist is of the same ilk as those astronomers who on account of their commitment to a geocentric model of the universe refused to countenance the Copernican proposal that the sun and not the earth lay at the center of the then known universe. The sheer revelatory pressure of the heliocentric reality itself, however, eventually brought about, a posteriori, that revolution in understanding that enabled a more adequate apprehension of the true nature of things. In the same way, I suggest, the resurrection itself gives rise to a radical reconception of the nature of history, in Wright's first sense of the term, and of the methodological dispositions needed in order to apprehend what has and is happening as God brings to fruition in our midst God's purposes for the world.

There are two central features of this changed disposition and the accompanying revisions of historical method that are necessary if we are to apprehend where God is at work in the world. The first, clearly enough, is openness to the possibility that God really is involved in the course of human history. Without deciding the matter in advance, the historian with such a disposition will be open to the possibility that, for instance, Paul's claim that "in Christ God was reconciling the world to himself" (2 Cor. 5:19) or the claim in the Letter to the Hebrews that "in these last days [God] has spoken to us by a Son" (Heb. 1:2) might in fact be more adequate explanations of what is going on through the career of Jesus of Nazareth than those explanations that confine themselves to naturalistic causes.

Methodological naturalists, and especially those interested in Jesus's career in Palestine two thousand years ago, might respond that such explanations properly belong to the realm of theology, while historians qua historians must confine themselves to presenting the facts that are discernible through naturalistic modes of historical inquiry. The obvious problem with that rejoinder is that scholars interested in the "historical Jesus" and purporting to be historians have consistently failed to comply with that description of the historian's task. They have formulated instead numerous portraits of Jesus, notorious in their variety, and claim as historians to have delivered the real Jesus into our hands. To take just one prominent and widely influential example, John Dominic Crossan's portrayal of Jesus as "a peasant Jewish Cynic" arrived at through the "stringent" application of his historical, anthropological, and literary methodology reveals, according to the back-cover blurb on Crossan's book, "the real Jesus—who he was, what he did, what he said." The blurb continues: "Using the strictest standards of research and scholarship, John Dominic Crossan provides us with the fullest presentation of the historical Jesus ever attained. The man who emerges is an intelligent and courageous Jewish peasant, both a revolutionary and a compassionate healer."[28] The "real Jesus" presented as the fruits of Crossan's methodologically naturalistic scholarship can be accounted for, apparently, without need of any theological reference.

---

28. Crossan, *Historical Jesus*.

The salient point for our purposes is that historians seeking to investigate the reality of Jesus according to the constraints of Western historiography, particularly its ontological and/or methodological naturalism, occupy a vastly different conceptual space than that occupied by the New Testament writers, who are convinced that in order to speak adequately of who Jesus is, and indeed of the reality of the resurrection, it is essential to recognize that God is at work in and through him. God is at work, that is, *within the terrain of human history*. Unfortunately, however, and as Brad Gregory explains, "To the extent that the modern social sciences and humanities are framed implicitly by the metaphysical naturalism of the modern natural sciences, they leave no room for the *reality* of the content of religious claims."[29]

The reality with which we are concerned in this book is the resurrection of Jesus from the dead. That reality, we have seen, cannot be accommodated within the naturalistic view of the world favored by modern Western historians. As was the case in the Copernican revolution when scientists and then the general population discovered that their conceptions of how the then known universe worked needed an entirely new center, a new point of orientation, so also the resurrection itself establishes and constitutes an entirely new point of orientation for our understanding of history.

The term *history* refers here to all four of the meanings identified by N. T. Wright.[30] It refers to actual happenings in the real world, to the task of investigating what has happened in the past, to the meaning discerned in the events, and to what we may write about what has happened. Christianly understood, the resurrection constitutes the utterly new starting point for our understanding of what is going on in the world. It reveals that God is at work through the course of human history overcoming the dread consequences of human sinfulness and making all things new. The redemptive and creative agency of God that will determine in the end the ultimate telos of human history is at work already among us and is definitively revealed in the resurrection of Jesus from the dead. This creative and redemptive agency is none other than divine agency. It does not originate within the usual run of natural causes that is the preferred realm of historical explanation. It comes from beyond; it is the utterly gratuitous gift of divine grace that reorders the world, precisely by setting it again on its trajectory to fullness of life in communion with the one who is its Creator and Redeemer.

29. Gregory, "The Other Confessional History," 137. Emphasis original.
30. See note 1 at the beginning of this chapter.

That is the meaning and the goal of history. That is the purpose to which all things are directed by the guiding hand of God, but this meaning and purpose cannot be discerned through a naturalistic mode of inquiry, nor is it intelligible within any conceptual framework other than that to which the resurrection itself gives rise. A transformation of one's understanding is needed. It is the kind of transformation for which the New Testament employs the term *metanoia*. *Metanoia* literally means the transformation of one's mind. It is the kind of transformation experienced by the disciples who first dismissed as an "idle tale" the news that Jesus had been raised (Luke 24:11). Through their encounters with the risen Lord himself, however, their minds were opened to the decisive action of God in the midst of human history making all things new. The resurrection thus became for them the starting point of a whole new way of understanding the world, a way of understanding that shed its light backward on all that Jesus had done among them and, indeed, on the whole of Israel's history.

Richard Hays thus affirms that "the resurrection of Jesus is the epistemological key to understanding the world and therefore the key to all history. If so, any history that does not begin from the vantage point of the resurrection of Jesus is perforce distorted because it denies or fails to grasp the true history of the world."[31] The disciples, the newly emergent church, and especially those who subsequently wrote the New Testament were able to discern afresh in the light of the resurrection where God is at work in the world. Such discernment will always elude those who look to understand the past through a naturalistic lens that allows no place for the agency of God.

Hays correctly observes that the resurrection requires of us a new conception of what history is, a new historiography, we might say. Such historiography is clearly evident in the New Testament itself. As Oswald Bayer explains, Paul's historiography works "from a key event that discloses the meaning of all events that come before and after it."[32] That event is, of course, the resurrection of Jesus from the dead. The point here is not that we should abandon historical inquiry. Quite the opposite, in fact. Biblical faith rests upon certain things having taken place through the course of human history. That is why throughout the Old Testament and into the New the people of God are repeatedly enjoined to remember what God has done among them.

31. Hays, "Knowing Jesus," 61.
32. Bayer, *Theology the Lutheran Way*, 200, quoted in Linebaugh, *Word of the Cross*, 47.

We began this chapter by noting that what God has done leaves traces in the fabric of human history. The instruction given by Jesus to the messengers sent by John the Baptist to inquire whether Jesus was the Messiah, "Go and tell John what you see and hear," confirms that there are signs of divine action discernible within the fabric of human history that can and should be a proper object of historical inquiry. The question arises, however, What is the appropriate conceptual framework for the interpretation of these signs? A naturalistic framework, and its associated historiography, will not do. We have need of modes of inquiry, discernment, and interpretation that are open to the possibility that God, the creator and sustainer of all things, is at work in the world making all things new. That work of renewal changes things; it leaves traces that are apprehensible through historical inquiry. But historical inquiry as recently practiced in the Western academy cannot provide the framework within which to recognize the reality to which those traces point. It cannot give us eyes to see. Seeing aright—seeing with the eyes of faith, we might say—is always to be understood as a divine gift. We cannot see without God's help. Intolerable though it may seem to the guild of determinedly secular historians, it might be appropriate to begin a genuinely open-minded inquiry into what actually happened in the career of Jesus of Nazareth with a prayer that the Holy Spirit of God would guide us into all truth.

7

Resurrection and Ethics

The infancy narrative in Matthew's Gospel presents the reader with a stark contrast between two kings: one, a politically appointed ruler of Judea; the other, a baby born in Bethlehem who is sought out by magi from the East who wish to pay homage to the one born "king of the Jews" (Matt. 2:2). The two kings represent two vastly different conceptions of how the world should be ordered and two vastly different conceptions of the good. The first king, Herod the Great, had become the king of Judea "through brutality and expeditious marriage into the Hasmonean family," and he ruled with an iron fist.[1] His loyalty to the Roman Empire did not endear him to his Judean subjects, while his "distrust of possible rivals led to the construction of inaccessible fortress palaces . . . and the murder of some of his own sons."[2] This is the background we need to be aware of when we read in Matthew's Gospel,

> In the time of King Herod, after Jesus was born in Bethlehem of Judea, wise men from the East came to Jerusalem, asking, "Where is the child who has been born king of the Jews? For we observed his star at its rising, and have come to pay him homage." When King Herod heard this, he was frightened, and all Jerusalem with him; and calling together all the chief priests and scribes of the people, he inquired of them where the Messiah was to be born. They told

1. Brown, *Introduction to the New Testament*, 58.
2. Brown, *Introduction to the New Testament*, 58.

him, "In Bethlehem of Judea." . . . Then Herod secretly called for the wise men and learned from them the exact time when the star had appeared. Then he sent them to Bethlehem, saying, "Go and search diligently for the child; and when you have found him, bring me word so that I may also go and pay him homage." (Matt. 2:1–5, 7–8)

The chilling pretense of Herod's words—"When you have found him, bring me word so that I may also go and pay him homage"—needs no further elaboration by Matthew. A king who would murder his own sons in order to suppress any threat of a rival is pitted against a child of lowly birth. Herod had wealth, power, and "all Jerusalem with him" (Matt. 2:3); the child had only his humble parents and their readiness to trust in the guidance of God (see 1:24; 2:14).

Matthew has left us in no doubt as to the drama that is being played out here. There are two kings who represent vastly different conceptions of the good. The first is represented by Herod, a brutal tyrant, and the second is embodied in the newborn child. Matthew has the wise men make the decisive choice: To whom should they give their allegiance? Will they fulfill Herod's command to tell him where the child lay (Matt. 2:8), or will they offer their gifts to the child and return home by another road (2:11–12)?

In Luke's Gospel too the narration of Jesus's birth indicates a radical subversion of the prevailing estimations of what is of value and what is good. Bearing in her womb the one who will be given the throne of his ancestor David (Luke 1:32), Mary sings,

> For the Mighty One has done great things for me,
>   and holy is his name.
> His mercy is for those who fear him
>   from generation to generation.
> He has shown strength with his arm;
>   he has scattered the proud in the thoughts of their hearts.
> He has brought down the powerful from their thrones,
>   and lifted up the lowly;
> he has filled the hungry with good things,
>   and sent the rich away empty.
>
>   (Luke 1:49–53)

This song of praise, like Matthew's announcement of two contrasting visions of kingly rule, reveals a moral framework that challenges the prevailing conceptions of what is good. In Mark's Gospel, the rival conceptions of what is good are played out in the recurring conflict between Jesus and the religious authorities, the scribes and the Pharisees. And in John, it is evident in the contrasts between darkness and light, blindness and sight.

It is striking that Matthew and Luke signal the impending competition between rival moral frameworks at the outset of their Gospels, in the midst of their respective accounts of Jesus's birth. Matthew in particular highlights the threat represented by Jesus to the distorted moral frameworks that typically prevail in a fallen world. The birth of a baby in Bethlehem sets fear into the heart of Herod the Great, the king whose wealth, power, and loyal service to imperial Rome have established his prerogative, so he believes, to determine what is good. Only he has confused what is good with what serves his own interests, even to the point of convincing himself of the virtue, so Matthew reports, of slaughtering all the male children under the age of two in an effort to extinguish any potential rival to his rule. There is no corroborating evidence for the massacre of the infants as reported in Matthew's Gospel, but Herod's well-attested killing of his own sons who were perceived as threats to his hold on power justifies the Matthean account of the brutal lengths to which tyrants may go in order to preserve their prerogative to determine what is good.[3] Abundant evidence provided through the course of human history supports Matthew's portrayal of the fear-filled brutality of tyrannical power and of a moral calculus that can justify the preservation of one's own interests at terrible cost to others. The sad story continues in our own time. As I write this chapter, the brutal assertion of Herodic power is being exercised through Vladimir Putin's invasion of Ukraine. The "special military operation," tragically supported by Patriarch Kirill of the Russian Orthodox Church, serves in Putin's mind to uphold a particular moral order centered on Russian nationhood. But Russia is not alone in adhering to a moral framework that has fear, mistrust, and violence at its heart. The same distorted moral calculus is evident in the fact that many nations' military budgets far exceed their spending on humanitarian aid.[4]

3. In 8 BC Herod accused his sons Alexander and Aristobulus of treason. They were subsequently found guilty in a Roman court and executed in 7 BC. Josephus writes of the "murderous mind" and the "barbarity" of the man who slaughtered his own sons. Josephus, *Antiquities* 16.11.8, quoted in Zeitlin, "Herod," 3.

4. In 2021, for instance, global military spending was in the order of 2.1 trillion USD, whereas global spending on humanitarian aid amounted to 31.3 billion USD, a mere 1.4 percent of the world's military budgets. The respective figures are taken from Tian et al., "Trends in World

Matthew's portrayal of such power, and the moral calculus that accompanies it, is no incidental detail in his Gospel. The good represented in the infant Jesus is a threat not only to Herod's political authority and supposed prerogative to determine what is good but also to the authority exercised by those responsible for upholding the religious order of the time. The four Gospels' portrayal of Jesus's encounters with the scribes and Pharisees, the teachers of the law, may border on caricature at points, but that such authorities saw Jesus as a threat to their conception of how the world should be ordered is a consistent theme and a recurring point of conflict throughout the Gospel accounts of Jesus's ministry. As we shall see further below, what was at stake for the teachers of the law was the defense of a theologically grounded moral order.

The Good on Trial

The conflict between competing moral frameworks is signaled, as we have seen, in the infancy narratives of Matthew and Luke, but it comes to a head in the drama of Jesus's passion and resurrection. The defenders of the existing order, variously identified in the Gospels,[5] gather as a council to bring Jesus to trial. Although they struggle to find compelling testimony against him (Matt. 26:59–60; Mark 14:55–56), they eventually find him guilty of blasphemy (Matt. 26:65; Mark 14:64; cf. Luke 22:70–71). It is clear, however, that the trial is merely a search for a pretext, "justifiable" in law, to condemn the man whose teaching and practice had exposed the defects in their own moral and theological framework. These are the religious authorities, but the political authorities—Pilate and, in Luke, also Herod Antipas[6]—are less interested in condemning Jesus. Pilate, the governor, whose permission is

---

Military Expenditure, 2022"; and Urquhart et al., "Global Humanitarian Assistance Report 2022."

5. The officials involved are identified as the high priest (Matthew, Mark, Luke), the chief priests (Matthew, Mark, Luke, John), the scribes (Mark, Luke), the elders of the people (Matthew, Mark, Luke), officers of the temple (Luke), and the Pharisees (John).

6. Herod the Great was no longer on the scene at the time of Jesus's crucifixion but had been succeeded by, among others, Herod Antipas, who had ordered the death of John the Baptist. Luke's Gospel includes a brief scene in which Jesus is brought before Herod, but, as Raymond Brown remarks, Luke "transmits early tradition about Herod Antipas—tradition that had a historical nucleus but had already developed beyond simple history by the time it reached Luke." Brown, *Death of the Messiah*, 1:785.

needed in order to carry out an execution under Roman law, can find nothing against Jesus (Luke 23:4, 13–16, 22; John 18:38, 19:4; cf. Matt. 27:22–23; Mark 15:12–14). Pilate is portrayed in the Gospels as a man faced with the same choice as the wise men in Matthew's infancy narrative. It is the choice of allegiance to a regime of violence or to a new order inaugurated in and through the person of Jesus. Pilate wonders and hesitates (Matt. 27:14; Mark 15:5), but he then capitulates to the crowd's demand that the regime of violence should be preserved. Having scourged Jesus, Pilate delivers him to be crucified (Matt. 27:26; Mark 15:15; Luke 23:25; John 19:16).

The political authorities of Jesus's day provide an example of a moral framework according to which the good consists in the preservation of one's own privilege and imperial power, by violent means if necessary. By contrast, the teachers of religious law—the chief priests, elders, and scribes—who "tie up heavy burdens, hard to bear, and lay them on the shoulders of others" (Matt. 23:4)—represent a misconstrual in legalistic terms of the goodness of God. This confusion of the good with strict observance of the law is a failing to which religious folk are especially prone. But Jesus reserves his harshest criticism for them: "Woe to you, scribes and Pharisees, hypocrites! For you tithe mint, dill, and cummin, and have neglected the weightier matters of the law: justice and mercy and faith. It is these you ought to have practiced without neglecting the others. You blind guides! You strain out a gnat but swallow a camel!" (Matt. 23:23–24). Jesus here echoes the denunciation by the prophet Isaiah of empty religious observance:

> What to me is the multitude of your sacrifices?
>   says the LORD;
> I have had enough of burnt offerings of rams
>   and the fat of fed beasts;
> I do not delight in the blood of bulls,
>   or of lambs, or of goats. . . .
>
> When you stretch out your hands,
>   I will hide my eyes from you;
> even though you make many prayers,
>   I will not listen;
>   your hands are full of blood.
> Wash yourselves; make yourselves clean;
>   remove the evil of your doings
>   from before my eyes;

cease to do evil,
    learn to do good;
seek justice,
    rescue the oppressed,
defend the orphan,
    plead for the widow.
          (Isa. 1:11, 15–17)

Jesus's own example, by contrast, introduces a conception of what is good that unmasks the principalities that hold sway in our world. In fact, it calls every one of us into question, probes the depths of our own hearts, and asks where our own moral allegiances lie. His way of being, his obedience to the Father, his inauguration of a kingdom in which the poor hear good news, captives are released, the blind are enabled to see, and the oppressed are set free (Luke 4:18) constitutes a radically different moral order, an order that, when taken up by the followers of Jesus in the early church, "[turns] the world upside down" (Acts 17:6). Those followers were dragged before the city authorities in Thessalonica and were accused of "acting contrary to the decrees of the emperor, saying that there is another king named Jesus" (17:7).

The conflict between rival conceptions of the good is played out throughout the Gospels, each in their distinctive ways, but in all four Gospels that conflict comes to a head in Jesus's crucifixion. The crucifixion enacts the religious and political condemnation of the kingdom proclaimed and inaugurated by Jesus. That kingdom must be opposed and ultimately extinguished, for it constitutes a threat to the existing order. How easily the crowd goes along with this verdict, being persuaded to demand that Jesus be killed, though they have no idea what evil he may have done (Matt. 27:20–23). And so it was that

the soldiers of the governor took Jesus into the governor's headquarters, and they gathered the whole cohort around him. They stripped him and put a scarlet robe on him, and after twisting some thorns into a crown, they put it on his head. They put a reed in his right hand and knelt before him and mocked him, saying, "Hail, King of the Jews!" They spat on him, and took the reed and struck him on the head. After mocking him, they stripped him of the robe and put his own clothes on him. Then they led him away to crucify him. (Matt. 27:27–31)

This defiant assertion of the prevailing morality, of a morality that wields violence in pursuit of the "good," is intended to extinguish the alternative morality proclaimed and embodied by Jesus. The verdict of death is thought to be the final word. Humanity has spoken and done its worst. Matthew puts the matter poignantly: "Then *the people as a whole* answered, 'His blood be on us and on our children!'" (Matt. 27:25, emphasis added). But there is another word still to be sounded, the divine word of resurrection and new life. The conflict between the two moral orders takes an unexpected turn. And it turns out that victory belongs to the lamb (Rev. 17:14; see also 7:10). The existing order of violence and death will not prevail, because God has raised Jesus from the dead. Humanity's choice of death, and the moral frameworks that lead to and justify death, have been overturned. This point has been powerfully explored in Oliver O'Donovan's book *Resurrection and Moral Order: An Outline for Evangelical Ethics*, to which we now turn.

You Shall Have Life

O'Donovan contends that Christian ethics must begin with the resurrection because it is there that God makes known most clearly God's verdict on and purpose for creation, and so also for created human life.[7] "The meaning of the resurrection," O'Donovan explains, "is that it is God's final and decisive word on the life of his creature, Adam. It is, in the first place, God's reversal of Adam's choice of sin and death: 'As in Adam all die, so also in Christ shall all be made alive' (1 Cor. 15:22)."[8] "Adam" has the dual sense here of the individual referred to in the creation stories of Genesis and the whole of humankind gathered up symbolically in the life of the prototypical first human being. In the second place, and precisely because it is a reversal of Adam's choice of death, "the resurrection of Christ is a new affirmation of God's first decision that Adam should live."[9] It is the decisive act of God in which creation is set again on its path toward fullness of life rather than death, the life that was purposed for it in the beginning. O'Donovan explains further:

> The work of the Creator who made Adam, who brought into being an order of things in which humanity has a place, is affirmed once and for all by this conclusion. It might have been possible, we could say, before Christ rose from the dead, for someone to wonder whether creation was a lost cause. If the

7. O'Donovan, *Resurrection and Moral Order*, 13.
8. O'Donovan, *Resurrection and Moral Order*, 13–14.
9. O'Donovan, *Resurrection and Moral Order*, 14.

creature consistently acted to uncreate itself, and with itself to uncreate the rest of creation, did this not mean that God's handiwork was flawed beyond hope of repair? It might have been possible before Christ rose from the dead to answer in good faith, Yes.[10]

Before God raised Jesus from the dead, it might have appeared that there was no hope, or perhaps that there was only an otherworldly hope, a hope of escape from this world to some spiritual realm elsewhere. But that is not the Christian hope. For in fact Christ has been raised from the dead, reconstituting this world in its relation to God, renewing the creation that had been brought low by humanity's choice of death, and beginning thus the task of restoring it to its intended purpose. The fact of Christ's resurrection rules out an otherworldly hope and also gives reason to move beyond our hopelessness, for in Christ, whom Paul calls the last Adam (1 Cor. 15:45), the first is rescued. "The deviance of [humanity's] will, its fateful leaning towards death, has not been allowed to uncreate what God created."[11]

The resurrection is, of course, but one aspect of a wider drama that the Gospel narratives proclaim. The opening verses of John's Gospel put it well. The Word of God, who was in the beginning with God, and through whom all things came to be, has come among us, has become flesh as a subject within the world that was made through him (John 1:2, 14). The drama thus testified to is the fulfillment of God's promise once given to Israel: "My dwelling place shall be with them; and I will be their God, and they shall be my people" (Ezek. 37:27). As the drama of God's presence with God's people unfolds through the ministry of Jesus, we see consistently the in-breaking of a new order of things: the blind see, the lame walk, the poor have good news preached to them. As noted earlier in this volume, these are signs of creation's renewal, the establishment once more of God's purpose of life rather than death, freedom rather than bondage—God's ordering of things in contrast with our own. As the drama progresses, Jesus comes into increasing conflict with the protectors of the old order until finally, urged on by the crowds, they have their way at Calvary and assert once more the Adamic choice of death.

Here it is that a decisive feature of God's reordering of things comes starkly into view. The new creation does not come into being through coercion or through the exercise of some superior force set in opposition to and suppress-

---

10. O'Donovan, *Resurrection and Moral Order*, 14.
11. O'Donovan, *Resurrection and Moral Order*, 14.

ing the human opposition. It comes into being, rather, through the persistence of suffering love. Because love is God's motivation and goal, it is also the means by which he brings the new creation into being. Human sinfulness is not angrily suppressed. It is not defeated by some further violence, executed this time by God. The new creation is inaugurated instead by God's suffering through the world's violence, by God's taking upon Godself the dread consequences of human sin and breaking the hold that sin and death have over creation.

The crucifixion of Jesus is sometimes portrayed as a judgment. It is that, but not in the sense of an angry God bent on punishment. Rather, it is judgment in that a loving and merciful God lays bare the truth of things. The truth of humanity's sinfulness is that it leads to death. But that bad news is overcome by a further disclosure of the truth: God takes upon Godself the death that should be ours and remains with us, even when we do our worst, precisely in order that we might be freed for the living of a new life in conformity with Christ's own life. This interdependence of divine judgment and liberation is especially evident in the final resurrection appearance recorded in John's Gospel, the encounter between Peter and the risen Lord. Being asked three times by Jesus, "Do you love me?," Peter becomes painfully aware of his previous betrayal of Jesus, yet he simultaneously hears the word of forgiveness and grace (John 21:15–19). Or again, the crucifixion is sometimes spoken of as a sacrifice. But it is not a sacrifice made to appease an angry God; it is a sacrifice of love made by the God who will not give up on God's promise to dwell with us even in the greatest depths to which we may sink.

It is in the face of humanity's defiant assertion of its own word, its own purpose, that God undertakes the task of new creation. From out of the darkness of a sealed grave, when humanity has uttered its verdict and has done its worst, a new Word is heard. It is again God's Word, the same Word spoken from the foundation of the world; the Word is love, and thus also forgiveness and new life. In raising Jesus from the dead, God claims back the prerogative to shape the world according to the divine purpose, to bring forth life where we have chosen death. The resurrection of Jesus is thus, and decisively, a foreshadowing of the final act in the drama of history, the act in which death and evil and suffering will be no more.

It is abundantly clear that the final overcoming of all that threatens life is as yet an anticipation of things hoped for, a hope still to be realized in its fullness. But in the resurrection of Jesus Christ, God inaugurates the renewal of creation and calls the world again to take up God's gift of life. The task of Christian ethics, therefore, is simply to describe the content of that new life as it is made known and made possible in Christ. The task of Christian ethics is to interpret, from its center in the crucified and risen Christ, the new ordering of things that God is bringing about.

The resurrection, then, is God's verdict upon the contrasting moral visions represented in Matthew's infancy narrative and variously developed through each of the four Gospels. It is in the resurrection of Jesus from the dead that the nature of the good is actually and finally decided. The violent machinations of the political powers, the coercive legalism of the religious authorities, and the impassioned fervor of the crowd are unmasked. They do not lead to the good, after all, but only to death. The good, as it turns out, is not determined by human deliberation, which always bears the marks of sin, but consists rather in what God does in raising Jesus from the dead. Thus, as Bonhoeffer insists, "The question of the good becomes the question of participating in God's reality revealed in Christ"; and further: "The will to be good exists only as desire for the reality that is real in God."[12] Christian ethics is thus conceived as a participation in the work that God is doing. Sarah Bachelard explains that "moral responsiveness is . . . connected to . . . the possibility of participating in the dynamic and project of divine life. It is not primarily about making 'justifiable' moral choices, or managing competing claims and interests, or measuring up to our ideals, but is in the service of life's renewal and healing energised by God's active presence. To 'share Christ's risen life,' in the shorthand of the New Testament, is to share in a life 'where God is the only ultimate horizon—not death or nothingness.'"[13]

In John's Gospel, Jesus repeatedly describes his own action as a participation in the work of the Father: "Very truly, I tell you, the Son can do nothing on his own, but only what he sees the Father doing; for whatever the Father does, the Son does likewise" (John 5:19). The work of the Father is variously described throughout the New Testament, but it consists in essence in giving new life to the dead: "Indeed, just as the Father raises the dead and gives them life, so also the Son gives life to whomever he wishes" (5:21). This explanation is offered by Jesus following his healing of a disabled man at the pool of Beth-zatha. Giving life to the dead is a generic description of the transformations wrought by Jesus as he releases people from whatever holds them in

12. Bonhoeffer, *Ethics*, 50.
13. Bachelard, *Resurrection and Moral Imagination*, 56. The citation in the final line comes from Williams, *Wound of Knowledge*, 22.

bondage into the fullness of life that is God's intention from the beginning of creation. Christian ethics is thus a response to and participation in the action of God. The language of participation has been contested by some,[14] but if understood in terms of the Fourth Gospel's call to abide in Christ, or to abide in his love (John 15:9), then it is, I think, legitimate.[15]

The irreducible connection between divine action and ethics motivated Karl Barth to insist that "the dogmatics of the Christian Church, and basically the Christian doctrine of God, is ethics."[16] The task of Christian ethics according to Barth lies, as Michael Banner explains, in "the description of [the] human action called forth by the reality of the action of God."[17] Specifically, it is an account of the human action called forth and enabled by God's creation of light and life from the dark and formless void (Gen. 1:2–3) and from the darkness that came over the earth when Jesus was hung on a cross (Matt. 27:45).

Commanded to Be Free

That Christian ethics is concerned with those human actions that share in the divine project of giving life to the dead is confirmed and definitively revealed through the resurrection. Yet even this project and its ensuing ethical obligations commenced with the calling forth of light from darkness and life from the formless void at the dawn of creation. We recall O'Donovan's observation that the resurrection is a reiteration of God's first decision that the creature shall have life. The call to participate in this divine project is evident throughout the long story of God's dealings with Israel and is made explicit in the Deuteronomic injunction to choose life, to love the Lord our God, to obey and hold fast to God (Deut. 30:19–20). It lies also at the foundation of the law given to Moses, typically described in English as the "Ten Commandments." We do better, however, to follow the Hebraic description of Exodus 34:28, עֲשֶׂרֶת הַדְּבָרִים (the ten words), for the ten words begin not with a commandment but with a declaration of what God has done: "I am the LORD your God, who brought you out of the land of Egypt, out of the house of slavery" (Exod. 20:2). It is on account of this action of God that a particular

14. See, e.g., Webster, *Confessing God*, 170.
15. I owe this point to Alan Torrance, personal correspondence, March 1, 2023.
16. Barth, *Church Dogmatics* II/2, 515.
17. Banner, *Christian Ethics and Contemporary Moral Problems*, 3.

form of life then described in the further words is made possible. Once you were in bondage, God reminds Israel, once you were slaves in Egypt, but now you have been set free. The words that follow upon this word of grace are not to be understood as moralistic prohibitions but as descriptions of what free life looks like. In effect, God is saying, "I have set you free. Therefore, you shall have no other gods but me. You shall not make idols for yourself." Why? Because other gods enslave us—the gods of money, fashion, or prestige do not liberate but plunge us again into bondage. They do not offer the freedom into which God has called God's people.

The following commandments, or words, continue in the same vein: "Because you have been set free, do not kill, do not commit adultery, honor your father and mother, do not covet," and so on. This is what free life looks like. God is saying to Israel that to violate these commandments is to repeat Adam's choice of bondage and death rather than to participate in the new life that God had made possible by delivering God's people from slavery. Commonly, however, the ethical injunctions are abstracted from the preceding word of grace; the other words are isolated from the declaration of liberation, and as a result a legalistic conception of humanity's call to participate in the divine project is imposed in place of the joyous freedom of a people released from bondage into the new life that God gives.

Eberhard Jüngel makes the point that the commandments enjoin what should really be self-evident.[18] "This is what God has done for you. Is it not obvious now what kind of life is appropriate in the light of your release from slavery?" And yet, despite its self-evidence, Israel did not see. No sooner had they been released from Egypt than they were bowing down to the golden calf (Exod. 32:16). The transformation of the indicatives of free life into the imperative form ("You shall not . . .") is, as Jüngel observes, already an indication that it is too late. "Where, for example, it is necessary to command: '*You shall not kill*,' murder has already occurred."[19] The self-evidence of the indicative has been lost, and it is necessary now to command. Paul writes in Galatians 3:19 that the law is added because of transgressions. Because the indicatives of freedom have been forgotten, the imperatives have now to be issued.

This same logic of the indicative of grace preceding the imperative of the ethical command is apparent throughout the New Testament. Paul is at pains to point out that the redemption of humanity and its release from bondage

18. Jüngel, "Value-Free Truth," 212.
19. Jüngel, "Value-Free Truth," 212.

comes not through observance of the law but through the grace of God in Jesus Christ. The ethical imperatives of the gospel are not the conditions of salvation but the outcome, so Paul insists, of the liberation from sin and death accomplished for the believer by Christ. Echoing the logic of the "ten words" given to Moses, Paul writes, "For freedom Christ has set us free. Stand firm, therefore, and do not submit again to a yoke of slavery" (Gal. 5:1).

The freedom that lies at the heart of Christian ethics is not to be construed as an individual's prerogative to do whatever he or she pleases. Paul quickly disabuses the Galatian Christians of that notion. He writes, "For you were called to freedom, brothers and sisters; only do not use your freedom as an opportunity for self-indulgence, but through love become slaves to one another. For the whole law is summed up in a single commandment, 'You shall love your neighbor as yourself'" (Gal. 5:13–14). This is the new freedom into which we are delivered through Christ's overcoming of sin and death. Following the resurrection, the first Christian disciples looked back to the life and teaching of Jesus and began to understand at last the internal logic of the kingdom that Jesus both proclaimed and inaugurated. It was a logic determined by freedom and love.

The same logic had been present in the Torah, Israel's law, but had been obscured through an obsessive concentration on the letter of the law. That obsession was exposed by Jesus in his dealings with the scribes and the Pharisees. These stewards of the law took exception, for instance, to Jesus healing on the Sabbath. The law prescribed that the Sabbath should be a day of rest. It should be a day to enjoy the fullness of God's creation and to worship the Creator. To work without rest is a form of bondage that is contrary to the will of God. Provision for Sabbath rest in the law given by God is yet one more expression of the freedom that God intends for the creature. What better expression of this vision of freedom and rest can there be than to release from bondage those who are sick, lame, blind, or otherwise suffer from affliction?

In one such instance of Sabbath healing, Jesus justifies his healing of a man who had been ill for thirty-eight years by declaring, "My Father is still working, and I also am working" (John 5:17). We have noted earlier that this work of the Father is the work of new creation. It is the work of giving new life to those who have been deprived of the fullness of life that God intends.[20] In healing on the Sabbath, Jesus fulfills the spirit of the command to keep the

---

20. This is the central theme of the theology of work developed by Miroslav Volf in his book *Work in the Spirit*.

Sabbath holy against the objections of those whose obsession with the letter had blinded them to the law's intent. Christian ethics, following the logic of resurrection and the giving of new life, is directed toward liberation from bondage and the granting of rest to those who labor and are heavy laden.

That logic is evident throughout Jesus's practice, through all of his encounters with others, and in his teaching. In Matthew 18:23–35 Jesus tells a story about a king who wished to settle the debts owed to him by his servants. One of the servants owed ten thousand talents, more than fifteen years' wages, and well beyond his capacity to repay. The king responded to his anguished plea for mercy, however, by canceling the debt. That same servant then went out, came upon one of his fellow servants who owed him one hundred denarii (i.e., one hundred days' wages) and seized him by the throat, demanding that he pay. In consequence of this action, the ungrateful servant was condemned in uncompromising terms.

It was not that the servant had violated the law (according to the law, debts ought to be repaid); it was that he failed to see how life should be different in light of the freedom that had been granted to him. He had not understood the logic of grace. Upon hearing the news of the forgiven servant's own lack of mercy, the king "summoned him and said to him, 'You wicked slave! I forgave you all that debt because you pleaded with me. Should you not have had mercy on your fellow slave, as I had mercy on you?' And in anger his lord handed him over to be tortured until he should pay his entire debt" (Matt. 18:32–34).

The consequence appears to be extremely harsh, but good storytellers often deal in hyperbole in order to stress a point. Jesus is drawing attention, I think, to the tragedy of a person who does not understand the logic of forgiveness and refuses to participate in the freedom and new life that has been granted to them. Such refusal plunges the servant back into the bondage from which he had earlier been released. Jesus concludes his story by urging his hearers to forgive one another from their hearts. That is not a new law; it is a description, rather, of what new life looks like in the light of God's forgiving and re-creative love, the same forgiving and re-creative love that is shown forth in the resurrection of Christ.

Another story told by Jesus is about some laborers in a vineyard (Matt. 20:1–16). A landowner hires some workers for his vineyard, and, after agreeing with them on the day's wage, he sends them to work. A couple of hours later, at 9:00 a.m., more workers arrive, and he sets them to work as well. This happens again at noon, at 3:00 p.m., and at 5:00 p.m.: more workers arrive and are given jobs. When evening comes, those who arrived last are paid first, and each receives a full day's wage. When those who worked all day come for their wages, they think that they should receive more, but the landowner pays them the same full day's wage that they initially agreed on. Then we read:

> When they received it, they grumbled against the landowner, saying, "These last worked only one hour, and you have made them equal to us who have borne the burden of the day and the scorching heat." But he replied to one of them, "Friend, I am doing you no wrong; did you not agree with me for the usual daily wage? Take what belongs to you and go; I choose to give to this last the same as I give to you. Am I not allowed to do what I choose with what belongs to me? Or are you envious because I am generous?" (Matt. 20:11–15)

This parable speaks of a different ordering of things, an order not governed by a system of just deserts but by consideration of what each person needs to feed a family, to maintain their freedom and dignity, and to sustain life as it was created to be by God. The abundant generosity of the vineyard owner gives a glimpse, Jesus suggests, of what free life looks like according to God's ordering of things. Christian ethics isn't a set of rules abstracted from the news of the gospel. It is an account of what the world looks like when turned upside down by the abundant generosity of God. And it makes sense, this different ordering of things, only in the light of the trustworthiness of God in providing for all God's creatures and under the assurance of new life to those who do not cling to the old order.

A Prodigal Son Returns

One of the best known of Jesus's parables, commonly named the parable of the prodigal son, hammers home the point. The parable begins with the younger of two sons asking his father to give him "the share of the property that will belong to me" (Luke 15:12). We should note the enormity of this request. The offense committed against the father is relational. In requesting that the inheritance that would otherwise come to him after his father's death be given to him now, the son is proposing that the family should behave as if his father were already dead. That defiance of the filial relationship is accentuated further by the language used by the son in making his request.

We miss it in the English translation, but in Greek the son asks not merely for his share of the property but for the "μέρος τῆς οὐσίας," "share of the being," that will fall to him. The father then divides between them "τὸν βίον," "his life." The father is giving up his life to his son. The "property" requested is more than mere chattels. The *being* and the *life* that the son receives from the father the son squanders. And in squandering these things the son finds himself in bondage, a servant in a distant land, competing with pigs for a morsel to eat.

Out of the midst of his misery, and determined to exploit his father even further,[21] the son hatches a plan to return to his father's house as an employee, for even his father's hired hands "have bread enough and to spare" (Luke 15:17). The son thus resolves, "I will get up and go to my father, and I will say to him, 'Father, I have sinned against heaven and before you; I am no longer worthy to be called your son; treat me like one of your hired hands'" (15:18–19). Note that the son does not propose, nor does he anticipate, a return to the status and privilege of sonship in his father's house. That *bios*, that life, has been lost. The son's logic is impeccable.

But when the son returns home, we see an astonishing reversal—exactly the opposite of what we think should happen. He has squandered half of the family's wealth, blown it all; and he has squandered his identity as a son as well. Then he comes skulking back home hoping for a job as a hired hand. By all conventional logic, he doesn't deserve it! And the elder brother is standing by to make exactly that point. But—and here is the central point of the parable—God, who is represented by the father in Jesus's parable, does not operate according to the conventional logic according to which people get what they deserve. God operates, rather, according to a logic of forgiveness and grace. The father thus instructs his slaves to "bring out a robe—the best one—and put it on [the son]; put a ring on his finger and sandals on his feet" (Luke 15:22). The robe and the ring are symbols of authority (e.g., Gen. 41:42). The robe is even a symbol of salvation. Isaiah 61, the chapter from which Jesus preaches in the synagogue at the beginning of his ministry in Luke,[22] reads,

> I will greatly rejoice in the LORD,
> my whole being shall exult in my God;

---

21. I am grateful to Alan Torrance for pointing this out. Personal correspondence, March 1, 2023.
22. See Luke 4:16–21.

> for he has clothed me with the garments of salvation,
> he has covered me with the robe of righteousness.
>
> (Isa. 61:10)

Righteousness (צְדָקָה) means to be restored to right relationship. It is a reversal of the relational damage done by the son in demanding that he take leave of his father and be given the father's being and life to do with as he pleases. The sandals too indicate a return to a position of privilege and authority in the father's house. They are a sign, so Kenneth Bailey explains, of the son's "being a free man in the house, not a servant. Derrett writes regarding the servants, 'They put his sandals on as a sign that they accept him as their master—indeed no order could have expressed this more conclusively.'"[23] The father then orders that the fatted calf be killed so that they may eat and celebrate. Why? It is because "this son of mine was dead and is alive again" (Luke 15:24). Resurrection has occurred!

The ethic of the kingdom is on display again here in Jesus's teaching. It is an ethic directed toward resurrection and new life. We, like the older son, have the choice to participate in it—or not. But the older son in Jesus's parable is instructive in another respect as well. Unlike his prodigal brother, the older son has remained in the father's house pulling his weight, as it were, and contributing to the economic well-being of the household. But his own description of those years of service is telling: "Listen!," he says to his father, in protest at the good things being lavished on his brother, "For all these years I have been working like a slave for you, and I have never disobeyed your command; yet you have never given me even a young goat so that I might celebrate with my friends" (Luke 15:29). The older son apparently perceives his participation in the father's household according to the old logic of just deserts. His sonship and the entitlements that go with it have been earned, he supposes, through his own labor. Like the Pharisees and the scribes to whom Jesus tells this parable (15:2–3), the older son imagines that his observance of the law of familial obligation ought to secure his father's (God's) favor.

The moral life of the Christian can also be (mis)construed in this way. Goodness is mistakenly conceived as a state that we must strive to attain in order to win God's favor. That logic issues, however, in the resentment of the

---

23. Bailey, *Poet and Peasant*, 185. The citation comes from Duncan and Derrett, "Law in the New Testament," 66.

older son, who is unable to share his father's joy that his brother who was dead has come to life, that the one who was lost has been found (Luke 15:32). It issues in the grumbling of the Pharisees and the scribes who are perturbed that Jesus should "welcome sinners and eat with them" (15:2). It issues in the self-righteousness of the Pharisee in another of Jesus's parables who goes up to the temple to pray and gives thanks that he is not like other men (18:1–8). But perhaps more frequently still, it issues in despair at the realization of one's own failure to be "good." Such despair leaves one bereft of hope and afflicted by a sense of profound unworthiness.

Jesus's parable offers one further antidote to this troublesome logic. It is offered in the father's response to his son: "Son, you are always with me, and all that is mine is yours" (Luke 15:31). The father's favor is not contingent at all upon the son's labor. The son is assured of it simply in virtue of the fact that he is a beloved son. "All that is mine is yours," says the father. Understood in theological terms, "all that is mine" includes the goodness and righteousness that belongs to God alone but is given to humanity in Christ. We do not attain that goodness for ourselves. It comes to us as gift. Thus Sarah Bachelard writes, "No amount of trying to be good, to possess a goodness of our own, will take us to true Goodness. That is because the only true goodness is God's. We are enabled to participate in it as we receive it as gift, letting go of our projects of self-making, our desire to secure our own righteousness."[24] Making the same point, but in his characteristically angular fashion, Søren Kierkegaard speaks of "the upbuilding that lies in the thought that in relation to God we are always in the wrong."[25]

The realization that we are neither expected nor able to achieve goodness on our own is itself a liberation into a new way of being, a way of being in which we are drawn by the Spirit to participate in the divine life. The burden of striving to be good and the despair that commonly follows failure are removed because my life is yielded into the life of Christ; "It is no longer I who live, but it is Christ who lives in me" (Gal. 2:20). The removal of the burden of making oneself righteous is precisely the "upbuilding" to which Kierkegaard refers. Kierkegaard himself recognizes that the removal of such a burden is cause for great joy. The sermon to which we have referred is preceded by the following prayer.

---

24. Bachelard, *Resurrection and Moral Imagination*, 98–99.
25. This is the title of a "sermon" that concludes Kierkegaard's work *Either/Or*, 339.

Father in heaven! Teach us to pray rightly so that our hearts may open up to you in prayer and supplication and hide no furtive desire that we know is not acceptable to you, nor any secret fear that you will deny us anything that will truly be for our good, so that the laboring thoughts, the restless mind, the fearful heart may find rest in and through that alone in which and through which it can be found—by always joyfully thanking you as we gladly confess that in relation to you we are always in the wrong. Amen.[26]

It is such a prayer that, prayed daily, sets the believer on the road of Christian moral life.

26. Kierkegaard, *Either/Or*, 342.

8

Life in Community

Every year at the beginning of the seven days of the Passover festival, millions of Jews around the world share together a family meal called the Seder. At this meal, special foods symbolic of Israel's deliverance from slavery in Egypt are eaten, and a liturgy called the Haggadah is recited. The word *Haggadah* simply means "recital." In the Bible the people of Israel are instructed to "tell" (וְהִגַּדְתָּ, Exod. 13:8) their children the story of Israel's exodus from Egypt.[1] As part of the Passover Haggadah the children seated around the table ask a series of questions: "Why does this night differ from all other nights? For on all other nights we eat either leavened or unleavened bread; why on this night only unleavened bread? On all other nights we eat all kinds of herbs: why on this night only bitter herbs?"[2] and so on.[3] The questions are followed by the *maggid*, in which the Exodus story is retold and commentary is made on its meaning for the present and future. The eating of unleavened bread recalls the haste with which the people of Israel left their homes in Egypt to set out on their journey of deliverance (Exod. 12:39). The bitter herbs recall the long years of suffering under the yoke of slavery

---

1. Raphael, *Feast of History*, 11.
2. This and the following citations of the Haggadah are taken from Glatzer, ed., *Passover Haggadah*, here 25.
3. Glatzer includes four questions in the Haggadah but advises that there were originally three recorded in the Palestinian Mishnah. See Glatzer, *Passover Haggadah*, 26.

(Exod. 1:13–14). The guiding theme as the Haggadah liturgy is recited is the instruction given in Exodus 13:8: "You shall tell your child on that day, 'It is because of what the LORD did for me when I came out of Egypt.'"

The Passover Haggadah does not function for Jews merely as an inspiring story from the past. It is their story now, the story in which they belong and that continues in the present day. It is the story of divine deliverance and liberation, of God's love and mercy and faithfulness, not only to their ancestors but also to them. It is the story of Jewish identity. It defines who they are. That is the principal reason why, as one anthropologist has put it, "All communication that takes place at the Seder must be available to everyone."[4] Whatever ambiguities there may be in providing a legal or a sociological response to the question "Who is a Jew?,"[5] or even an answer determined by religious observance, the theological answer is emphatic: a Jew is a person whom God has delivered from bondage. Thus an old rabbinic saying from the Haggadah reads, "In every generation let each man look on himself as if *he* came forth out of Egypt."[6] And a little later it states; "It was not only our fathers that the Holy One, blessed be he, redeemed, but us as well did he redeem along with them. As it is written, 'And he brought us out from thence, that he might bring us in, to give us the land which he swore to our fathers' (Deut. 6:23)."[7]

The Jewish sense of identification with their ancestors, especially with their suffering and subsequent deliverance, has become even more acute since the Holocaust. Writing in 1972, Chaim Raphael explains, "For those of us who have lived through the drama of the last decades, the most powerful feeling emerging from the Haggadah is not that we are following mutely in the steps of our ancestors but that a revolution and a miracle has transformed this kinship."[8] Raphael explains further, "The Haggadah, leading us on to think about our history, makes us aware also, as nothing else can, of the transformation that has come into our lives."[9] Thus, the Passover Haggadah itself begins with an expression of anguish and shame as Jews remember the days of suffering, and it concludes with praise and gratitude to God for their delivery

---

4. Fredman, *Passover Seder*, 10, quoted in Bokser, *Origins of the Seder*, 81.
5. On which see Raphael, *Feast of History*, 16–23.
6. Glatzer, *Passover Haggadah*, 59, emphasis original. I have retained the gendered language of Glatzer's edition, but note that inclusive language editions have recently become available. See the story in Berger, "Giving a Haggadah a Makeover."
7. Glatzer, *Passover Haggadah*, 59.
8. Raphael, *Feast of History*, 13.
9. Raphael, *Feast of History*, 13.

from oppression.[10] The Haggadah, writes Abraham Bloch, is "the classical Jewish manifesto of freedom."[11]

Eucharistic Identity

The soteriological drama of transformation from shame and anguish to joyous praise following God's liberation of God's people from bondage reaches its high point, so Christians believe, in the death and resurrection of Jesus. The continuity with Israel's proclamation of divine deliverance seemed obvious to the early Christians, and so each of the four evangelists takes care to point out that the death and resurrection of Jesus took place at the time of the Passover celebration. Matthew, Mark, and Luke suggest, but not without some ambiguity, that Jesus shares a Passover meal with his disciples (Matt. 26:17–20; Mark 14:12–17; Luke 22:7–14). Noting the ambiguity, Alasdair Heron explains that "it is even today not entirely certain whether or not the Last Supper was a Passover meal. The main reason for this uncertainty is that the Gospels themselves seem to disagree on the point. Mark 14.12–16 leads up to the story of the Last Supper by describing the preparations 'for the Passover which I will eat with my disciples' (v. 14), and Matt. 26.17–19 and Luke 22.7–13 are similar. Of the institution narratives proper, however, only Luke's refers explicitly to the Supper as a Passover, while John 18.28 states that the Passover *followed* Jesus' arrest."[12]

Despite the widespread influence of Joachim Jeremias's work *The Eucharistic Words of Jesus*, in which he argues that the Last Supper was a Passover meal and that all the sayings ascribed to Jesus should be interpreted against that background, the meal as recorded in the Gospels does not follow very precisely the usual form of the Passover meal. While there are similarities, notably an opening blessing, the dipping of bread in the cup, didactic elements, and a closing hymn, it is clear that the meal that Jesus shared with his disciples departs in substantial detail from the Seder.[13] The Gospel writers, it

10. I take the point from Bloch, *Jewish Customs and Ceremonies*, 234.
11. Bloch, *Jewish Customs and Ceremonies*, 229.
12. Heron, *Table and Tradition*, 17.
13. This has been observed by numerous scholars including, for example, the Jewish scholar Chaim Raphael in his *Feast of History*, 82–85, and Christian scholars Alasdair Heron and David Stubbs. Heron has argued that Jeremias's work reads rather too much into the Passover setting of the Last Supper. See Heron, *Table and Tradition*, 9. Stubbs has likewise argued that "the

appears, were concerned to evoke comparison with the Passover rather than to insist that Jesus and his disciples shared all the elements of a Seder complete with the recitation of the Haggadah. We turn our attention, accordingly, to what the evangelists may have been trying to convey by linking the passion narratives to the Passover.

We note first of all that in the Gospels of Matthew and Mark, Jesus approves the suggestion of the disciples that they prepare for the Passover meal (Matt. 26:17; Mark 14:12). Luke alone reports that Jesus initiated the needed preparations (Luke 22:8). The reports then offered by the Gospel writers of how the meal unfolded tell of a supper that retained some elements of the Seder but also diverged substantially from the usual order and content. If Luke's report is veridical, what might have been Jesus's purpose in linking his own institution of what Christians now call the Eucharist, the Mass, or the Lord's Supper with the Jewish Passover meal? What justification might there be for the evocation of the Jewish Passover in the context of Jesus's impending death and resurrection, and for the reinterpretation of the bread and wine as symbols of his own body and blood?

The setting of Jesus's passion within the context of the Passover meal places Jesus himself in the same tradition of divine deliverance and liberation that Jews tell of through the Haggadah. The evocation of Passover is an expression of the belief that God is at work again in the death and resurrection of Jesus, liberating God's people from the bondage of sin and death. Just as the Passover story is central to the identity of the Jewish people, central to who they are, so too the Lord's Supper and the story there told are key to the identity of Christians. Who is a Jew? A Jew is one whom God has delivered from bondage in Egypt. And who is a Christian? A Christian is one whom God has delivered from the bondage of sin and death and who has entered into the fellowship of Christ's body. When Christians celebrate the Lord's Supper, they are telling the story of who they are, a people whose identity is determined by the liberation accomplished for them by Jesus the Christ.

While there is undoubtedly considerable divergence from the Seder in the New Testament reports of the Last Supper, we may also note some important

---

eucharist is not merely a transformation of a Passover Seder meal." Stubbs, *Table and Temple*, 35. Having made the point that the supper Jesus celebrated with his disciples was not a simple transformation of the Seder, he then explains the important connections that are nevertheless drawn in the New Testament between the Jewish Passover meal and the Christian Eucharist. Stubbs, *Table and Temple*, 225–36.

similarities. Two points in particular are of special importance. First is the fact that the Seder included the Haggadah, the interpretation of the meal and its components. This provides a likely setting for Jesus's words of reinterpretation. The unleavened bread and the cups of wine that feature in the Seder are given new symbolic resonance as Jesus links them to his own suffering and death: "While they were eating, [Jesus] took a loaf of bread, and after blessing it he broke it, gave it to them, and said, 'Take; this is my body.' Then he took a cup, and after giving thanks he gave it to them, and all of them drank from it. He said to them, 'This is my blood of the covenant, which is poured out for many. Truly I tell you, I will never again drink of the fruit of the vine until that day when I drink it new in the kingdom of God'" (Mark 14:22–25).

The second feature is that the Seder itself is a meal of remembrance, present celebration, and hope. This is true also of the Christian celebration of the Lord's Supper. It looks back in remembrance at what has been done by God in delivering God's people from bondage. It celebrates the present identity of the people—a people for and to whom Christ has given his life and who live now in covenant relationship with God. And it looks forward in hope to that day when Christ will come again and drink new wine with his people in the kingdom of God. These features are maintained through the New Testament's various reports of the Last Supper, although the precise words differ across the three Synoptic Gospels and in Paul's report in 1 Corinthians 11:23–26.

The gestures and symbols of the Seder that tell the story of the exodus are not replicated exactly, but they are alluded to in the New Testament records. They are alluded to in order to make clear that God is at work again delivering people from bondage, but this time God's work of deliverance extends to the whole creation. How is this message conveyed? We shall first consider the bread over which Jesus says, "This is my body, which is given for you. Do this in remembrance of me" (Luke 22:19). We should note first the passive form. Although Jesus himself certainly acts here, he is also "given." This is not a drama that can be accounted for at the human level alone. As he has done throughout the Gospel narratives, Jesus speaks of his own action as the action of God the Father. The gift we are concerned with here, and the act of giving, is the work of the holy Father who gives his Son to enter into the midst of the world's evil and sin. It is not just Jesus who gives. He is also given by the Father for the sake of humankind.[14]

---

14. On which, see Heron, *Table and Tradition*, 23–24.

Jesus takes the bread and breaks it, as is the Jewish custom. In Christian thought, the breaking of bread is commonly regarded as a representation of the breaking of Jesus's body on the cross. The parallel suggests itself clearly enough, but in the Passover meal the main emphasis was on the dividing (breaking) of the bread so that the blessing of God could be distributed among all who had gathered for the meal. The distribution of the broken bread made clear as well that all who eat the bread are included in the drama of the exodus. We recall the rabbinic saying: "In every generation let each man look on himself as if *he* came forth out of Egypt."[15] The sharing of the broken bread binds them together with their ancestors as one people. Paul picks up the same theme when in 1 Corinthians he writes, "The bread that we break, is it not a sharing in the body of Christ? Because there is one bread, we who are many are one body, for we all partake of the one bread" (1 Cor. 10:16–17). Those who share bread together are bound together as one people under God's blessing.

Again and again through the course of his ministry, Jesus prompts outrage among the religious authorities because of his insistence on eating with sinners, outcasts, and the despised. In doing so he makes them one with himself, and he one with them. One of the most poignant moments in the Gospels is when Jesus, sitting at the Last Supper with his disciples, takes a piece of bread, dips it in the cup, and gives it to Judas, the one who will betray him (John 13:26; cf. Matt. 26:23; Mark 14:18; Luke 22:21). Sinners are not excluded from companionship with the Lord. As Stefan Alkier has put it, "Judas, the traitor, and Peter, the denier, are both guests at the table of the Lord, and no one doubts their belonging there."[16] Note that the word *companion* comes from the Latin *com panis*, which literally means "with bread." The old French word *compaignon* means "one who breaks bread with another."

The unleavened bread of the Passover meal is described as the bread of affliction that the Jews' ancestors ate in Egypt. It is the same bread—unleavened on account of the haste needed as God led the Israelites out of Egypt—that was eaten during the exodus. To this day, those who share the Seder are eating the same bread of affliction. Alasdair Heron observes that the claim "'This is the bread of affliction which our fathers ate' is not 'mere metaphor' but solemn description."[17] Christians see a link here with the affliction and suffering of Jesus, but those who share now in the Eucharist enter into this same drama

---

15. Glatzer, *Passover Haggadah*, 59. Emphasis original.
16. Alkier, *Reality of the Resurrection*, 260.
17. Heron, *Table and Tradition*, 26.

of suffering and death, and so also into the drama of deliverance through resurrection. The new life given by God comes by way of affliction and death.

The fellowship of believers with Christ established through their sharing in the one loaf is reinforced by their reception of the cup over which Jesus says, "This cup that is poured out for you is the new covenant in my blood" (Luke 22:20; cf. Matt. 26:28; Mark 14:24; 1 Cor. 11:25).[18] These words again point to the new identity of the people who share in this meal. Reference to the new covenant recalls the promise of Jeremiah 31, now being fulfilled through the life, death, and resurrection of Jesus:

> The days are surely coming, says the Lord, when I will make a new covenant with the house of Israel and the house of Judah. It will not be like the covenant that I made with their ancestors when I took them by the hand to bring them out of the land of Egypt—a covenant that they broke, though I was their husband, says the Lord. But this is the covenant that I will make with the house of Israel after those days, says the Lord: I will put my law within them, and I will write it on their hearts; and I will be their God, and they shall be my people. No longer shall they teach one another, or say to each other, "Know the Lord," for they shall all know me, from the least of them to the greatest, says the Lord; for I will forgive their iniquity, and remember their sin no more. (Jer. 31:31–34)

The key point for my purposes here is that the new covenant establishes a relationship that determines the identity of the people: "I will put my law within them, and I will write it on their hearts; and I will be their God, and they shall be my people." The new identity is given and established by God. When the church gathers to celebrate the Eucharist, it shares in an act of thanksgiving (*eucharistia*) for the new identity given to it as the people of God. "Once you were not a people, but now you are God's people; once you had not received mercy, but now you have received mercy" (1 Pet. 2:10). The new identity is characterized by freedom and is manifest in a new form of life. Thus the author of 1 Peter goes on to stress, "As servants of God," you are to "live as free people" (1 Pet. 2:16), a people called and enabled to "follow in [Christ's] steps" (1 Pet. 2:21).

A third element of the Passover meal that is linked with the Eucharist in the New Testament is the sacrifice of the Passover lamb. We need not pursue in detail here the ways in which Christ is identified as the paschal lamb by New

---

18. The word *new* is omitted in some manuscripts of Matthew and Mark.

Testament writers, either directly or through allusion, but it is important to note that the lamb sacrificed at the Passover festival was not a sin offering. Rather, the offering of an unblemished lamb was a symbol of Israel's total offering of itself and of its total dedication to God. In the context of the Passover meal, the renewal of Israel's dedication to God is prompted by remembrance of the exodus. David Stubbs confirms the point: "The Passover sacrifice is not about atonement for sin. Instead it is a celebration of being saved from powers of oppression and being saved for a specific vocation, to be a priestly people."[19] Richard Hays concurs: "The Passover festival has nothing to do with atonement for sin," he says, "and everything to do with deliverance from the powers of oppression."[20] While there are texts elsewhere in the New Testament that portray the crucifixion of Jesus as a sacrifice for sin, the eucharistic references to the paschal lamb (e.g., 1 Cor. 5:6–8) have another purpose in view. They point to the crucifixion as an offering of the unblemished one in total dedication to God. Christ alone is worthy and makes the one true offering of total dedication to God. The resurrection may then be seen as God's acceptance and approval of Jesus's offering of himself on behalf of all humanity. We may truly say then that through the sacrifice of Christ, humanity is released into the fullness of life that God intends for the whole creation.

Gathered into Communion

One of the distinctive characteristics of both meals—the Passover and the Lord's Supper—is that they are celebrated as a community; they cannot be celebrated alone. They are celebrated, furthermore, by the community formed by God's saving action. Israel is the community formed by God's promise to Abraham and Sarah and called out of bondage in Egypt. The church is the community delivered by God from the bondage of sin or, we might say, the bondage of disrupted relationships, for that is essentially what sin is. Sin is commonly construed as moral failure or misdemeanor, but that is merely a symptom of sin. The more fundamental problem that the term *sin* indicates is the disruption of relationships—with God, with our neighbors, and with the rest of the created order. The call of Christ is best understood, therefore, as a call to share in the mending and rebuilding of relationships. It is a call to

19. Stubbs, *Table and Temple*, 223.
20. Hays, *First Corinthians*, 90–91.

share in a new community, a community characterized above all by love. The trouble is, of course, that those who are called into this community are themselves in need of restoration and repair. They are the outsiders, the sinners, the non-law-abiding. These are the people whom Jesus searched out in his own ministry as narrated in the Gospels and whom he continues to seek out today.

Thus, when they come together in community—into the community called church—those gathered by Christ into communion with him and with one another turn out to be a rough lot. They are still sinners, works in progress, and that means that the church is a place where there is much need for grace and forgiveness. There is much need for the exercise of compassion because those gathered into the community of the church aren't necessarily the people whom others gathered into that same body of Christ would choose as their friends. The people gathered into communion are gathered precisely because God has transformative work to do with them, both individually and as a community.

Christian life is inconceivable apart from this community. For Christian life simply is a life lived in reconciled communion with God, one another, and indeed all of God's creation. It is not a private form of existence to be lived out by individuals. It is a new way of being—in loving communion with God and with one's neighbor. One often hears complaints about the church, about the awkward and annoying people to be found there. But that is surely the point. The church is gathered together because God has transformative work to do with every one of us. God is in the business of raising people from the dead, of gathering home lost prodigals, and of building a new community. It is a work in progress that will be completed only when the Son hands over the kingdom to the Father and God will be all in all (1 Cor. 15:24, 28). Those who seek to be part of that transformative community, therefore, should not expect perfection. They should expect, rather, to be apprenticed—discipled—in the practices of forgiveness, reconciliation, and grace. They should expect to be trained in the art of love, not only for their neighbors but for their enemies too.

The new community gathers regularly for worship, and at the heart of its worship is a table on which are laid bread and wine, symbols of the body of Christ given for us and the blood of Christ poured out for many for the forgiveness of sin. That gathering around the table is itself a powerful symbol of the communion to which the church is called. It is a communion in which, according to Paul, there is neither Jew nor Greek, slave nor free, male nor female, for all are made one in the body of Christ (Gal. 3:28). The church is to be, therefore, a community in which the divisions of race, social class, and gender are broken down. Why is that? It is because the community is formed of those who have heard and responded to the news that God has delivered them from bondage. They are not formed because of their particular interests or hobbies. They are not formed because of some common characteristic such as their nationality, race, or economic status. Nor are they formed because of some prior affection for one another. They are gathered together solely in virtue of the fact that they have heard and responded to the call of Christ. They are the *ekklēsia*, the ones whom Christ has "called out" to be his people. In this they are equal, and, precisely in virtue of this equality, every division between them must be set aside.

It is for that reason that Paul is so disturbed by the abuse of the Lord's Supper that he sees in the church in Corinth.

Now in the following instructions I do not commend you, because when you come together it is not for the better but for the worse. For, to begin with, when you come together as a church, I hear that there are divisions among you; and to some extent I believe it. Indeed, there have to be factions among you, for only so will it become clear who among you are genuine. When you come together, it is not really to eat the Lord's supper. For when the time comes to eat, each of you goes ahead with your own supper, and one goes hungry and another becomes drunk. What! Do you not have homes to eat and drink in? Or do you show contempt for the church of God and humiliate those who have nothing? What should I say to you? Should I commend you? In this matter I do not commend you! (1 Cor. 11:17–22)

The essential failure that Paul complains of here is that some members of the church in Corinth have failed to grasp the radical transformation of social relations that ought to take place among the followers of Jesus. There are divisions in the community (v. 18). Some go ahead with their own supper, while others go hungry, and some become drunk (v. 21). Richard Hays explains that "Paul's vision of community comes into conflict with the Corinthians' conventional social mores, which require distinctions of rank and status to be recognized at table; the more privileged members expect to receive more and better food than others."[21]

Those guilty of this preservation of their own privilege and the accompanying insensitivity to the needs of others had the audacity, it seems, to suppose that their drunken feasting constituted a celebration of the Lord's Supper.

21. Hays, *First Corinthians*, 194.

"Paul regards this as a humiliation for the community and as an abuse of the Supper of the Lord, whose own example contradicts such status divisions."[22]

It is possible, because language can have several layers of meaning, that when Paul admonishes the Corinthians for failing to discern the *body* (1 Cor. 11:29), he has in mind the body of Christ represented in the bread broken and shared at the Lord's Supper. But in the context of his consternation at the Corinthians' failure to grasp the gospel's radical challenge to the prevailing social order, it seems likely that Paul's reference to the "body" here is also, if not primarily, a reference to the people called into community as the "body of Christ." The community gathered into companionship with the risen Christ is called into a new way of being, one of the marks of which is discernment of the body—discernment, that is, of those to whom is due compassion and honor regardless of their ethnicity, gender, socioeconomic status, and indeed of all those particularities of individual human beings that so readily become a pretext for exclusion. Paul's condemnation of such exclusion and of the associated social hierarchies echoes the words of Jesus to the disciples who were arguing over "which of them was to be regarded as the greatest" (Luke 22:24). Jesus said to them, "The kings of the Gentiles lord it over them; and those in authority over them are called benefactors. But not so with you; rather the greatest among you must become like the youngest, and the leader like one who serves" (22:25–26).

The Practice of *Koinōnia*

Those called into community with the risen Christ are called into a new way of being. They are called into what the New Testament frequently refers to as κοινωνία, *koinōnia*. *Koinōnia* means "communion." It was commonly used of the marriage relationship to indicate the deep bond of love that binds the two partners of a marriage together.[23] Its root is used in the description of the gathering of believers following the day of Pentecost: "All who believed were together and had all things in common [κοινά]" (Acts 2:44). *Koinōnia* was further expressed through a set of distinctive practices: "They would sell their possessions and goods and distribute the proceeds to all, as any had need. Day by day, as they spent much time together in the temple, they broke bread

22. Hays, *First Corinthians*, 194.
23. See references in Arndt and Gingrich, *Greek-English Lexicon*, 439.

at home and ate their food with glad and generous hearts, praising God and having the goodwill of all the people" (Acts 2:45–47).

But this communion of the church is not simply the communion that believers have with one another. As Robert Jenson points out, "The communion that is the church . . . is primarily God's communion with us in the incarnate Christ; and because the God who thus admits us to communion is in himself a *koinonia*, the *perichoresis*, the 'mutual inhabiting,' of Father, Son and Spirit, we are drawn also to mutual love of one another."[24] Paul made this clear at the beginning of his letter to the believers in Corinth: "God is faithful; by him you were called into the fellowship [κοινωνίαν] of his Son, Jesus Christ our Lord" (1 Cor. 1:9). The pneumatological dimension of Jenson's summary claim is evident in the benediction of 2 Corinthians 13:13: "The grace of the Lord Jesus Christ, the love of God, and the communion [κοινωνία] of the Holy Spirit be with all of you." Jenson has earlier pointed out the importance of recognizing that the communion that is constitutive of the ecclesial community is neither initiated nor sustained by the people who come together to be the church.[25] The *koinōnia* of Father and Son, sustained by the Spirit, precedes the calling of the church and is the *koinōnia* into which the church is called. John 17:21–22 displays the intrinsic order: "As you, Father, are in me and I am in you, may they also be in us, so that the world may believe that you have sent me. The glory that you have given me I have given them, so that they may be one, as we are one." So also 1 John 1:3: "We declare to you what we have seen and heard so that you also may have fellowship [κοινωνίαν] with us; and truly our fellowship [κοινωνία] is with the Father and with his Son Jesus Christ." Jenson observes further: "When the church prays to the Father, believing the Son's promise that he is there to pray with them (Matthew 18:20), this human gathering participates in the Son's obedience to the Father, the very obedience by which he is in fact God the Son. All this *is* simply the free action of the Spirit, the very action by which he is the *viniculum amoris*, the 'bond of love' by which Father and Son are free for each other."[26]

James Torrance aptly contends, therefore, that "the worship of the church [is] the gift of participating through the Holy Spirit in the incarnate Son's communion with the Father."[27] This understanding of worship attests to the

---

24. Jenson, "The Church and the Sacraments," 215.
25. See Jenson, "The Church and the Sacraments," 215.
26. Jenson, "The Church and the Sacraments," 217.
27. Torrance, *Worship, Community and the Triune God of Grace*, 9.

presence of the Son and Spirit wherever two or three are gathered in Jesus's name (Matt. 18:20). The church may be defined, therefore, as the community gathered by the Spirit into the presence of the risen Christ.

The Presence of Christ

Although the church ought not to make any exclusive claim on the presence of Christ and the Spirit, for that would be a violation of divine freedom, the church lives nevertheless in confidence that Christ will be with his people whenever they gather in his name. The modes of Christ's presence are several. He is present in the sacrament of the Lord's Supper, where Christ himself is host.[28] He is present too as Word, declaring himself, as John Webster has said, through the words of Holy Scripture. As Webster further points out, Christ does not resign his office of self-communication following his resurrection and ascension; he does not hand it over to the texts of Scripture, which are "henceforth in and of themselves his voice in the world."[29] Rather, Scripture and the preaching of the biblical word are precisely the instrument of Christ's self-communicative presence. Thus, Christ is present through the ministries of Word and sacrament. But also, and no less important, Christ is present through the ministry of service, through *diakonia*. Jesus's teaching in Matthew 25:31–46 attests his presence in and as the stranger in need, in the sick, the naked, the imprisoned, the hungry, and the thirsty. Insofar as anyone shows compassion to these "little ones" or these "least" (ἐλαχίστων), says Jesus, you do it to me (Matt. 25:40).

Called to Serve

It is true to say that the church is constituted through Word and sacrament, through the hearing of God's Word in Scripture and proclamation, and by entering into the body of Christ through baptism and Eucharist. But it is equally

28. There have been, of course, endless debates in the church about the manner of Christ's presence in the Eucharist, particularly through the elements of bread and wine. As Henri De Lubac has pointed out, the debates concerning the real presence of Christ in the Eucharist have frequently undermined the unity that is affirmed as Christians gather to share in the eucharistic meal. See De Lubac, *Catholicism*, 171. A comprehensive survey of the debates over the presence of Christ in the Eucharist, and suggestions toward a recovery of the unity symbolized through the Eucharist, can be found in Hunsinger, *Eucharist and Ecumenism*.

29. Webster, "On Evangelical Ecclesiology," 189. See also Webster, *Holy Scripture*.

true that the church is constituted by its participation through the Spirit in Christ's ministry of service to the poor, the outcast, the lost, and the lonely. The church is summoned to share in the life of the crucified and risen Son and to participate in the mission of the triune God who gives life to the world. This aspect of the church's being as the body of Christ is easily forgotten, especially when the "church," now in name only, becomes comfortably aligned with and complicit in a world in which there is injustice, poverty, violence, and oppression. The church may continue in such circumstances with its ritualistic observance of liturgical life, but in so doing it will have ceased to attend deeply to the Word of God, while its celebration of the "Lord's Supper" will have become a Corinthian sham, undertaken without discerning the body. It will have become a "church" in need of the prophetic admonition:

> What to me is the multitude of your sacrifices?
>   says the LORD;
> I have had enough of burnt offerings of rams
>   and the fat of fed beasts;
> I do not delight in the blood of bulls,
>   or of lambs, or of goats.
>
> When you come to appear before me,
>   who asked this from your hand?
>   Trample my courts no more;
> bringing offerings is futile;
>   incense is an abomination to me. . . .
> Wash yourselves; make yourselves clean;
>   remove the evil of your doings
>   from before my eyes;
> cease to do evil,
>   learn to do good;
> seek justice,
>   rescue the oppressed,
> defend the orphan,
>   plead for the widow.
>   (Isa. 1:11–12, 16–17)

Throughout the course of Christian history, it has commonly been the poor, the marginalized, and the oppressed who, having recognized the presence of the risen Christ among them, have reminded the church that the risen

Lord is to be found among those whom the world has left for dead—like a man who fell into the hands of robbers and was stripped and beaten and left lying by the road (Luke 10:30). The church comes into being because of the resurrection, but it comes into being to share in the work of Christ Jesus, who continues to do the work of his Father and so is engaged still in seeking out the lost and lonely and giving new life to the dead. Jon Sobrino thus explains that "the Church that comes into existence [because of the resurrection] is not simply the depository of the truth *about* the resurrection of Christ but is itself the very expression, at the historical level, of the newness that has come in Christ."[30] Sobrino goes on to quote Jürgen Moltmann: "Without new life, without the ability to love and the courage to hope in the Lordship of Christ, faith in the resurrection would decay into belief in particular facts, without any consequences."[31]

Elsewhere too among the marginalized and oppressed, the liberating power of the resurrection in the midst of the concrete realities of prejudice, injustice, and oppression has been recognized and gladly received. Mercy Amba Oduyoye, for example, summarizes the insights of African women as they reflect on the resurrection of Christ: "African women are heard loud and clear singing the redemptive love of Jesus the liberator. Jesus accomplishes God's mission by setting women free from sexism, oppression, and marginalisation through his death and resurrection, and both women and men are made members of God's household and of the same royal priesthood as men. In *Talitha Qumi!* we read: 'The ultimate mission of Jesus was to bring healing, life and dignity to the suffering. Jesus came to give voice to the voiceless.'"[32]

The resurrection of Jesus from the dead establishes a missional imperative to participate in the divine project of giving life to the world. That includes making disciples, baptizing them in the name of the Father and of the Son and of the Spirit, and teaching them to obey everything that the Lord has commanded (Matt. 28:19–20). It also includes offering hospitality to strangers (Rom. 12:13), remembering the poor (Gal. 2:10), forgiving sins (Luke 6:37), making peace (Matt. 5:9), doing good, seeking justice, rescuing the oppressed,

---

30. Sobrino, *The True Church and the Poor*, 87.
31. Moltmann, *Church in the Power of the Spirit*, 98.
32. Oduyoye, "Jesus Christ," 156. Incorporating the words of Jesus as he called Jairus's daughter back from death (Mark 5:41), the work *Talitha Qumi! Proceedings of the Convocation of African Women Theologians* is a collection of essays edited by Mercy Amba Oduyoye and M. R. A. Kanyoro. The embedded quotation is from Kanyoro, "Daughter Arise: Luke 8:40–56," 59.

defending orphans, and pleading for widows (Isa. 1:17). The missional imperatives stemming from the resurrection, and consistent with God's deliverance
of God's people from bondage throughout the biblical narrative, are directed
toward the actualization of the kingdom and toward the fulfillment of the
divine promise that the world shall have life in its fullness (see John 10:10).
Sarah Bachelard observes this missional imperative taking shape with the
early Christian community:

> The resurrection, they [the disciples] are adamant, is something that happens
> to Jesus, but it both reveals and makes available a new life, a new creation. This
> new life is characterised by freedom, even in the face of fear and persecution,
> forgiveness, and trust in the inexhaustible hospitality, the grace of God. It begins
> to be lived out in the earliest Christian communities in the form of proclaiming
> the "good news" of God's acceptance and forgiveness, invitation into a life of
> discipleship and transformation, provision and care for those in need, and a
> ministry of healing and social inclusion. . . . Through the Spirit poured out by
> the risen Jesus, this is the pattern that characterises the early Christian com-
> munity and makes it a community of resurrection.[33]

Baptism

We have emphasized in this chapter that the resurrection of Jesus from the dead
establishes a new community, a community that lives in company with the risen
one and is drawn through the Spirit into his communion with the Father. To
live in communion with this triune God is to participate in this God's creative
and redemptive purposes for the world. It is to participate in this God's work of
giving life to the world, first and continually as people who are recipients of new
life themselves and then also as those commissioned to go "and make disciples
of all nations, baptizing them in the name of the Father and of the Son and of
the Holy Spirit" (Matt. 28:19). Baptism is the symbol of entry into this new
life. It is the symbol of dying and rising with Christ, and so of the beginning of
a new life. Those who have been baptized live no longer under the dominion,
or lordship, of sin and death but under the lordship of the risen Christ.

The believer's dying and rising with Christ, as recognized and accepted in
baptism, is made possible only on account of Jesus Christ himself having been

---

33. Bachelard, *Resurrection and Moral Imagination*, 45.

baptized. Three of the four Gospels report (though Mark and Luke do so only very briefly) that at the beginning of Jesus's ministry, Jesus himself submitted to the baptism of John. What is remarkable about this is that John offered a baptism for repentance and the forgiveness of sin, which Jesus himself had no personal need of. He was, we are told in the Epistle to the Hebrews, "without sin" (Heb. 4:15; see also Heb. 7:26; John 8:46; Acts 3:14; 2 Cor. 5:21; 1 Pet. 1:19). As I have explored elsewhere, the Gospel writers (Matthew excepted) tend to downplay this aspect of the baptism offered by John and submitted to by Jesus.[34] The evangelists focus instead on the anointing of the Spirit and the voice from heaven declaring Jesus to be God's beloved Son (Mark 1:9–11; Luke 3:21–22; John 1:32).

Only Matthew notes the incongruity of Jesus being baptized by John and records John's protest that Jesus should be baptizing him, rather than the other way around (Matt. 3:13–17). Responding to John's reluctance to baptize him, Jesus says in Matthew 3:15, "Let it be so for now; for it is proper for us in this way to fulfill all righteousness [δικαιοσύνην]." Light is shed on this somewhat enigmatic saying when we consider the term *righteousness* (δικαιοσύνη). This term has to do with the restoration of that which has been disrupted, with putting things right after some offense has occurred, with the doing of justice. We may see in this light that Jesus's submission of himself to the baptism of John for repentance and forgiveness of sin is a decisive moment in Jesus's total identification with our human situation. As he is submerged in the waters of the Jordan so too he submerges himself in the totality of our broken humanity, precisely in order to repair it and to make things right. Jesus puts himself in the place of humanity, in the place of those who have chosen the ways of death rather than life, in the place of those needing to repent.[35] The baptism is thus to be understood as the beginning of his passion,[36] in which he journeys through the agony of godforsakenness and the darkness of death. Through his life of obedience to his Father's will, Jesus offers to God a true faithfulness and a true repentance undistorted by the propensity of all other human beings to disobedience and pretense. It is in this way that Jesus "fulfills all righteousness." Sustained and empowered by the Spirit, who descends on him at his baptism, Jesus enacts and brings to fruition the covenant faithfulness and

---

34. See Rae, "Baptism of Christ," 121–37.
35. The vicarious repentance offered by Christ on behalf of all humanity is profoundly explored by John McLeod Campbell in his influential work *The Nature of the Atonement*.
36. On which see Moorman, *Luke, I–IX*, 482.

steadfast love of God for God's people—even when they do their worst—and thus restores humanity to right relationship with the Father. The resurrection is to be understood, therefore, as God's acceptance and vindication of this human life of perfect oblation, of perfect offering to God.

Those baptized into Christ, therefore, are baptized into this drama of obedience, redemption, and new life. Their baptism represents their dying and rising with Christ, their transformation from old life to new. As the drama of Jesus's baptism plays out through the course of his life of total obedience to the Father and total identification with fallen humanity, he remarks to the disciples, "Are you able to drink the cup that I drink, or be baptized with the baptism that I am baptized with?" (Mark 10:38). Jesus asks the question having just explained to the disciples that he will suffer and die but that after three days he will rise again (10:33–34). As C. E. B. Cranfield points out, "The only true answer [to Jesus's question] was, of course, No!"[37] But the disciples, patently unaware at this stage of what they are saying, answer that they are able. Jesus agrees, however, that they will drink the cup (of suffering and death) that he will drink, and they will be baptized with the baptism with which he is baptized (10:39). But within the scope of the biblical narrative as a whole we recognize that the disciples will do this only insofar as they are incorporated by grace into the death and resurrection of Christ (Rom. 6:3–5; Col. 2:12). They, and we, cannot offer the life of perfect obedience that Jesus offers to the Father; nor can they, or we, endure the abyss of godforsakenness that Jesus endures. But having identified himself completely with humanity through the incarnation, and having confirmed that total identification through submission to John's baptism, Jesus's passion, his death, and his resurrection are undertaken for us—and in a carefully defined sense, *by* us—just insofar as Jesus is one of us, sharing fully our human nature and taking our burden of alienation from God upon himself. To be baptized, then, in the name of the Father and of the Son and of the Holy Spirit is to be incorporated into the drama of death and resurrection. It is to become a participant in God's creative and redemptive purposes for the world. It is to be incorporated into the abundant life of *koinōnia* that is creation's true purpose and its promised end.

37. Cranfield, *Mark*, 339.

9

Resurrection
and Christian Hope

Many times throughout the earlier chapters of this book, we have spoken of the resurrection of Jesus from the dead as an event that opens up a new future, that sets creation again on its trajectory to fullness of life in reconciled relationship with God, that releases creation from its travail and humanity from its bondage to sin and death. Yet the realization of these outcomes remains a work in progress. The work of God in bringing creation to fruition is not yet complete. Looking to what was not yet present in its fullness, the disciples were enjoined by Jesus to pray "Your kingdom come" and to be on the lookout for its coming. This posture of prayerful expectancy remains the posture of his disciples still. The significance of the resurrection, then, is not that it finally accomplishes all that God has promised, but rather that it reveals, as the firstfruits, the end, or *telos*, to which all things are directed. The resurrection is the dawn of a new day, a day full of promise. In this concluding chapter we will explore in more detail the content of that promise and the hope to which it gives rise.

The heart of Christian hope is found in the concept of the coming kingdom of God (or of heaven) and the rule of Christ over all things.[1] This hope

---

1. Jürgen Moltmann makes essentially the same point in Moltmann, *Theology of Hope*, 126.

is expressed by Paul in his letter to the church in Corinth: "Then comes the end, when he hands over the kingdom [βασιλείαν] to God the Father, after he has destroyed every ruler and every authority and power. For he must reign until he has put all his enemies under his feet. The last enemy to be destroyed is death. For 'God has put all things in subjection under his feet.' . . . When all things are subjected to him, then the Son himself will also be subjected to the one who put all things in subjection under him, so that God may be all in all" (1 Cor. 15:24–28).

The term *kingdom* (βασιλεία) is a political term; it refers to a polity, to the ordering of life in community under royal rule. Richard Bauckham explains that "the kingdom of God, the subject of much of Jesus' preaching, offers a political and social image of the perfection of human society in full accord with the will of God."[2] To speak of the kingdom of God, then, is to speak of God's ordering of things and of the divine rule over all things. In order to retain and properly emphasize the personal involvement of God in this ordering, we might do better, as R. T. France has suggested,[3] to translate βασιλεία as "kingship" rather than "kingdom," thus preserving Paul's declaration that when the kingdom is complete, God will be "all in all." France's recommendation is apposite also because fellowship with the king turns out to be a central feature of the new ordering of things to which the Bible testifies when it speaks of the kingdom of God. We will retain the standard nomenclature, "*kingdom* of God," in what follows, but we will remain mindful as well of France's observation that the nature and form of the kingdom is wholly determined by the one whose kingdom it is.

The nature and form of God's kingdom, of the divine order and rule, is the principal subject matter of the teaching and the example of Jesus. Mark's Gospel presents Jesus's declaration that the kingdom has come near as the first of Jesus's public utterances (Mark 1:15).[4] Frequently in Jesus's teaching we hear, "The kingdom of God/heaven is like . . ." He then goes on to describe an ordering of things that challenges conventional expectations and turns the present order upside down. Thus, in Matthew 22:1–14, for instance, Jesus declares that "the kingdom of heaven may be compared to a king who gave

2. Bauckham, "Eschatology," 320.
3. France, "Kingdom of God," 420–22.
4. "The kingdom of God" or an equivalent occurs seventy times in the Synoptic Gospels but only twice in John. It may be argued, however, that John is equally interested in Jesus's proclamation of the coming realization of God's purposes but frames it in terms of new creation rather than the kingdom.

a wedding banquet for his son" (22:2). As the parable unfolds we learn that the guests at this wedding turn out to be the least likely of characters. They are those gathered up off the streets whose qualification for attendance at the wedding feast amounted to nothing more than their readiness to accept the invitation when summoned by the king.

Jesus's portrayal of the kingdom fits exactly with his own practice of seeking out the lost and the lonely, the outcast and the despised in order to share a meal with them (Matt. 9:10–13; Mark 2:15–22; Luke 5:29–32). The result, as is made explicit in the story of Jesus's encounter with Zacchaeus, is personal transformation and entry into a new way of being (Luke 19:1–10). This particular beneficiary of Jesus's companionship submits himself to the rule of the Lord, repents and makes amends for his earlier fraudulent commercial endeavors, and begins to attend to the needs of the poor. It is a striking feature of the story that after "trying to see who Jesus was" at the beginning of the narrative (Luke 19:3), Zacchaeus proceeds at the end to address Jesus as "Lord" (v. 8). Zacchaeus's discovery of who Jesus is prompts his participation in what Jesus is doing. It prompts his participation in the coming kingdom of God.

Much more could be written here about the content of the kingdom that Jesus proclaims and for whose coming Christians are taught to pray, but suffice for now to recall the central features of the kingdom recurringly emphasized in Jesus's teaching and consistently identified among the priorities of God throughout the Bible. They are justice and righteousness (Isa. 9:7; 32:16–17; Jer. 23:5–6), mercy (Luke 6:36), blessing for the poor (Luke 6:20), freedom from disease and affliction (Matt. 9:35), and compassion for the despised and the marginalized (Zeph. 3:19; Matt. 21:31). The kingdom is to be characterized as well by the peaceful ordering of relationships among all God's creatures (Isa. 11:1–9) and the flourishing of the whole creation (Rom. 8:21). The appearance of these characteristics of the kingdom through the course of Jesus's ministry are a sign that Jesus himself is the long-awaited king who will bring God's purposes to completion. "The blind receive their sight, the lame walk, the lepers are cleansed, the deaf hear, the dead are raised, and the poor have good news brought to them" (Matt. 11:5; Luke 7:22). These signs provide confirmation in response to John the Baptist's inquiry that Jesus is "the one who is to come" (Matt. 11:3; Luke 7:20) and justify Jesus's repeated assertion that the kingdom of God has come near (Matt. 4:17; Mark 1:15).

A Present and Future Reality

It is clear enough, however, that the signs of the kingdom that were apparent in Jesus's ministry are not yet pervasive in the way that is hoped for when Christians pray, "Your kingdom come . . . on earth as it is in heaven" (Matt. 6:10). We still await the fulfillment of that hope. The kingdom of heaven has come near, according to Jesus, but it is still and also a future reality. What then is the basis for the Christian hope that the kingdom of God will one day be fulfilled and "God will be all in all"? The ground of Christian hope is that the crucified one has been raised from the dead. The one who was himself poor, despised, and executed among criminals has been raised by God from death, thereby giving hope that the death-dealing ways of this world, along with all the forces that oppress and extinguish life, will finally be overcome. The last word does not go to the principalities and powers that orchestrate death, but rather to the God who raised Jesus from the dead. The resurrection is thus God's promissory note: the kingdom of this world will become the kingdom of our Lord and of his Messiah, and he will reign forever and ever (Rev. 11:15). This is the future that is proclaimed when the church remembers that Jesus has been raised from the dead.[5]

The present life of the Christian church is determined both by its remembering and by its hope. Precisely by remembering that Jesus has been raised, the church looks forward in hope to the final overcoming of sin and death and to the full realization of the divine promise that the creature shall have life in all its fullness. In this time between the times, the church proclaims the good news of Christ's victory over sin and death and watches for the signs of that victory that are already evident in the present age. We come back to the point that the kingdom proclaimed and enacted by Jesus is both present and yet to come. The determination of the church's existence through remembrance and hope corresponds to the reality of the coming kingdom, which is both "already and not yet." "The kingdom of God has come near," according to Jesus's teaching (Mark 1:15), and there are signs already present that indicate that "the kingdom has come to you" (Matt. 12:28) and is "among you" (Luke 17:21), yet Jesus also speaks of entry to the kingdom as a future reality (e.g., Matt. 7:21). And, as has already been noted, Jesus teaches the disciples to pray, "Your kingdom come," which suggests that it is not yet present in its

5. Karl Barth declares that "the future can be proclaimed only in the form of recollecting the resurrection of Christ." Barth, *Church Dogmatics* I/2, 54.

fullness. This tension between the now and the not yet has led theologians
to speak of the signs of the coming kingdom, supremely the resurrection, as
events of the eschatological future breaking into the present. As Bauckham
puts it, Jesus's "ministry, death and resurrection constitute God's definitive
promise for the eschatological future of all things. . . . It is promise in the form
of concrete anticipation. What has happened to Jesus is what will happen to
the whole creation."[6]

Following the lead of Geerhardus Vos, as developed in his 1930s book *The
Pauline Eschatology*, many theologians have spoken of the "already but not
yet" character of the kingdom of God in terms of inaugurated eschatology.[7]
The eschatological future has begun in and through Jesus but is not yet complete. There are certainly biblical texts, as referenced above, that justify this
kind of language, but there is a necessary qualification: there has never been a
time when God has not been sovereign. God's rule upholds creation from the
beginning (e.g., 1 Chron. 29:11; Ps. 103:19; 1 Tim. 6:15; Heb. 1:3, 10–12). It is
incorrect, therefore, to suggest that the divine kingship commenced sometime
during Jesus's ministry or even with the resurrection.

What is distinctive about Jesus's ministry, however, is that the divine Son
and ruler of all things located himself, became incarnate, in the midst of history to secure the victory over sin and death that will one day be complete.
In this sense, it is legitimate to speak of the future eschatological age having
begun with Jesus. The life, death, and resurrection of Jesus was not the inauguration of God's kingship but the decisive and future-determining manifestation of his kingship in the midst of human history. Because of Christ and his
resurrection from the dead, and because of the signs of the kingdom already
present wherever forgiveness and reconciliation take place in our world and
the forces of sin and death are overcome, the full realization of God's rule
over all things is "a possible object of confident hope."[8]

The dual aspect of the coming kingdom of God as a reality that is both
present and yet to come is evident also in the propensity of the apostle Paul
to speak of the Christian community as a people who already share in the
resurrection of Christ. In virtue of their baptism, they have passed through

6. Bauckham, "Eschatology," 309.
7. Vos, *Pauline Eschatology*. Others who have contributed to the widespread acceptance of
the concept of inaugurated eschatology include Fuller, *Mission and Achievement of Jesus*, and
Jeremias, *Parables of the Kingdom*.
8. I take this phrase from Moltmann, *Theology of Hope*, 229.

death and are beneficiaries already of Christ's resurrection. Thus, in Romans 6:4–7, Paul writes, "Therefore we have been buried with him by baptism into death, so that, just as Christ was raised from the dead by the glory of the Father, so we too might walk in newness of life. For if we have been united with him in a death like his, we will certainly be united with him in a resurrection like his. We know that our old self was crucified with him so that the body of sin might be destroyed, and we might no longer be enslaved to sin. For whoever has died is freed from sin."

We have surveyed already in chapter 3 Paul's expectation that the life of the Christian community should itself be a sign of the resurrection. Christians have been freed from death and are enabled now to "walk in newness of life." Of course, Paul also understands that this is a work in progress for each of us individually and for the community. This newness of life has begun, but it is yet to be realized in its fullness.[9]

The Spirit Poured Out

When considering the basis and content of Christian hope, we must speak first of the resurrection of Jesus, but then also of the coming of the Holy Spirit. In Jewish expectation, the pouring out of the Spirit is understood to be a sign of the coming eschatological age. Joel 2:28–29 provides the most well-known expression of this hope.

> I will pour out my spirit on all flesh;
>> your sons and your daughters shall prophesy,
>> your old men shall dream dreams,
>> and your young men shall see visions.
> Even on the male and female slaves,
>> in those days, I will pour out my spirit.

This is the text quoted by Peter on the day of Pentecost to explain what was happening when the followers of Jesus began to "speak in other languages" and to declare "God's deeds of power" (Acts 2:4, 11). "This," says Peter, "is what was spoken [of] through the prophet Joel" (Acts 2:16). The Spirit is repeatedly spoken of in Scripture as the giver of life. This refers to the breath,

---

9. On which, see Campbell, *Pauline Dogmatics*, 124–27.

or *ruach*, that sustains and animates the creature (e.g., Gen. 6:17; 7:15, 22; Ps. 104:29–30; Ezek. 37:9–10) and also to that fullness of life that transcends mere biological function and that has as its distinguishing feature intimate communion with God. The Spirit is the one who draws us into that communion, enabling us to cry "Abba! Father!" (Gal. 4:6; cf. Eph. 2:18). The Spirit is also the one who equips us for the living of a fully human life through the giving of gifts for the upbuilding of the community (1 Cor. 12:1–11) and the giving of "fruits" that emerge as God transforms us (Gal. 5:22–23). The completion of that project is again conceived of in Scripture as an eschatological reality, but the pouring out of the Spirit at Pentecost, as also the distribution of the gifts and fruits of the Spirit, is evidence that the project is underway and solid grounds for hope that it will be brought to fruition. The activity of the Spirit in the meantime is "to draw the world forwards"[10] to its eschatological completion in the coming kingdom of God.

Our participation in the reality of the coming kingdom is enabled by the Spirit, but it is the experience of every Christian that such participation is imperfect and certainly incomplete as yet. We remain resistant to the Spirit's work even while confessing belief. Hence the transferability of the prayer of Mark 9:24: "I believe; help my unbelief!" In the face of human resistance, God does not coerce. The Holy Spirit works through the faithful persistence of love, drawing us toward that day when we will resist no more but utter our glad Amen to all that God has done.

Imagining the End

The resurrection of Jesus from the dead provides a glimpse of the future to which the whole of creation is directed. We have spoken in earlier chapters of the cosmic scope of the eschatological vision given to us in Scripture. John of Patmos, for example, includes in his account of the final victory of God over sin and death a vision of "a new heaven and a new earth" (Rev. 21:1). There has been much debate in Christian theological tradition about the fate of this material world of space and time. John's recounting of his vision of a new heaven and a new earth continues: "for the first heaven and the first earth had passed away" (21:1). And this prompts the question, "With regard to

10. I take this point from Gunton, "Holy Spirit," 305.

the nonhuman material world, does John the Seer envisage an eschatological annihilation of the cosmos, and its replacement with something else, or does he instead envisage an eschatological renewal of the present cosmos, which despite its significant experience of transformation, stands in some kind of material continuity with the present order of things?"[11]

Mark Stephens, the author of the words just quoted, goes on to survey the varied responses to this question in Christian tradition and concludes that while both the annihilationist and the transformational views are present in the tradition, there are good reasons within the book of Revelation itself to favor the transformational view. Stephens refers us to Revelation 4 and 5, which envisage the whole of creation gathered in praise of the Creator and the Lamb:[12]

> Then I heard every creature in heaven and on earth and under the earth and in the sea, and all that is in them, singing,
>
>> "To the one seated on the throne and to the Lamb
>> be blessing and honor and glory and might
>> for ever and ever!" (Rev. 5:13)

Although the contrary annihilationist view is certainly present in Christian tradition, the transformational view has generally found more widespread favor. Paul Althaus says of "Catholic orthodoxy": "Transformation, not annihilation—that is the unanimously held doctrine from Irenaeus onwards, by way of Augustine and Gregory the Great, Aquinas and the whole of mediaeval theology, down to the present-day Catholic dogmatics."[13] Jürgen Moltmann likewise contends that the predominant view in theological tradition has been the transformative one.[14]

While there is certainly room for further discussion of this matter, and while proponents of each view can adduce supportive texts from Christian Scripture, particular weight should be given, I suggest, to the clearest clue we have about the nature of eschatological reality—namely, the resurrection of Jesus. Although some have argued differently, there can be little doubt—as

---

11. Stephens, *Annihilation or Renewal?*, 1–2.
12. See Stephens, *Annihilation or Renewal?*, 190.
13. Althaus, *Die letzten Dinge*, 350, quoted in Moltmann, *Coming of God*, 268.
14. Moltmann, *Coming of God*, 268–69. I have cited this conclusion found in Althaus and Moltmann in a fuller discussion of the matter in Rae, *Architecture and Theology*, chap. 4.

has been argued earlier in this volume—that when the New Testament authors speak of Jesus's resurrection, they are referring to a reality that involves Jesus's body, the same and yet transformed body that was crucified on Good Friday.[15] It was the same in virtue of its recognizability (Luke 24:31; John 20:20), though the recognition was not always immediate among those to whom the risen Jesus appeared, in virtue of its still bearing the wounds of crucifixion (Luke 24:40; John 20:24–27), and in virtue of its having some of the same capacities as the pre-resurrection body. Those include the capacity to be touched, for example (Matt. 28:9; Luke 24:39; John 20:27), and to eat food (Luke 24:42–43). Yet the resurrection body was also different. It could appear seemingly out of nowhere (Luke 24:36; John 20:19) and disappear just as suddenly (Luke 24:31).

We see in the resurrected Christ both continuity and discontinuity. His body bears still the wounds of crucifixion, and yet it has been transformed in some way.[16] This reality gives us reason to affirm a transformative rather than an annihilationist vision of the new heaven and new earth in the age to come. There is, in my view, a preponderance of evidence, both biblical and theological, supporting an eschatological vision of the creation as a whole redeemed and perfected and enabled at last to flourish in peace as was intended from the beginning. This biblical vision is to be distinguished, however, from the post-Enlightenment confidence in humankind's inevitable progression toward perfection, such as was expressed by Herbert Spencer, the English sociologist who proclaimed in the mid-nineteenth century, "Progress is not an accident but a necessity. Surely must evil and immorality disappear; surely must men become perfect."[17] Such confidence was nourished by impressive advances in science and technology in the modern age. It was also given considerable impetus by the French Revolution, begun in 1789, in which the old oppressive hierarchies of the "*ancien régime*" were dismantled, to be replaced, or so it was hoped, by democratic and egalitarian social and political institutions. In a poem originally titled "The French Revolution as It Appeared to Enthusiasts at Its Commencement," the Romantic poet William Wordsworth (1770–1850) gave further expression to the intoxicating sentiments of the

15. See, again, Wright's analysis of the New Testament writings in *Resurrection of the Son of God*.
16. For a profound exploration of the resurrection body and the maintenance of personal identity through transformation, see Whitaker, *Perfect in Weakness*.
17. Spencer, *Social Statics*, 32.

age: "Bliss was it in that dawn to be alive."[18] The engine of change driving us toward a utopian future was thought to be human prowess and ingenuity, which "in that dawn" was supposed to have no bounds.

Richard Bauckham regards this expectation of a better future as a secularization of Christian hope, but it was a hope that "abandoned transcendence, trusting instead the immanent possibilities of the historical process itself."[19] As Bauckham further points out, it was also a hope that "offered no redemption from the past and no hope for the dead."[20] The wounds of history are not healed, and the "kingdom" realized through this vision serves only those fortunate enough to be born once the utopian dream has been accomplished.

This is not the Christian hope, which is characterized instead by the healing of all the wounds of history, the resurrection of the dead, the reconciliation of all things, and the wiping of all the tears of history from our eyes. The driving force of this transformation is the God who raised Jesus from the dead. The resurrection does not reveal a life-giving power at work within the realm of immanent causality; it reveals rather the power of God to create ex nihilo and the steadfastness of a divine love that will not abandon the creature to the ruinous consequences of human sin. By raising Jesus from the dead, God acts in the midst of human history to heal and redeem the whole, and to direct it again toward its *telos* of fullness of life in communion with God.

We have therefore to speak, when articulating the Christian hope, of the repair of all that has been broken through humanity's defiance of God's will. We have to speak of the wiping away of the tears of all who have wept throughout the course of human history. We have to speak of the resurrection of all the victims of violence and brutality. We have to speak of the shining of divine light into all the places of darkness into which God's creatures have fallen or to which they have been consigned.

This is what we must intend when we repeat the words of Paul, who looks to that day when "God will be all in all" (1 Cor. 15:28). This is what we must mean when we speak of divine sovereignty and of God as Lord of all. No part of God's good creation, expansive in time and space, can be consigned

---

18. Wordsworth, "1805 Prelude," 360. Wordsworth's enthusiasm for the French Revolution was prompted by a visit to France on the first anniversary of the storming of the Bastille, although he would later become disillusioned about the prospects for transformation.

19. Bauckham, "Eschatology," 312.

20. Bauckham, "Eschatology," 312.

to the dust heap of history. Only those things that, in virtue of their complete contravention of God's purposes for creation, never had any life in them will finally be done away with.

In further explanation of the point, Richard Bauckham writes, "In distinction from any kind of immanent utopianism, a holistic Christian eschatology expects an eschatological future for the past. What God through new creation takes into eternity is not simply what creation will be at the end of the temporal process, but all that has ever been. Nothing of value will be lost. In relation to individual humans, resurrection surely implies not merely that they will continue to live beyond death, but also that the whole of the life they have lived up to death will be gathered, redeemed, and transfigured into their eschatological identity."[21]

David Fergusson likewise explains that the Bible typically envisages the coming kingdom of God "not as a release from our present mode of physical existence, but as a transformation of the entire created order."[22] We may add that the eschatological future involves not an escape *from* history but the redemption *of* history.

Personal Resurrection

It is within this expansive vision of heaven and earth transformed and made new that we may speak also of the Christian hope for the individual beyond death. Again, our starting point must be the resurrection of Jesus from the dead. In anticipation of his own resurrection, the Jesus of John's Gospel says, "Because I live, you will live also" (John 14:19). Paul uses the same logic to declare, "Christ has been raised from the dead, the first fruits of those who have died"; and further, "As all die in Adam, so all will be made alive in Christ" (1 Cor. 15:20, 22). Or as 2 Timothy 2 puts it, "The saying is sure: If we have died with him, we shall also live with him; if we endure, we will also reign with him" (2 Tim. 2:11–12). Paul's account of the Christian hope of resurrection, especially as set out in 1 Corinthians 15, makes clear that hope for the resurrection of the dead is not based on a general expectation of an eschatological resurrection, much less on the Greek notion of the immortality of the soul, but rather on the very particular manifestation of this hope

21. Bauckham, "Eschatology," 315.
22. Fergusson, "Eschatology," 237.

in the midst of human history: "If Christ has not been raised, your faith is futile" (1 Cor. 15:17).[23]

It is worth pursuing further here the claim made by Jesus in John's Gospel: "Because I live, you will live also." Jesus goes on to say, "On that day you will know that I am in my Father, and you in me, and I in you" (John 14:20).[24] That is, perhaps, the most profound description in all of Scripture of the content of the Christian hope for the individual. Jesus here describes a reality that is true already but will be realized in its fullness with the final resurrection of the dead. He offers the most complete assurance possible that beyond death, for us and for all others who have learned to trust their lives to God, all will be well. I leave open here the question of whether, for some people, that learning begins beyond death itself. We do not know, but we can hope.

The eschatological fulfillment of our being in Christ, who is in turn "in the Father," has profound implications for human existence. It reveals that human existence is constituted relationally. Our identity as human beings is determined by the fact that Christ has entered into the midst of human life and restored it to its proper place in communion with the Father. To borrow here from Karl Barth, "Our human existence is no longer alone. It is no longer left to itself. But in Jesus Christ it is received and adopted into the deity of God. In him it has already been raised and cleansed and transfigured into the divine likeness. . . . In Jesus Christ we see our own existence wide open to heaven, irradiated, purified, held and sustained from above, not rejected by God, but in a love that interpenetrates all things affirmed by Him in the way in which He affirms Himself."[25]

The dialectic between the "already" and the "not yet" must be invoked again here. Barth contends that our humanity has already been "raised and cleansed and transfigured." To put it in colloquial terms: it is a done deal. Jesus has seen to it that humanity's future is secure; that has radically changed our status and existence in the present. There simply is no doubt any longer that, despite our continuing sinfulness, human beings belong to God, are loved by God, and are destined to share fully in the loving communion of the divine life as was intended

---

23. On which, see Novakovic, *Resurrection*.

24. Commentators frequently note that while the locution "on that day" (ἐν ἐκείνῃ τῇ ἡμέρᾳ) has strong eschatological overtones—as used, for instance, in Mark 13:32—John appears here to be referencing Jesus's resurrection appearances. Using the phrase to refer to the resurrection does not exclude the eschatological overtones, of course. See, e.g., Barrett, *John*, 387–88; and Marsh, *Saint John*, 509.

25. Barth, *Church Dogmatics* II/2, 558.

from the beginning. That means, as Paul insists, that "neither death, nor life, nor angels, nor rulers, nor things present, nor things to come, nor powers, nor height, nor depth, nor anything else in all creation, will be able to separate us from the love of God in Christ Jesus our Lord" (Rom. 8:38–39). Not even death! Paul knows that because Jesus who was crucified has been raised by God from death, the gates of eternal life have been opened to all who trust their lives to him. This reality is to be realized in full in the future, but as Paul contends in 2 Corinthians 5:17, it has already begun: "If anyone is in Christ, there is a new creation: everything old has passed away; see, everything has become new!"

Resurrection of the Body

That which has been said above about Jesus's resurrection applies also to the general resurrection of the dead: resurrection involves bodies. There is a striking difference, of course, between Jesus and all others who are raised from death. No others who have died appear in the flesh after their deaths. They do not cook fish on the lakeshore or show up at meals. They are not available to be seen and touched in the way that Jesus was according to the Gospel reports. We may say, however, that the bodily appearances of Jesus following his resurrection were necessary in a way that is not true of anyone else. They were necessary to make it known that death has been overcome, that it does not have the last word. They were necessary to make it known that the one who proclaimed the coming kingdom, who took it upon himself to forgive sins, who spoke of his own intimate communion with the Father, and who was crucified as a blasphemer was vindicated by God. The appearances of the risen Christ were necessary in order to confirm God's verdict on all that happened through the course of Jesus's ministry, but such appearances are not necessary in the case of anyone else. It is sufficient for us to know that because Christ lives, we will live also. Or, as Paul puts it, "If we have been united with him in a death like his, we will certainly be united with him in a resurrection like his" (Rom. 6:5). Thus does the Christian church declare, in the words of the Apostles' Creed, "I believe in the resurrection of the body."

Belief in bodily resurrection is consistent with the biblical presumption that when speaking of the human being, we are speaking of an entity that is irreducibly composed of body and spirit or soul. Commenting on Genesis 2:7, particularly the phrase "and the man became a living being," Claus

Westermann writes, "This sentence is very important for the biblical understanding of humanity: a person is created as a נֶפֶשׁ חַיָּה; a 'living soul' is not put into one's body. The person as a living being is to be understood as a whole and any idea that one is made up of a body and soul is ruled out."[26] This contrasts markedly with the dualistic Greek notion of an eternal soul that is constitutive of our true humanity and is separable from the body. This kind of dualism, says E. Jacob, is never found in the Old Testament.[27] Nor is it in the New. To suppose, then, that the resurrection does not involve the body is to envisage an anthropology that is utterly foreign to biblical ways of thinking.

How that bodily resurrection occurs is, of course, much more difficult to say. Paul in 1 Corinthians 15 is at pains to point out a qualitative difference between the perishable bodies we now inhabit and the imperishable bodies that we are destined to attain. Though he appears to come close to a dualistic conception of the physical and the spiritual in verse 44 ("if there is a physical body, there is also a spiritual body"), he is nevertheless talking about the existence of *bodies* in each realm, and he later affirms that it is indeed "this perishable body" that "must put on imperishability" (1 Cor. 15:53). A spiritual body is not to be understood, therefore, as a nonphysical kind of body, but as a body transformed from being a body of death to one that is made fully alive through the indwelling Spirit of God.[28]

Douglas Farrow's observation concerning Paul's claim that "flesh and blood cannot inherit the kingdom" (1 Cor. 15:50) is also pertinent here:

> Paul did not mean to exclude flesh and blood from the kingdom (a most un-Jewish idea) but rather to make clear to Jews, and Gentiles too, that access to the kingdom does not come by human strength, or by ethnic identity, or by any means available to mortal man. This is the discontinuity Paul had in view: that the old man must be displaced by the new . . . through a transformation already determined for him in Jesus Christ. And this is the continuity: that what is transformed is the whole man; the perishable is clothed with the imperishable, "the mortal with immortality."[29]

---

26. Westermann, *Genesis 1–11*, 207. Westermann means here that body and soul are not two entities that could in principle exist apart.

27. Jacob, "Anthropology of the Old Testament," 623.

28. Gunton gives a helpful account of the matter in Gunton, *Christian Faith*, 153.

29. Farrow, "Resurrection and Immortality," 216. Rather than *man*, I prefer to use the more inclusive term *human*, but I have preserved Farrow's original usage here.

As has been intimated above, the Christian doctrine of the resurrection must be clearly distinguished from the Greek notion of the immortality of the soul. Despite their frequent conflation, the two notions are very different. The Greek notion of an immortal soul proposes that eternal life is an innate feature of human existence and that it is this immortal soul, entirely independent of any bodily existence, that constitutes our essential humanity. It is "beyond all doubt then," according to Socrates in Plato's *Phaedo*, that "soul is deathless and imperishable, and our souls will in truth exist in Hades."[30]

This Socratic idea is expressed in the well-known song originating during the American Civil War that celebrates the abolitionist John Brown:

> John Brown's body lies a mouldering in the grave.
> His soul's marching on![31]

That this was thought to be a Christian idea is revealed in a subsequent verse of the song, which says of John Brown, "He's gone to be a soldier in the army of the Lord." The idea here is that our essential humanity—the immaterial soul—is not subject to death after all but simply "goes marching on." There would be, if this were true, no need for resurrection; and there would be no need for God to be involved, other than, perhaps, as the one who created human beings this way in the first place. Socrates and Plato, who made the idea of an immortal soul popular in Western thought, did not think that such divine agency was required in order to effect the survival of the soul beyond death.

Against this confusion of resurrection with a Platonic doctrine of the immortality of the soul, Farrow explains, "Now to abolish death as the means of bringing life and immortality to light is not at all the same thing as to conduct an argument such as Plato's. . . . It is to perform an act, a miracle on a par with the miracle of creation . . . , and to invite belief, not in the afterlife of the soul, but in 'the resurrection of the body and the life of the world to come.'"[32]

Priestly Intercession

We have stressed several times that the biblical witness speaks of the kingdom of God as a reality that is both present already and yet still to come in its

30. Plato, *Phaedo*, 107a, 161.
31. "John Brown Song."
32. Farrow, "Resurrection and Immortality," 213.

fullness. We live, it is sometimes said, "between the times," between the time of Jesus's resurrection as the firstfruits and the gathering in of the full harvest and the restoration of abundant life to the creation as a whole. This time between the times is, we might say, a time of grace in which God gives us space and time to respond in faith to the initiative taken on our behalf when Jesus offered himself on the cross as a perfect sacrifice of obedience and praise to the Father. We have been given time to offer our own thanks and praise and to repent of the resistance we continue to show to the steadfast love of God.

To live within the tension of the "already" and the "not yet" is not easy. Speaking first of the personal level, all of us know the tension that exists between the person we know ourselves to be and that which we are called to be in Christ. Paul knew of that inner tension and struggle. The same Paul who declares "I have been crucified with Christ; it is no longer I who live, but it is Christ who lives in me" (Gal. 2:19–20) can also confess, "I do not do the good I want, but the evil I do not want is what I do" (Rom. 7:19).

The same tension is evident in the stories of numerous biblical characters, notably in those who receive a new name as a signifier of the new identity to which they are called. The tension is evident in Jacob as he wrestles with "a man" at Peniel. The struggle is in a certain sense a struggle with God, but it is also a struggle within himself between the fugitive Jacob, who has burned many bridges in his past and is now returning to face his brother's fury, and the man Israel, who prevails as the bearer of the divine promise (Gen. 32:22–31).[33] It is the tension painfully evident for Peter when, following his threefold denial of Jesus before the crucifixion, he is met by the risen Lord who asks him three times, "Simon son of John, do you love me?" (John 21:15–17). The name *Simon* is a signifier of the old identity still driving Peter to denial. Yet through the encounter with the living and forgiving Lord, his new identity as Peter, the one who will "tend [Jesus's] sheep," is lovingly restored (21:16). Paul, again, knew well that we have yet to grow into the fullness of the reality that is already ours as "God's chosen ones, holy and beloved"; there is work to be done yet before we are fully clothed, as Paul enjoins us to be, with compassion, kindness, humility, meekness, and patience (Col. 3:12).

In the meantime, there is one who intercedes for us, a high priest who sympathizes with our weaknesses, for he too has been tested (Heb. 4:15). The crucified and risen Christ has now "ascended to heaven and is seated at the

---

33. I owe the point to Geoff New, as delivered in a sermon at Flagstaff Community Church on March 12, 2023.

right hand of the Father," as the Nicene Creed puts it. There he intercedes for us. There is something to be said here for Dorothee Sölle's account of Christ as our representative, for he is the one who holds our place for us in the coming kingdom.[34] The ascended Christ, at the Father's side, is now already at the place where we have not yet arrived. He is the forerunner, the pioneer and perfecter of our faith (Heb. 12:2), awaiting our arrival into the fullness of life promised to the children of God. Sölle comments, "Our representative speaks for us, but we ourselves have to learn to speak. He believes *for* us, but we ourselves have to learn to believe. He hopes when we are without hope, but that is not the end of the story. The Spirit who intercedes for us with inarticulate groans does not intend to replace our own praying. But certainly he represents those whose only prayer is ignorance of what to pray for. By this representation he holds their place open for them lest they should lose it."[35]

The risen Christ is the forerunner and ground of Christian hope; and the ascended Christ, along with the Spirit (Rom. 8:26), maintains the cogency of that hope by interceding for us before the Father while we await the final "redemption of our bodies," when we will, at long last, "obtain the freedom of the glory of the children of God" (Rom. 8:23, 21).

Let Justice Roll Down

The eschatological fulfillment of the kingdom of God is often referred to in Scripture as "the day of the LORD." One of the characteristics of that day and of divine kingship is, as already noted, justice. We see this in the words of the psalmist, who declares that "righteousness and justice are the foundation of [God's] throne" (Ps. 89:14). We see it also in the prophet Amos, who looks forward to that day when justice will "roll down like waters" (Amos 5:24). These biblical writers are aware that with justice comes judgment, a laying bare of the truth of things. Psalm 98:9 declares, for example, that the Lord "is coming to judge the earth. He will judge the world with righteousness, and the peoples with equity." Justice involves truth-telling. If we are to hope, therefore, that justice will indeed roll down like waters, then we have to be prepared also for the truth to be told about our human sinfulness. We have to be prepared to hear God's verdict on our resistance to the divine command.

34. Sölle, *Christ the Representative*.
35. Sölle, *Christ the Representative*, 104.

Amos thus speaks of the day of the Lord as a dark day: "Is not the day of the LORD darkness, not light?" (Amos 5:20).

If, as I have argued above, the eschatological realization of God's purposes for creation involves the gathering up and redemption of the whole of human history, rather than simply the dawning of some utopian era for those fortunate enough to be present at the end, then the kingdom cannot come without all the cries of history's victims being heard; it cannot come without their wounds being healed; it cannot come without the evil that has been done to them being confronted and finally defeated; it cannot come without the truth being told and without the wheat finally being sorted from the chaff. Speaking of the heavenly Jerusalem, John of Patmos tells us, "Nothing unclean will enter it, nor anyone who practices abomination or falsehood," and "nothing accursed will be found there any more" (Rev. 21:27; 22:3). Judgment is a necessary feature, therefore, of the coming of God's kingdom.

But here again, we have to speak of a kingdom that has already dawned and that is already present in the midst of human history. It is present in the rule of the one who makes his way to Calvary and exposes once and for all the desperate truth of humanity's alienation from God. The death of Jesus on the cross is itself the act of divine judgment—not the act of an angry God demanding blood in order to be appeased, but rather the act of a profoundly loving God shining divine light into the depths of human defiance and sin, exposing our sinfulness for what it really is. The judgment and the verdict become abundantly clear: to act in defiance of God, now by crucifying God's own beloved Son, is to choose godforsakenness and death. There is no future judgment that will make things any clearer than they have been made already by the events of that day when darkness came over the face of the earth and Jesus breathed his last (Luke 23:44, 46).

We may call this day "the day of the LORD," for in it God's final verdict was declared upon the reality of human sin. But also on that day, a prayer was uttered. Out of the darkness of godforsakenness and death, Jesus prayed, "Father, forgive them; for they do not know what they are doing" (Luke 23:34). One day—again we may call it "the day of the LORD"—we will know. On that day, all that has been hidden will be revealed, and all that has been secret will come to light (Luke 8:17). What are we to hope for on that day? Surely our hope can only be that on that day the prayer of the crucified, risen, and ascended Lord will be answered once and for all. Then shall we see, face-to-face at last, the glory of the Lord.

Bibliography

Adams, Samuel V. *The Reality of God and Historical Method: Apocalyptic Theology in Conversation with N. T. Wright.* Downers Grove, IL: IVP Academic, 2015.

Alkier, Stefan. *The Reality of the Resurrection: The New Testament Witness.* Translated by Leroy A. Huizenga. Waco: Baylor University Press, 2013.

Allison, Dale C., Jr. *The Resurrection of Jesus: Apologetics, Polemic, History.* London: T&T Clark, 2021.

Althaus, Paul. *Die letzten Dinge: Entwurf einer christlichen Eschatologie.* Gütersloh: C. Bertlesmann, 1922.

Arndt, William F., and F. Wilbur Gingrich. *A Greek-English Lexicon of the New Testament and Other Early Christian Literature.* Chicago: University of Chicago Press, 1957.

Athanasius. *On the Incarnation.* Christian Classics Ethereal Library. https://www.ccel.org/ccel/athanasius/incarnation.ii.html.

Avery-Peck, Alan J. "The Doctrine of God." In *The Blackwell Companion to Judaism*, edited by Jacob Nuesner and Alan J. Avery-Peck, 212–29. Oxford: Blackwell, 2000.

Bachelard, Sarah. *Resurrection and Moral Imagination.* London: Routledge, 2016.

Bailey, Kenneth E. *Poet and Peasant: A Literary-Cultural Approach to the Parables in Luke.* Grand Rapids: Eerdmans, 1976.

Banner, Michael. *Christian Ethics and Contemporary Moral Problems.* Cambridge: Cambridge University Press, 1999.

Barclay, John. *Obeying the Truth: Paul's Ethic in Galatians.* Minneapolis: Fortress, 1988.

———. *Paul: A Very Brief History.* London: SPCK, 2017.

Barrett, C. K. *A Critical and Exegetical Commentary on the Acts of the Apostles.* Vol. 1. Edinburgh: T&T Clark, 1994.

———. *The Gospel according to John: An Introduction with Commentary and Notes on the Greek Text*. London: SPCK, 1955.

Barth, Karl. *Church Dogmatics*. Edited by G. W. Bromiley and T. F. Torrance. Translated by G. W. Bromiley, G. T. Thomson, et al. Four volumes in 13 parts. Edinburgh: T&T Clark, 1936–77.

Bauckham, Richard. "Eschatology." In *The Oxford Handbook of Systematic Theology*, edited by John Webster, Kathryn Tanner, and Iain Torrance, 306–22. Oxford: Oxford University Press, 2007.

———. *God Crucified: Monotheism and Christology in the New Testament*. Carlisle, UK: Paternoster Press, 1998.

———. *Gospel of Glory: Major Themes in Johannine Theology*. Grand Rapids: Baker Academic, 2015.

Bayer, Oswald. *Theology the Lutheran Way*. Edited and translated by J. G. Silcock and M. C. Mattes. Grand Rapids: Eerdmans, 2007.

Becker, Jürgen. *Jesus of Nazareth*. Berlin: de Gruyter, 1998.

Bellinger, William H., Jr., and William R. Farmer, eds. *Jesus and the Suffering Servant: Isaiah 53 and Christian Origins*. Eugene, OR: Wipf & Stock, 1998.

Berger, Joseph. "Giving a Haggadah a Makeover." *New York Times*, April 8, 2011.

Berger, Peter. *The Sacred Canopy—Elements of a Sociological Theory of Religion*. New York: Anchor Books, 1967.

Bird, Michael F., and Preston M. Sprinkle, eds. *The Faith of Jesus Christ: Exegetical, Biblical, and Theological Studies*. Milton Keynes, UK: Paternoster, 2009.

Bloch, Abraham P. *The Biblical and Historical Background of Jewish Customs and Ceremonies*. New York: Ktav, 1980.

Bokser, Baruch M. *The Origins of the Seder: The Passover Rite and Early Rabbinic Judaism*. Berkeley: University of California Press, 1984.

Bonhoeffer, Dietrich. *Ethics*. Vol. 6 of *Dietrich Bonhoeffer Works*. Edited by Clifford J. Green. Translated by Reinhard Krauss, Charles C. West, and Douglas W. Scott. Minneapolis: Fortress, 2005.

Brock, Ann Graham. *Mary Magdalene, The First Apostle: The Struggle for Authority*. Cambridge, MA: Harvard University Press, 2003.

Brown, Francis, S. R. Driver, and Charles A. Briggs, eds. *A Hebrew and English Lexicon of the Old Testament*. Boston: Houghton Mifflin, 1907.

Brown, Jeannine K. "Creation's Renewal in the Gospel of John." *The Catholic Biblical Quarterly* 72 (2010): 275–90.

Brown, Raymond. *The Death of the Messiah*. Vol. 1. New York: Doubleday, 1994.

———. *The Gospel according to John I–XII*. Anchor Bible Commentary. New York: Doubleday, 1966.

———. *An Introduction to the New Testament*. New York: Doubleday, 1997.

Brueggemann, Walter. *Hopeful Imagination: Prophetic Voices in Exile*. London: SCM, 1986.

————. *Theology of the Old Testament: Testimony, Dispute, Advocacy*. Minneapolis: Fortress, 1997.

Buber, Martin. *Der Jude und sein Judentum*. Cologne: Joseph Melzer, 1963.

Campbell, Douglas A. *Pauline Dogmatics: The Triumph of God's Love*. Grand Rapids: Eerdmans, 2020.

————. *The Quest for Paul's Gospel: A Suggested Strategy*. London: T&T Clark, 2005.

Campbell, John McLeod. *The Nature of the Atonement and its Relation to Remission of Sins and Eternal Life*. London: Macmillan, 1895.

Charlesworth, James. *The Beloved Disciple: Whose Witness Validates the Gospel of John?* Valley Forge, PA: Trinity Press International, 1995.

Cheng, Ling. *The Characterisation of God in Acts: The Indirect Portrayal of an Invisible Character*. Eugene, OR: Wipf & Stock, 2015.

Chilton, Bruce D. *Resurrection Logic: How Jesus' First Followers Believed God Raised Him from the Dead*. Waco: Baylor University Press, 2019.

Coakley, Sarah. "The Identity of the Risen Jesus: Finding Jesus Christ in the Poor." In *Seeking the Identity of Jesus: A Pilgrimage*, edited by Beverly Roberts Gaventa and Richard B. Hays, 301–19. Grand Rapids: Eerdmans, 2008.

Collingwood, R. G. *The Idea of History: With Lectures 1926–1928*. Rev. ed. Edited with an introduction by Jan van der Dussen. Oxford: Oxford University Press, 1993.

Conzelmann, Hans. *Acts of the Apostles*. 2nd ed. Hermeneia. Philadelphia: Fortress, 1987.

Craddock, Fred B. *Luke*. Interpretation. Louisville: Westminster John Knox, 1990.

Craig, William Lane. *Reasonable Faith: Christian Truth and Apologetics*. 3rd ed. Wheaton: Crossway, 2003.

Cranfield, C. E. B. *The Gospel according to Mark*. Cambridge: Cambridge University Press, 1959.

————. *Romans: A Shorter Commentary*. Grand Rapids: Eerdmans, 1985.

Crossan, John Dominic. *The Historical Jesus: The Life of a Mediterranean Jewish Peasant*. Edinburgh: T&T Clark, 1991.

Crowe, Brandon D. "The Chiastic Structure of Seven Signs in the Gospel of John: Revisiting a Neglected Proposal." *Bulletin for Biblical Research* 28, no. 1 (2018): 65–81.

Crüsemann, Frank. "Scripture and Resurrection." In *Resurrection: Theological and Scientific Assessments*, edited by Ted Peters, Robert John Russell, and Michael Welker, 89–102. Grand Rapids: Eerdmans, 2002.

Dalferth, Ingolf U. *Crucified and Resurrected: Restructuring the Grammar of Christology*. Translated by Jo Bennett. Grand Rapids: Baker Academic, 2015.

Davies, Margaret. *Matthew*. 2nd ed. Sheffield: Sheffield Phoenix, 2009.

Davies, W. D., and Dale C. Allison Jr. *A Critical and Exegetical Commentary on the Gospel according to St. Matthew*. Vol. 3. Edinburgh: T&T Clark, 1997.

De Lubac, Henri. *Catholicism: Christ and the Common Destiny of Man*. London: Burns and Oates, 1962.

Duff, Paul B. *Moses in Corinth: The Apologetic Context of 2 Corinthians 3*. Boston: Brill, 2015.

Duncan, J., and M. Derrett. "Law in the New Testament: The Parable of the Prodigal Son." *New Testament Studies* 14 (1967): 56–74.

Du Rand, Jan A. "The Creation Motif in the Fourth Gospel: Perspectives on Its Narratological Function within a Judaistic Background." In *Theology and Christology in the Fourth Gospel: Essays by the Members of the SNTS Johannine Writings Seminar*, edited by G. Van Belle, J. G. Van der Watt, and P. Mentz, 21–46. Leuven: Leuven University Press, 2005.

Evans, C. Stephen. *The Historical Christ and the Jesus of Faith: The Incarnational Narrative as History*. Oxford: Oxford University Press, 1996.

Farrow, Douglas. "Resurrection and Immortality." In *The Oxford Handbook of Systematic Theology*, edited by John Webster, Kathryn Tanner, and Iain Torrance, 212–35. Oxford: Oxford University Press, 2007.

Fergusson, David. "Eschatology." In *The Cambridge Companion to Christian Doctrine*, edited by Colin E. Gunton, 226–44. Cambridge: Cambridge University Press, 1997.

Filson, Floyd V. *The Gospel according to Matthew*. Peabody, MA: Hendrickson, 1960.

Fitzmyer, Joseph A. *The Gospel according to Luke X–XXIV*. Anchor Bible Commentary. Garden City, NY: Doubleday, 1983.

France, R. T. *The Gospel of Matthew*. Grand Rapids: Eerdmans, 2007.

———. "Kingdom of God." In *Dictionary for Theological Interpretation of the Bible*, edited by Kevin J. Vanhoozer, Craig G. Bartholomew, Daniel J. Treier, and N. T. Wright, 420–22. Grand Rapids: Baker Academic, 2005.

Fredman, Ruth. *The Passover Seder*. Philadelphia: University of Pennsylvania Press, 1981.

Fuller, R. H. *The Mission and Achievement of Jesus: An Examination of the Presuppositions of New Testament Theology*. London: SCM, 1954.

Glatzer, Nahum N., ed. *The Passover Haggadah: Introduction and Commentary Based on the Studies of E. D. Goldschmidt*. New York: Schocken Books, 1953.

Gorman, Michael. *Apostle of the Crucified Lord: A Theological Introduction to Paul and His Letters*. Grand Rapids: Eerdmans, 2004.

Green, Joel B. *The Gospel of Luke*. Grand Rapids: Eerdmans, 1997.

Gregg, Robert E., and Dennis E. Groh. "The Centrality of Soteriology in Early Arianism." *Anglican Theological Review* 59, no. 3 (1977): 260–78.

Gregory, Brad. "The Other Confessional History: On Secular Bias in the Study of Religion." *History and Theory* 45 (2006): 132–49.

Gregory Nazianzus. "To Cledonius the Priest against Apollinarius, Epistle 101." In *Cyril of Jerusalem, Gregory Nazianzen*. Vol. 7 of *Nicene and Post-Nicene Fathers, Second Series*. Translated by Charles Gordon Browne and James Edward Swallow. Edited by Philip Schaff and Henry Wace. Buffalo, NY: Christian Literature, 1894. Revised and edited for New Advent by Kevin Knight. https://www.newadvent.org/fathers/3103a.htm.

Gunton, Colin E. *The Christian Faith: An Introduction to Christian Doctrine*. Oxford: Blackwell, 2002.

———. *Father, Son and Holy Spirit: Toward a Fully Trinitarian Theology*. London: T&T Clark, 2003.

———. "Holy Spirit." In *The Oxford Companion to Christian Thought: Intellectual, Spiritual, and Moral Horizons of Christianity*, edited by Adrian Hastings, Alistair Mason, and Hugh Pyper, 304–6. Oxford: Oxford University Press, 2000.

Haacker, Klaus. *Der Brief des Paulus an die Römer*. Leipzig: Evangelisches Verlagsanstalt, 1999.

Hagner, Donald. "Jesus and the Synoptic Sabbath Controversies." In *Key Events in the Life of the Historical Jesus*, edited by Darrell L. Bock and Robert L. Webb, 251–92. Grand Rapids: Eerdmans, 2010.

Hamlin, E. John. *Ruth: Surely There Is a Future*. Grand Rapids: Eerdmans, 1996.

Haskins, Susan. *Mary Magdalen*. London: HarperCollins, 1993.

Havard-Williams, P., ed. *Marsden and the New Zealand Mission: Sixteen Letters*. Dunedin: University of Otago Press, 1961.

Hays, Richard B. *First Corinthians*. Interpretation. Louisville: Westminster John Knox, 1997.

———. "Knowing Jesus: Story, History and the Question of Truth." In *Jesus, Paul and the People of God: A Theological Dialogue with N. T. Wright*, edited by Nicholas Perrin and Richard B. Hays, 41–61. Downers Grove, IL: IVP Academic, 2011.

———. *The Moral Vision of the New Testament: A Contemporary Introduction to New Testament Ethics*. San Francisco: HarperSanFrancisco, 1996.

Healy, Mary. *The Gospel of Mark*. Grand Rapids: Baker Academic, 2008.

Hengel, Martin. "The Prologue of the Gospel of John as the Gateway to Christological Truth." In *The Gospel of John and Christian Theology*, edited by Richard Bauckham and Carl Moser, 265–94. Grand Rapids: Eerdmans, 2008.

Heringer, Seth. *Uniting History and Theology: A Theological Critique of the Historical Method*. Lanham, MD: Lexington / Fortress Academic, 2018.

Heron, Alasdair I. C. *Table and Tradition: Toward an Ecumenical Understanding of the Eucharist*. Philadelphia: Westminster, 1983.

Hunsinger, George. *The Eucharist and Ecumenism*. Cambridge: Cambridge University Press, 2008.

Irenaeus. *Against Heresies*. Edited by Alexander Roberts and James Donaldson. *Ante-Nicene Fathers* 1. Peabody, MA: Hendrickson, 1885.

———. *Libros quinque adversus haereses*. Edited by W. Wigan Harvey. 2 vols. Cantabrigiae: Typis academicis, 1857.

Jacob, E. "ψθχη: B. The Anthropology of the Old Testament." In Vol. 9 of *Theological Dictionary of the New Testament*. Edited by Gerhard Kittel and Gerhard Friedrich. Translated by G. W. Bromiley, 617–31. Grand Rapids: Eerdmans, 1974.

Jenson, Robert W. "The Church and the Sacraments." In *The Cambridge Companion to Christian Doctrine*, edited by Colin E. Gunton, 207–25. Cambridge: Cambridge University Press, 1997.

———. *Systematic Theology*. Vol. 1, *The Triune God*. Oxford: Oxford University Press, 1997.

Jeremias, Joachim. *The Parables of the Kingdom*. New York: Scribner, 1961.

Jewett, Robert. *Romans: A Commentary*. Hermeneia. Minneapolis: Fortress, 2007.

"John Brown Song." Mississippi State University Institutional Repository. Scholar's Junction. Accessed September 26, 2023. https://scholarsjunction.msstate.edu/fvw -manuscripts-nicolay-and-hay-documents/17/.

Jüngel, Eberhard. "Value-Free Truth: The Christian Experience of Truth in the Struggle against the 'Tyranny of Values.'" In *Theological Essays II*, edited by J. B. Webster. Translated by Arnold Neufeldt-Fast and J. B. Webster, 191–215. Edinburgh: T&T Clark, 1995.

Just, Arthur A., Jr. *Luke 9:51–24:53*. Concordia Commentary. Saint Louis: Concordia, 1997.

Kant, Immanuel. *Kritik der reinen Vernunft*. Edited by Jens Timmermann. Hamburg: Meiner Verlag, 1998.

Kanyoro, M. R. A. "Daughter Arise: Luke 8:40–56." In *Talitha Qumi! Proceedings of the Convocation of African Women Theologians*, edited by Mercy Amba Oduyoye and M. R. A. Kanyoro, 54–62. Ibadan: Daystar, 1989.

Käsemann, Ernst. *Commentary on Romans*. Translated by G. W. Bromiley. Grand Rapids: Eerdmans, 1990.

Keener, Craig S. *A Commentary on the Gospel of Matthew*. Grand Rapids: Eerdmans, 1999.

Kelhoffer, James A. *Miracle and Mission: The Authentication of Missionaries and Their Message in the Longer Ending of Mark*. WUNT 2/112. Tübingen: Mohr Siebeck, 2000.

Kierkegaard, Søren. *Either/Or*. Part 2. Edited by and translated by Howard V. Hong and Edna H. Hong. Princeton: Princeton University Press, 1987.

———. *Philosophical Fragments*. Edited and translated by Howard H. Hong and Edna H. Hong. Princeton: Princeton University Press, 1985.

Knight, Douglas. *The Eschatological Economy: Time and the Hospitality of God*. Grand Rapids: Eerdmans, 2006.

Knox, John. *Chapters in a Life of Paul*. Rev. ed. London: SCM, 1950.

Kuhn, Thomas. *The Structure of Scientific Revolutions*. 2nd ed. Chicago: University of Chicago Press, 1970.

Lee, Dorothy A. *Creation, Matter and the Image of God: Essays on John*. Adelaide: ATF, 2020.

Lessing, Gotthold. "On the Proof of Spirit and of Power." In *Lessing's Theological Writings*, translated by Henry Chadwick, 51–56. Stanford: Stanford University Press, 1956.

Levy, Thomas E., Thomas Schneider, and William H. C. Propp, eds. *Israel's Exodus in Transdisciplinary Perspective: Text, Archaeology, Culture and Geoscience*. Cham: Springer, 2015.

Leyser, Henrietta. "Mary Magdalene." In *The Oxford Companion to Christian Thought: Intellectual, Spiritual, and Moral Horizons of Christianity*, edited by Adrian Hastings, Alistair Mason, and Hugh Pyper, 416–17. Oxford: Oxford University Press, 2000.

Linebaugh, Jonathan A. *The Word of the Cross: Reading Paul*. Grand Rapids: Eerdmans, 2022.

Longenecker, Bruce W. *The Triumph of Abraham's God: The Transformation of Identity in Galatians*. Edinburgh: T&T Clark, 1998.

Longenecker, Richard N. *Studies in Paul, Exegetical and Theological*. Sheffield: Sheffield Phoenix, 2004.

Lunn, Nicholas P. *The Original Ending of Mark: A New Case for the Authenticity of Mark 16:9–20*. Cambridge: James Clark, 2015.

Luther, Martin. *D. Martin Luthers Werke*. Weimar: Hermann Böhlaus Nachfolger, 1930–85.

———. *Luther's Works*. Edited by Jaroslav Pelican and Helmut T. Lehman. 55 vols. Philadelphia: Fortress; St. Louis: Concordia, 1955–86.

Luz, Ulrich. *Matthew 21–28: A Commentary*. Hermeneia. Minneapolis: Augsburg Fortress, 2005.

Marsh, John. *Saint John*. Harmondsworth: Penguin Books, 1968.

Matera, Frank J. *New Testament Christology*. Louisville: Westminster John Knox, 1999.

Molnar, Paul D. *Divine Freedom and the Doctrine of the Immanent Trinity*. London: T&T Clark, 2002.

Moltmann, Jürgen. *The Church in the Power of the Spirit: A Contribution to Messianic Ecclesiology*. Translated by Margaret Kohl. London: SCM, 1977.

———. *The Coming of God*. Translated by Margaret Kohl. Minneapolis: Fortress, 1996.

———. *Theology of Hope: On the Ground and Implications of a Christian Eschatology*. Translated by James W. Leitch. London: SCM, 1967.

——. *The Way of Jesus Christ: Christology in Messianic Dimensions.* Translated by Margaret Kohl. London: SCM, 1990.

Moore, Anthony M. *Signs of Salvation: The Creation Theme in John's Gospel.* Cambridge: James Clarke, 2013.

Moorman, John R. H. *The Gospel according to Luke, I–IX.* New York: Doubleday, 1981.

Neil, William. *The Acts of the Apostles.* Grand Rapids: Eerdmans, 1987.

Novakovic, Lidija. *Resurrection: A Guide for the Perplexed.* London: Bloomsbury T&T Clark, 2016.

O'Donovan, Oliver. *Resurrection and Moral Order: An Outline for Evangelical Ethics.* Leicester, UK: Inter-Varsity, 1986.

Oduyoye, Mercy Amba. "Jesus Christ." In *The Cambridge Companion to Feminist Theology,* edited by Susan Frank Parsons, 151–70. Cambridge: Cambridge University Press, 2002.

Oduyoye, Mercy Amba, and M. R. A. Kanyoro, eds. *Talitha Qumi! Proceedings of the Convocation of African Women Theologians.* Ibadan: Daystar, 1989.

Paget, James Carleton. "Quests for the Historical Jesus." In *The Cambridge Companion to Jesus,* edited by Markus Bockmuehl, 138–55. Cambridge: Cambridge University Press, 2001.

Painter, John. "Earth Made Whole: John's Rereading of Genesis." In *Word, Theology, and Community in John,* edited by John Painter, R. Alan Culpepper, and Fernando F. Segovia, 65–84. St. Louis: Chalice, 2002.

Pannenberg, Wolfhart. *Jesus—God and Man.* Translated by Lewis L. Wilkins and Duane A. Priebe. London: SCM, 1968.

Pervo, Richard I. *Acts: A Commentary.* Hermeneia. Minneapolis: Fortress, 2009.

Plato. *Phaedo.* Translated with an introduction and commentary by R. Hackforth. Cambridge: Cambridge University Press, 1955.

Rae, Murray A. *Architecture and Theology: The Art of Place.* Waco: Baylor University Press, 2017.

——. "The Baptism of Christ." In *The Person of Christ,* edited by Stephen R. Holmes and Murray A. Rae, 121–37. London: T&T Clark, 2005.

——. *History and Hermeneutics.* London: T&T Clark, 2005.

——. "Texts and Context: Scripture and the Divine Economy." *Journal of Theological Interpretation* 1, no. 1 (2007): 23–45.

——. "Theological Interpretation and Historical Criticism." In *A Manifesto for Theological Interpretation,* edited by Craig G. Bartholomew and Heath A. Thomas, 94–109. Grand Rapids: Baker Academic, 2016.

Raphael, Chaim. *A Feast of History: Passover through the Ages as a Key to Jewish Experience.* New York: Simon & Schuster, 1972.

Rauber, D. F. "The Book of Ruth." In *Literary Interpretations of Biblical Narratives*, edited by Kenneth R. R. Gros Louis, James S. Ackerman, and Thayer S. Warshaw, 163–76. Nashville: Abingdon, 1974.

Ricci, Carla. *Mary Magdalene and Many Others: Women Who Followed Jesus*. Translated by Paul Burns. Minneapolis: Fortress, 1994.

Rowe, C. Kavin. "Acts 2.36 and the Continuity of Lukan Christology." *New Testament Studies* 53 (2007): 37–56.

———. *Early Narrative Christology: The Lord in the Gospel of Luke*. New York: de Gruyter, 2006.

Salmond, Anne. *Between Worlds: Early Exchanges between Maori and Europeans, 1773–1815*. Auckland: Penguin Books, 1997.

Sánchez M., Leopoldo A. "The Church Is the House of Abraham: Reflections on Martin Luther's Teaching on Hospitality toward Exiles." *Concordia Pages* 7 (2022). https://scholar.csl.edu/cgi/viewcontent.cgi?article=1006&context=concordiapages.

Sanders, E. P. *Jesus and Judaism*. Philadelphia: Fortress, 1985.

Schnabel, Eckhard J. *Acts: Exegetical Commentary on the New Testament*. Grand Rapids: Zondervan, 2012.

Schweitzer, Albert. *The Quest of the Historical Jesus*. 2nd ed. London: A&C Black, 1936.

Schweizer, Eduard. *The Good News according to Mark*. Translated by Donald H. Madvig. Atlanta: John Knox, 1970.

Seitz, Christopher R. *Word without End: The Old Testament as Abiding Theological Witness*. Grand Rapids: Eerdmans, 1998.

Sobrino, Jon. *The True Church and the Poor*. Translated by Matthew J. O'Connell. London: SCM, 1985.

Sölle, Dorothee. *Christ the Representative*. London: SCM, 1967.

Song, Choan-Seng. *The Compassionate God: An Exercise in the Theology of Transposition*. London: SCM, 1982.

Spencer, Herbert. *Social Statics*. London: Williams and Norgate, 1892.

Stephens, Mark B. *Annihilation or Renewal? The Meaning and Function of New Creation in the Book of Revelation*. WUNT 2/307. Tübingen: Mohr Siebeck, 2011.

Stubbs, David L. *Table and Temple: The Christian Eucharist and Its Jewish Roots*. Grand Rapids: Eerdmans, 2020.

Stuhlmacher, Peter. "Isaiah 53 in the Gospels and Acts." In *The Suffering Servant: Isaiah 53 in Jewish and Christian Sources*, edited by Bernd Janowski and Peter Stuhlmacher, 147–62. Grand Rapids: Eerdmans, 2004.

Thompson, James W. *The Church according to Paul: Rediscovering the Community Conformed to Christ*. Grand Rapids: Baker Academic, 2014.

Tian, Nan, Diego Lopes da Silva, Xiao Liang, Lorenzo Scarazzato, Lucie Béraud-Sudreau, and Ana Carolina de Oliveira Assis. "Trends in World Military Expenditure,

2022." Stockholm: Stockholm International Peace Research Institute, 2023. https://www.sipri.org/sites/default/files/2023-04/2304_fs_milex_2022.pdf.

Tiede, David L. *Luke*. Augsburg Commentary on the New Testament. Minneapolis: Augsburg, 1998.

Torrance, James B. *Worship, Community and the Triune God of Grace*. Downers Grove, IL: InterVarsity, 1996.

Torrance, T. F. *Atonement: The Person and Work of Christ*. Edited by Robert T. Walker. Downers Grove, IL: IVP Academic, 2009.

———. *The Christian Doctrine of God: One Being Three Persons*. Edinburgh: T&T Clark, 1996.

Troeltsch, Ernst. "Historical and Dogmatic Method in Theology." In *Religion in History: Ernst Troeltsch*, 11–32. Edinburgh: T&T Clark, 1991.

Tyrrell, George. *Christianity at the Crossroads*. London: Longmans, Green, 1910.

Urquhart, Angus, Fran Girling, Erica Mason, and Suzanna Nelson-Pollard. "Global Humanitarian Assistance Report 2022." Bristol, UK: Development Initiatives, 2023. https://devinit.org/documents/1193/GHA2022_Digital_v8_DknWCsU.pdf.

Vistar, Deolito V., Jr. *The Cross and Resurrection*. Tübingen: Mohr Siebeck, 2019.

Volf, Miroslav. *Work in the Spirit: Toward a Theology of Work*. Oxford: Oxford University Press, 1991.

Vos, Geerhardus. *The Pauline Eschatology*. Grand Rapids: Baker, 1930.

Watson, Francis. *Text, Church and World: Biblical Interpretation in Theological Perspective*. Grand Rapids: Eerdmans, 1994.

Webb, Robert L. "The Historical Enterprise and Historical Jesus Research." In *Key Events in the Life of the Historical Jesus*, edited by Darrell L. Bock and Robert L. Webb, 9–93. Grand Rapids: Eerdmans, 2010.

Webster, John B. *Confessing God: Essays in Christian Dogmatics II*. London: T&T Clark, 2005.

———. *Holy Scripture: A Dogmatic Sketch*. Cambridge: Cambridge University Press, 2003.

———. "On Evangelical Ecclesiology." In *Confessing God*, 153–93.

———. "Prolegomena to Christology." In *Confessing God*, 131–49.

———. "Resurrection and Scripture." In *Christology and Scripture: Interdisciplinary Perspectives*, edited by Andrew T. Lincoln and Angus Paddison, 138–55. London: T&T Clark, 2008.

Westermann, Claus. *Genesis 1–11: A Commentary*. Translated by John J. Scullion. London: SPCK, 1984.

Whitaker, Maja I. *Perfect in Weakness: Disabilty and Human Flourishing in the New Creation*. Waco: Baylor University Press, 2023.

White, Richard. *Remembering Ahanagran: Storytelling in a Family's Past*. New York: Hill and Wang, 1998.

Williams, Rowan. *Arius*. 2nd ed. London: SCM, 2002.

———. *The Wound of Knowledge: Christian Spirituality from the New Testament to Saint John of the Cross*. 2nd ed. Cambridge, MA: Cowley Publications, 1991.

Williams, Travis B. "Bringing Method to the Madness: Examining the Style of the Longer Ending of Mark." *Bulletin for Biblical Research* 20, no. 3 (2010): 397–418.

Williamson, Lamar, Jr. *Mark*. Interpretation. Atlanta: John Knox, 1983.

Wordsworth, William. "The 1805 Prelude." In *The Norton Anthology of English Literature*. Vol. 2. 7th ed. Edited by M. H. Abrams, Stephen Greenblatt, and Jack Stillinger, 305–83. New York: Norton, 2000.

Wright, N. T. *History and Eschatology: Jesus and the Promise of Natural Theology*. London: SPCK; Waco: Baylor University Press, 2019.

———. *Jesus and the Victory of God*. London: SPCK, 1996.

———. "The Meanings of History: Event and Interpretation in the Bible and Theology." *Journal of Analytic Theology* 6 (2018): 1–28.

———. *The New Testament and the People of God*. London: SPCK, 1992.

———. *The Resurrection of the Son of God*. London: SPCK, 2003.

Zeitlin, Solomon. "Herod: A Malevolent Maniac." *The Jewish Quarterly Review* 54, no. 1 (1963): 1–27.

Scripture Index

Author and Subject Index